Advancing Higher Education

To Tonya Fehrenbach —

Advancing Higher Education

*New Strategies for Fundraising,
Philanthropy, and Engagement*

Edited by Michael J. Worth and
Matthew T. Lambert

Welcome Back home to William & Mary — we are excited to have you as the first point of contact for all our donors and alumni!

Matthew T. Lambert

ROWMAN & LITTLEFIELD
Lanham • Boulder • New York • London

Published by Rowman & Littlefield
An imprint of The Rowman & Littlefield Publishing Group, Inc.
4501 Forbes Boulevard, Suite 200, Lanham, Maryland 20706
www.rowman.com

6 Tinworth Street, London SE11 5AL

British Library Cataloguing in Publication Information Available

Library of Congress Cataloging-in-Publication Data

Names: Worth, Michael J., editor. | Lambert, Matthew T., 1977– editor.
Title: Advancing higher education : new strategies for fundraising, philanthropy, and engagement / Edited by Michael J. Worth, Matthew T. Lambert.
Description: Lanham, Maryland : Rowman & Littlefield, [2019] | Includes bibliographical references and index. |
Identifiers: LCCN 2019010820 (print) | LCCN 2019017748 (ebook) | ISBN 9781475845037 (Electronic) | ISBN 9781475845013 (cloth : alk. paper) | ISBN 9781475845020 (pbk. : alk. paper)
Subjects: LCSH: Education, Higher—Aims and objectives--United States. | Educational fund raising—United States. | Endowments—United States. | Universities and colleges—Planning—United States.
Classification: LCC LB2322.2 (ebook) | LCC LB2322.2 .A33 2019 (print) | DDC 378/.01—dc23
LC record available at https://lccn.loc.gov/2019010820

♾ ™ The paper used in this publication meets the minimum requirements of American National Standard for Information Sciences Permanence of Paper for Printed Library Materials, ANSI/NISO Z39.48-1992.

Printed in the United States of America

Contents

Acknowledgments

As coeditors, we are grateful, first and foremost, to the chapter authors who have contributed cutting-edge insights and trends. All contributors are distinguished experts on the topics they address as well as active professionals with significant responsibilities. Each brings a unique perspective and has worked diligently with us to develop a rich and forward-looking assessment of the noble and crucial work of the advancement field. Their investment of thought, effort, and time represents an important commitment to our profession.

We thank Thomas F. Koerner, vice president and publisher of education at Rowman & Littlefield, for his encouragement of this project. We acknowledge the capable editorial assistance of Miranda Hines, a graduate student at the George Washington University, Trachtenberg School of Public Policy and Public Administration, for attending to every detail.

Michael is grateful to his colleagues at the George Washington University, both current and former; to his students at GW, from whom he learns; and to clients, who have provided him with opportunities to see innovative fundraising in action. He thanks his wife, Maria, for her understanding and support.

Matthew is grateful to the many devoted colleagues at William & Mary who conceived and operationalized many of the concepts covered in this book and contribute significantly to imagining the future of our profession. His wife, Karen, once again provided her never-ending patience, support, and love; she puts up with his absence more nights and weekends than he cares to count. His boys, William and Harrison, are his joy, and they give him hope for the future of our wider world.

Michael J. Worth and Matthew T. Lambert

Introduction

Michael J. Worth and Matthew T. Lambert

The Council for Advancement and Support of Education (CASE) defines advanced professionals as individuals "who share the goal of championing education to transform lives and society" (CASE, n.d.). Advancement encompasses the disciplines of alumni relations (increasingly also named *alumni engagement*); communications and marketing; fundraising (development); and advancement series. In some institutions, advancement professionals also hold responsibility for government relations and career services programs.

Principles of advancement have been addressed in various books over the last five decades. A. Westley Rowland served as editor of the *Handbook of Institutional Advancement*, the first book to define many of the concepts of the field when it was published in 1974. A second edition of Rowland's handbook was published in 1986; a third edition, edited by former CASE president Peter McE. Buchanan, was published in 2000.

Other edited books have addressed specific advancement disciplines. Two such examples include *Educational Fund Raising: Principles and Practice* (1993) and *New Strategies for Educational Fund Raising* (2002). Michael Worth, coeditor of this volume, served as the editor of both. In addition, there have been many books that focus on specific advancement topics and disciplines within the field.

Significant technological, social, economic, and political changes have created a new environment in the second decade of the twenty-first century, and the advancement field has continued to grow and adapt with increasing speed. This book highlights some implications of such changes for advancement practice on the threshold of the century's third decade.

Unlike earlier handbooks, this volume is not an exhaustive compilation of knowledge in the field. Although it may be of interest to newcomers in the field, as well as seasoned practitioners, it is not intended as a textbook or a how-to manual. The intended audience is thoughtful advancement practitioners at any stage of their careers who are looking to the future and seeking to understand the new ideas and challenges that are shaping our profession.

This volume is also of interest to other leaders in higher education, including presidents and chancellors, board members, and senior administrators who recognize the importance of effective advancement efforts to their institution's ability to thrive.

Chapter authors take different approaches to their work. Some offer case studies of successful programs, while others take a broader approach to discussing principles related to their topics. Some offer prescriptive advice, while others are more philosophical and reflective. All address such questions as "What is working now?" "Where are we going?" and "What will the future of advancement look like?"

Chapter authors are innovative and seasoned practitioners and influencers in advancement. Most hold leadership positions in institutions; some are working as consultants; and some are in academic roles, engaged in research related to the field.

This book is focused on higher education, although many of the topics it considers are also important to independent schools and other types of institutions. Chapter authors include one practitioner from outside the United States, but the book emphasizes advancement from the perspective of American colleges and universities. Of course, the topics also are relevant to the practice of advancement around the world, subject to their unique environments.

OVERVIEW OF THE BOOK

The book's twenty chapters are organized in seven parts. Part I includes two chapters that provide context for the balance of the book, summarizing the forces shaping higher education now and the history of the advancement profession. Three chapters in part II establish the foundation for advancement by addressing strategic planning, marketing and communications, and the importance of an integrated advancement program.

Part III includes four chapters that discuss engaging and raising funds from individuals and the state-of-the-art in core fundraising programs. The two chapters in part IV discuss campaigns and fundraising for programs and projects, including corporate and foundation relations. Part V includes four chapters that discuss engaging new generations, underrepresented communities, women in philanthropy, and international and global fundraising from the perspective of colleges and universities in the United States.

The American system of higher education encompasses a variety of institutional models, and advancement professionals work in various settings. The three chapters in part VI provide insights on the unique challenges and opportunities facing advancement in some of those environments. Advancement programs have grown dramatically in size and scope and today require a significant commitment of institutional resources. This has increased the emphasis on management. Two chapters in part VII discuss important topics—structuring and managing advancement staff and advancement services, the backbone of any effective advancement organization.

Colleges and universities are among the most enduring and crucial institutions in our society, providing individuals with opportunities that last throughout their lives and supplying the talent and new ideas that will create a better world for all. Those who work to advance higher education are engaged in noble and important work. It is our hope that readers will find the chapters in this book interesting, stimulating, and helpful in thinking about the current and future state of their profession and that the insights the authors provide will inspire as well as inform.

REFERENCES

Buchanan, Peter McE., ed. 2000. *Handbook of Institutional Advancement*. 3rd ed. Washington, DC: CASE.
CASE (Council for Advancement and Support of Education). n.d. "About CASE." Accessed April 9, 2019. https://www.case.org/about-case.
Rowland, A. Westley, ed. 1974. *Handbook of Institutional Advancement*. 1st ed. San Francisco: Jossey-Bass.
———, ed. 1986. *Handbook of Institutional Advancement*. 2nd ed. San Francisco: Jossey-Bass.
Worth, Michael J., ed. 1993. *Educational Fund Raising: Principles and Practice*. Phoenix: Oryx Press, American Council on Education.
———, ed. 2002. *New Strategies for Educational Fund Raising*. Westport, CT: Praeger, American Council on Education.

I

Advancement in Higher Education

This book is not intended as an academic work but rather as a resource for thoughtful advancement practitioners and other higher-education leaders who are interested in new strategies for advancement practice and trends affecting the future of the field. However, the two chapters in this opening section establish a broader context by considering the present and future of higher education and the origins and growth of advancement as a profession.

The new strategies discussed in this book are necessary because of changes in the environment of higher education itself. It is not possible to be an effective leader in institutional advancement today without understanding the place of higher education in society and the forces shaping the past, present, and future of colleges and universities.

As Matthew Lambert describes in chapter 1, this is a time of economic and political challenge. Some observers are questioning the value of higher education, even as technology and globalization are making education even more essential to achieving success in life and career. These and other forces are driving change and perhaps leading to a new type of university—a hybrid of private and public, reliant on resources from both sectors and increasingly interactive with the marketplace. As Lambert writes, the "future of higher education—whether you work at a public or private institution—is a public–private partnership. This partnership requires the essential skills of strategic planning, engagement, communications, fundraising, and leading—all with an eye toward advancing our institutions forward."

Fully understanding the present and preparing for the future also requires an appreciation of the past. In chapter 2, Michael Worth describes the historical roots of advancement in America's earliest colleges and universities, the development of its core disciplines, its emergence as a professional field in the twentieth and twenty-first centuries, and its growing scale and importance in the United States and elsewhere in the world. Like Lambert, Worth notes the expansion of advancement from its roots in private higher education to a central place in both private and public institutions, which now rank among the top in campaign and fundraising achievement.

As Worth's historical review illustrates, higher education has faced challenges in the past, and advancement strategies have been invented and reinvented as the times demanded. Worth concludes that "advancement will remain a central focus of higher education in the future."

ONE

The Present and Future of Higher Education

Matthew T. Lambert

Higher education is seemingly under assault today from all sides—legislators, students and their parents, the media, and the public at large. Meanwhile, much like the crew of the *Titanic*, most institutions have been gently moving the deck chairs around during the past twenty-five years without trying to make any dramatic changes.

Today, the forces of globalization and financial instability are straining even some of the most prestigious universities, leading boards of trustees and presidents to begin thinking about new modes of teaching and learning and delivery of our "product," recruitment of new and more diverse student populations, exploration of new revenue models, and searching for greater productivity and efficiency.

Societal turmoil in a period of deep political divisions has made the American college campus a new front in the culture wars. Educational quality and the relevance and value of higher education are being openly questioned—often by college graduates themselves. With much to fear and loathe, is the future of higher education one where institutions will slowly glide into mediocrity and poverty while robots and artificial intelligence (AI) take over the jobs of even the most capable knowledge workers? No! But we must work now to change in order to advance our institutions forward into a new era.

Some of the most dramatic change, support, and innovation in higher education have come during some of the darkest days of our republic. Let us not forget the Morrill Act, which spurred massive growth in the scale and number of public institutions; it was passed by Congress and signed by President Lincoln just one month after the Civil War battle of Shiloh, where 25,000 men lost their lives. Or the GI Bill and the National Defense Education Act, which unleashed massive growth in student populations, broad-based higher education, and spending on a research infrastructure in colleges and universities across the nation. The GI Bill was passed by Congress just two weeks after the D-Day invasions during World War II.

The creativity, innovation, and entrepreneurial thinking that is beginning to blossom at some of America's colleges and universities today is more exciting than at any point in the past century. Technology is enabling great leaps in reimagining the way we teach our students and, more importantly, how they learn.

The diversity of institutions of higher education—today numbering more than five thousand in the United States—allows for opportunities for more students to achieve a postsecondary education than ever before in human history. This includes those from backgrounds previously excluded or who were unable to afford college. Whether that education culminates in a particular credential, such as a degree or certificate, or is just retraining of a new skill or fulfilling a desire for lifelong learning, it provides even more opportunities.

THE SECOND AMERICAN REVOLUTION

In 1985, the Association of American Colleges wrote, "We have reached a point at which we are more confident of the length of a college education than its content and purpose" (AAC 1985). While this statement appears in a national report written more than thirty years ago, it just as easily could have been lifted from the headlines of the *New York Times* today. We are facing another massive shift in the workforce that has not truly been seen on the same scale since the Industrial Revolution, when large numbers of workers had to retrain in order to move from farms to factories.

Today, it is technology that is forcing workers in almost every sector of the economy to retrain for what Joseph Aoun (2017) calls "robot-proof" jobs, including many knowledge workers. Robot-proofing our higher-education system entails thinking anew about the skills, abilities, and tools that we must teach our students. We must now enable them to thrive in an era of AI, where robots are not only delivering packages to our doors and driving our cars but also writing articles and deciphering the best financial investment options.

Why, you might ask, is this relevant to those of us who work in the many disciplines of institutional advancement? Why is this our problem if we are presidents or chancellors or deans or board members? We're not responsible for the problems of higher education today writ large or the woes befalling other segments of our industry; we're just supposed to deal with our specific institution and focus on engaging alumni and asking them for money, right? Wrong.

As you will read throughout this book, our roles are essential for the future of higher education—a future that will require us to engage effectively with of a wide variety of constituents, rally all parties together around a shared mission and set of goals, communicate central messages about where our institutions are headed, and work with philanthropists to secure that future. If we do our part, this future will be even brighter than the past four hundred years of higher education in America.

The future of higher education is a public–private partnership. This partnership requires the essential skills of strategic planning, engagement, communications, fundraising, and leading—all with an eye toward advancing our institutions. Advancing our institutions requires harnessing all these skills with the right external partners as well as effective corralling and partnership with internal colleagues.

THE FOUR HORSEMEN OF ACADEMIC REFORM

The desire for and drive toward change in higher education often come back to four overarching themes. These are familiar to almost anyone who has ever been at a cocktail party and had to answer such questions as "Why does college cost so much?" "Why can't my child get into your university when she has perfect grades?" and "When is tenure going to end?"

These questions and many more always boil down to the not-quite-as-scary-as-they-sound "Four Horsemen of Academic Reform," as Robert Zemsky (2009) named the persistently perplexing and complicated themes of access, affordability, accountability, and quality. Our collective challenge in the decades ahead is to build a model of higher education that grapples with these four horsemen and makes them our rallying cry for the longevity, value, and relevance of higher education in the twenty-first century and beyond.

Robert Gates (2013), former secretary of defense, once mused, "[If] colleges and universities don't reform themselves to contain costs, improve access, and increase graduation rates, federal and state governments will step in. That can only be bad news because, like the dinosaur, government has a heavy foot, a small brain, and no fine motor skills." We—the leaders and practitioners working together to advance our institutions—must work doggedly to achieve such reform.

After the most immediate effects of the Great Recession had passed, Thomas Friedman made a prediction that remains prescient today. In order to turn around the significant loss of middle-class jobs, which occurred mostly as a result of globalization, we "will require a new level of political imagination—a combination of educational reforms and unprecedented collaboration between business, schools, universities and government to change how workers are trained and empowered to keep learning" (Friedman 2012).

Indeed, the crucial role of advancement professionals today is to bring forward the imagination, creativity, and inspiration required to galvanize industry, government, philanthropists, and higher education in a common mission of advancing the longest-lasting and most successful sector in our country—colleges and universities.

THE HYBRID UNIVERSITY

Much as our cars are evolving with greater numbers of hybrids on the road each year, so, too, are our universities becoming hybrid institutions. Mark Yudof (2002), among others, has described the evolution of our higher-education institutions that once were mostly supported by the church, tuition-paying students, or the state into newer forms of hybrids, where both public and private institutions today have a mix of funding sources.

Elite private universities receive billions of dollars in public funding, mostly in the form of research grants, and public universities receive billions of dollars in private funding, mostly in the form of philanthropy. The students who attend these universities, both private and public, bring millions of additional public dollars in the form of educational grants and student-loan subsidies.

Tuition has increased and become a larger source of revenue for both private and public institutions. The traditional divisions of public and private are blurring. As discussed in chapter 2 of this book, we are seeing rapidly increasing numbers of public universities conduct multibillion-dollar campaigns and diversify their funding models.

The hybrid university today requires everyone to pull their own oar in the waters of higher education. Governments will have to provide more autonomy and stable, even if diminished, funding. Faculty and staff will need to work toward new models of employment with a greater focus on cost reduction, efficiency, and productivity. Students and their parents will have to pay more of the actual cost of their education in the form of tuition. The lifetime value to a college graduate has been calculated as millions of dollars more than a high school graduate. Much like buying a house, that expense is worth the long-term amortization of the cost.

Finally (and perhaps most crucially for advancement professionals), alumni, corporations, foundations, and other donors will be called upon for ever-increasing philanthropy, which now has surpassed state support at many public institutions and is a growing share of total revenue at almost all institutions. Engaging each of these partners in the hybrid university requires the strategic approach of an integrated and thoughtful advancement operation at a university (Lambert 2014).

PRIVATIZATION: OUTSOURCING, PARTNERING, AND CONTRACTING

The word *privatization* is something of a Rorschach test: Each person sees what they want to see in it (sometimes scary, sometimes exhilarating, but rarely reality). Christopher Bradie's (2012) research on outsourcing in higher education found that a majority of institutions outsource at least one nonacademic service already, and the number and variety of services are growing rapidly.

While some purists will see this negatively as a corporatization of the college campus, it reflects today's necessity of finding new ways of financing the core academic mission. Private funding and partnership endeavors can enable the essential work of faculty and students—what those of us working in the advancement profession seek to support through our work.

Derek Bok (2003) thoughtfully reflected the value of such partnerships, noting,

> The obvious attraction of most commercial ventures to their university sponsors is the prospect of bringing substantial new revenues to the university. In the hands of academic officials, such funds have the ennobling quality of being used, not to line the pockets of private investors, but to help fund scholarships, purchase library books, pay for new laboratory equipment, or support any one of a number of worthy educational purposes.

Keep Bok's words in mind as we set out even more aggressively in the years ahead to seek sustainable support for our institutions' core missions.

The privatization movement in the United States took hold among some policy makers beginning in earnest in the 1970s and led to new conceptions of which services might be managed by private enterprise instead of solely by government. Roads, prisons, and even portions of the military have been outsourced, with varying levels of success. Within higher education, the 1990s saw another wave of declining state support and constraints on tuition, leading institutions to accelerate the outsourcing of bookstores, food service, housing, and parking.

None of these areas is what most reasonable people would consider part of the core academic mission. "Is Outsourcing Right for You?" (2005) explains the decision to privatize a service: "The basic rationale for a college or university to outsource to a vendor could be summed up this way: I can't do this, others can, I think I'll let them." Not only can others do something, but also they often can do it at lower cost with higher quality because it is their specialty and not ours.

The education and training of higher-education leaders prepared them for teaching, research, and management but not for understanding parking services or food service management or bookstore management. As noted in chapter 2, many of the earliest fundraising endeavors were outsourced to private firms that worked on behalf of the university to solicit gifts, and only later did institutions begin to hire full-time advancement staff. Even today, many advancement operations employ large numbers of consultants to provide specialized expertise in everything from marketing to feasibility studies to phone-a-thons to event management to wealth assessment and many other functions.

Beyond these most explicit forms of outsourcing, partnerships and sponsorship agreements are common across higher education and are growing in complexity. Athletics departments, alumni associations, and intellectual property and technology transfer offices are all engaged in a variety of privatization partnerships that allow for the funding of core business.

As advancement professionals, our objective is to seek partners that both share our institutional values and can maximize revenues in perimeter (as opposed to core) functions, thus allowing that funding to flow into the core of the institution—student learning and engagement, teaching, and research.

Privatization, when properly planned and executed in its many forms on college campuses, represents the essence of effective public–private partnerships. When working properly, privatization helps to tackle Zemsky's (2009) "Four Horsemen of Academic Reform" and enables institutions to focus resources and energy on increasing access, ensuring affordability, mandating accountability, and improving teaching and learning quality and quantity.

ADVANCING HIGHER EDUCATION

While predictions about the future of higher education are as numerous as the proliferation of rankings publications, there is reason for concern in an industry that has, for too long, not been sufficiently responsive to students, employers, legislators, or the external marketplace.

Colleges and universities are full of innovation and inspiration. If properly harnessed, we will see a new revolution, one that will help to prepare our students for careers that will take many turns through jobs that have yet to be invented.

At the same time that we must face these realities, we also must more effectively educate our alumni, students, parents, faculty and staff, legislators, and donor communities about the realities involving the costs associated with a college education. Our costs are mostly in our people. Faculty, staff, and students represent, on many campuses, 80 percent or more of the expenses.

Like other industries where increasing costs have outpaced inflation (such as medicine), we have a highly educated workforce, which is not cheap and is increasingly mobile. Faculty and staff are no longer bound by geography, industry, or allegiance to the institution. As much as we all wish it did not cost so much to educate a student, the facts are what they are.

CONCLUSION

This era of rising expenses and shrinking revenues makes the work of advancement professionals all the more crucial and exhilarating. Our goal is to advance our institutions. That requires that we find and engage friends of the university who believe in the mission and want to support it. It requires that we clearly and effectively communicate that mission to more and varied audiences. It calls upon us to lead, drive, focus, and serve as a check on institutional strategic planning. It requires that we form partnerships with state and federal governments, wherever possible, to provide greater public financing. It demands that we draw ever closer to those philanthropists who are inspired to align their passions with our mission for the fulfillment of the greater good our institutions provide.

The responsibility for addressing today's challenges extends to board members, presidents, and all advancement professionals—whether they serve as gift officers, alumni-engagement specialists, government-affairs liaisons, communications experts, or in other roles. It applies to advancement rookies and veterans and to those who serve elite private institutions, as well as those who serve regional public institutions. Advancement professionals must think constantly about the challenges and opportunities facing higher education and about how they can help to bring forward solutions, partners, and friends interested in achieving shared goals.

REFERENCES

AAC (Association of American Colleges). 1985. *Integrity in the College Curriculum: A Report to the Academic Community.* Washington, DC: AAC.
Aoun, Joseph E. 2017. *Robot-Proof: Higher Education in the Age of Artificial Intelligence.* Boston: MIT Press.

Bok, Derek. 2003. *Universities in the Marketplace: The Commercialization of Higher Education.* Princeton, NJ: Princeton University Press.

Bradie, Christopher. 2012. "More Than Just One Breath: Exploring How Three Universities Decided Whether to Outsource Their Campus Bookstores." PhD diss., University of Pennsylvania.

Friedman, Thomas. 2012. "Hope and Change: Part Two." *New York Times*, November 7, 2012. https://www.nytimes.com/2012/11/07/opinion/friedman-hope-and-change-part-two.html.

Gates, Robert E. 2013. "Charter Day Remarks." Speech, William & Mary, February 8, 2013, Williamsburg, VA. https://www.wm.edu/news/stories/2012/robert-gates-charter-day-remarks123.php.

"Is Outsourcing Right for You?" 2005. *University Business*, February 5, 2005. https://www.universitybusiness.com/article/outsourcing-right-you.

Lambert, Matthew T. 2014. *Privatization and the Public Good: Public Universities in the Balance.* Boston: Harvard Education Press.

Yudof, Mark. 2002. "Higher Tuitions: Harbinger of a Hybrid University?" *Change* 34, no. 2: 16.

Zemsky, Robert M. 2009. *Making Reform Work: The Case for Transforming American Higher Education.* Piscataway, NJ: Rutgers University Press.

TWO

History and Growth of Institutional Advancement

Michael J. Worth

Institutional advancement has become a global profession, but its roots can be identified in the history of higher education in the United States. Many early American colleges were sponsored by religious congregations and operated free of government control, although some did receive public funds.

When public colleges and universities were created in the United States in the nineteenth and twentieth centuries, their governance was modeled on that of existing independent institutions. Their boards were designed to be one step removed from direct control by state government. As a result of this history, American colleges and universities— both independent and public—always have operated as relatively autonomous institutions, competing for students, faculty, and resources.

ADVANCEMENT'S HISTORICAL ROOTS

In 1641, William Hibbens, Hugh Peter, and Thomas Weld set sail from Boston to London on a mission to solicit gifts for a young American college. Their stated purpose was to raise money for the college to "educate the heathen Indian," a cause viewed as worthy by wealthy British citizens of the time (Cutlip 1965, 4).

Weld remained in England, never to return to America. So, too, in a manner of speaking, did Peter, who was hanged for crimes committed under British law. Only Hibbens returned to America, a year later, with £500 to support the struggling institution—Harvard College. As historian Scott Cutlip dryly observes, "Such were the rewards of early fund raisers" (1965, 4).

Throughout the eighteenth and nineteenth centuries, fundraising methods remained primitive by today's standards, mostly consisting of "passing the church plate, of staging church suppers or bazaars, and of writing 'begging letters'" (Cutlip 1965, 7). Early colleges were often connected with a sponsoring church, and their fundraising reflected a religious zeal, with gifts being solicited for the purpose of advancing Christianity in a young nation. The blending of religion and higher education was exemplified in the preaching tours of George Whitfield, who raised money for Harvard, Dartmouth, Princeton, and the University of Pennsylvania, as well as for "the poor" (Cutlip 1965, 6).

Alumni interest and loyalty to alma mater also was evident early in the history of higher education in the United States. About the same time that Hibbens, Peter, and Weld left for their fundraising journey in England, Harvard alumni began returning to attend commencements and renew old acquaintances. Yale began organizing alumni by class in 1792, and the first meeting of the Society of Alumni of Williams College was held in 1821 (CASE 2013).

The first organized fundraising programs in higher education came in the area of alumni annual giving. Formal alumni funds appeared in the 1800s, often promoting the concept of alumni as a "living endowment" for the institution (Ransdell 1986, 374).

Educational fundraising before the twentieth century was generally amateur and personal, a transaction between two individuals, with no role for organization, strategy, or professional managers. However, some early fundraising efforts do reveal the seeds of modern techniques. For example, in 1829, a Philadelphia fundraiser named Mathew Carey introduced the ideas of rated prospect lists and advance promotion of the fundraising appeal, concepts that Cutlip calls "in embryo, the elements of modern fund raising" (1965, 8). Despite such examples, the beginning of a professional approach to fundraising and the other advancement disciplines we know today came in the early years of the twentieth century.

EMERGENCE OF A PROFESSIONAL APPROACH

YMCA executive Lyman L. Pierce had begun a campaign in 1902 to raise $300,000 toward construction of a new YMCA in Washington, DC. With the help of a $50,000 gift from John D. Rockefeller and other donors, his campaign had come within $80,000 of its goal, when it stalled in 1905. Pierce then called on Charles Sumner Ward, a fellow YMCA executive from Chicago who had gained attention for his fundraising skills. Ward came to Washington to help Pierce complete the floundering campaign.

As Cutlip recounts, "The collaboration of Ward and Pierce produced the first modern fund raising campaign techniques: careful organization, picked leaders spurred on by team competition, prestige leaders, powerful publicity, a large gift to be matched, . . . careful records, report meetings, and a definite time limit" (1965, 74). Ward became "widely acknowledged as the prime originator" of what became known as the Ward method of fundraising (Cutlip 1965, 40). He went on to found a consulting firm and extended the campaign method into higher education in 1914, directing a $3 million campaign for the University of Pittsburgh.

In contrast to the early college fundraisers, who relied on their personal charisma and relationships to solicit gifts, Ward introduced the idea that fundraising could be based on an established methodology. The task of solicitation was carried out by volunteers and institutional leaders, with Ward providing overall direction of the campaign but not directly raising funds himself. With his emphasis on strategy, methods, and process, Ward was one of the first fundraising professionals. It would be decades before such professionals became common on the staffs of colleges and universities.

In the first half of the twentieth century, most college and university campaigns were directed by consultants from firms like those founded by Ward and his contemporaries. The firm would send a resident manager, who would work with the institution for a period of months to complete the campaign and then move on to the next assignment at another college or university, remaining an employee of the consulting firm, not the institution.

Depending on which historical account one accepts, the term *development* was introduced at Northwestern University or the University of Chicago in the 1920s (Kelly 1998). The university determined that its continued growth would require an ongoing structure for the cultivation of relationships with donors rather than episodic campaigns directed by outside consultants. The purpose was to make fundraising a strategy for continuous institutional development, for which *development* became an abbreviation. A new office was created to manage this process, called the "department of development" (Kelly 1998, 150).

As programs became continuous, more institutions came to recognize the value of having a fundraising professional as a full-time member of the college or university staff. The transition was a gradual one. A survey in 1949 found only two members with the title director of development. In 1952, another survey discovered only thirteen (Pray 1981, 2).

By the mid-1960s, the number of staff development officers had become so significant that many consulting firms began to change their emphasis from on-site resident management to part-time counseling. Today, every college or university employs fundraising professionals, and many large institutions have development staff members numbering in the hundreds.

In contrast to campus fundraisers, who emerged from the consulting world outside of higher education, the early predecessors of today's alumni-engagement professionals were institutional figures. Alumni secretaries often were well-known campus personalities, including some former professors, and served their colleges or universities for long periods of time.

Alumni relations efforts also became professionalized in the twentieth century, when H. S. "Dave" Warwick, the first full-time alumni secretary at The Ohio State University, led the transition to a more formalized approach. In 1913, Warwick organized a meeting of twenty-three alumni secretaries at Ohio State, which resulted in the establishment of the Association of Alumni Secretaries (AAS).

In 1925, Daniel Grant of the University of North Carolina at Chapel Hill spearheaded formation of the American Alumni Council (AAC) through the merger of AAS and two other organizations (CAE 2016). As mentioned previously, some people now prefer the term *alumni engagement* instead of *alumni relations*, a trend that is reflected in some other chapters in this book.

The ancestors of today's campus marketing and communications professionals were focused on gaining publicity, primarily coverage of their institutions in newspapers. The American Association of College News Bureaus (AACNB) was established in 1917 under the leadership of Theodore Thomas Frankenberg, the publicity director at Western College in Ohio (Reck 1976, 2). AACNB later became the American College Publicity Association and eventually the American College Public Relations Association (ACPRA; Reck 1976, xi).

The importance of communications and marketing professionals in higher education grew over the decades, as colleges and universities faced increasing competition for students and other resources. The increased competition for students was driven in part by changes in federal student aid programs starting in the 1960s. New programs made students empowered consumers, with choices about where to apply their benefits under grant and loan programs.

One milestone was the 1972 publication of an article by A. R. Krachenberg, a professor at the University of Michigan, who argued for the application of marketing principles from business to help colleges address enrollment declines in the 1970s (Larson 2013a). Another breakthrough was a 1976 article by John Maguire, the dean of admissions at Boston College, who introduced the concept of enrollment management and described how marketing principles could be applied in the recruitment and retention of students (Larson 2013b). Today, colleges and universities engage in marketing and branding in much the same way as commercial businesses.

INSTITUTIONAL ADVANCEMENT

The functions then identified as alumni relations, development, and public relations were organized separately on many campuses throughout most of the twentieth century. The need for coordination among these functions came to be recognized by members of AAC and ACPRA in the 1950s. In 1958, representatives of the two organizations met at the Greenbrier Resort in West Virginia. The product of that conference, the Greenbrier report, gave birth to the contemporary definition and concept of institutional advancement. As Michael Richards and Gerald Sherratt describe it,

> The Greenbrier report was a comprehensive effort to define and improve the management of institutional advancement and its elements, as they were conceived in 1958. The report advised institutions to elect an organizing pattern for their programs that would encourage coordi-

nation of all advancement functions and that would lighten the responsibilities of the president. (1981, 11)

The Greenbrier report recommended the appointment of an administrator at each institution who would work with the president to oversee
alumni relations, development, and public relations—essentially a chief
advancement officer.

The Greenbrier recommendations gained greater acceptance during
the 1960s and 1970s, as advancement programs were increasingly placed
under the direction of a single administrator, usually at the vice-presi-
dential level. In the culmination of the movement initiated at Greenbrier,
the AAC and ACPRA merged in 1974 to create the Council for Advancement and Support of Education (CASE).

Because *development* had become synonymous with *fundraising*, institutional advancement was adopted as the umbrella concept that could
encompass all of the related disciplines. In light of this history, it is ironic
that some today question whether *advancement* has become synonymous
with *fundraising* and suggest that an alternative term might better encompass alumni relations (or engagement), communications and marketing,
and fundraising (Cunningham 2015).

THE GROWTH OF ADVANCEMENT PROGRAMS

As mentioned earlier, the first American colleges and universities were
private institutions, and it was in the private sector that formal development programs originated. State universities and community colleges
were created much later, in the nineteenth and twentieth centuries, with
financial support coming primarily from state governments.

The history of philanthropic support for public institutions varies
across the country. In the Midwest, state universities were often the first
higher-education institutions founded, and they enjoyed considerable
prestige and support right from the start. For example, the Kansas
Endowment Association was established in 1891 to receive gifts from
grateful alumni of the University of Kansas (Worth 1985, 1). In the East,
however, state colleges and universities were newcomers in an area dom-
inated by the older private colleges. Their missions were initially limited
to agriculture, mechanical arts, and teacher training, often due to political
pressure from neighboring private institutions.

These institutions developed in an era of relatively generous state budgets and a national climate that placed a high priority on public funding for education. Before the 1970s, most public colleges and universities had neither the ability nor the need to seek significant private support.

However, as the missions and role of public colleges expanded, so, too, did their financial needs, which outstripped the willingness of state and local governments to respond. Those changes forced these institutions to seek new sources of support. They found one such source in philanthropy. By 2017, the top twenty universities in terms of total gift revenue included eight public institutions (CAE 2018). As Matthew Lambert describes in chapter 1, many institutions in both the independent and public sectors have, in effect, become hybrids that draw from both public and private resources.

Community colleges lagged behind four-year public institutions in moving into the fundraising arena. But, as Lauren Brookey discusses in chapter 17, many have expanded alumni relations and development programs and are experiencing positive results (Kreisel and Patterson 2013).

As Ivan Adames explains in chapter 15, in recent decades, colleges and universities in the United States have become more international, reaching out across the globe for donors and students, and many have developed programs for the continued engagement of alumni worldwide. In addition, higher-education institutions in many nations have faced reduced government support and have implemented advancement programs similar to the US model.

This growth in the profession has increased the need for trained advancement professionals around the globe, a trend reflected in the opening of CASE offices in London in 1994, in Asia in 2007, and in Latin America in 2011. In addition, CASE programs extend to Africa and other parts of the world (CASE n.d.).

EXPANDING ASPIRATIONS AND ACHIEVEMENTS

Historian Scott Cutlip cites three campaigns run by Harvard University to illustrate the dramatic growth in college and university fundraising goals in the twentieth century. Harvard's campaign of 1904–1905 sought $2.5 million for faculty salaries. A 1919–1920 campaign raised more than $14 million for Harvard's endowment. Writing in 1965, Cutlip describes

Harvard's 1956–1960 campaign as having raised the "staggering sum of $82,775,553" (480).

Surely, Cutlip would have found it more than staggering when commitments to Harvard's campaign exceeded $9.1 billion in 2018 (Halper and Wang 2018). As mentioned previously, public colleges and universities now compete with independent institutions at the highest levels of fundraising. For example, in 2016, the University of Washington was engaged in a campaign for $5 billion (Seltzer 2017), and the University of Virginia announced a $5 billion campaign goal in 2018 (McCance 2018).

Along with higher campaign goals have come gifts of extraordinary magnitude, some in the hundreds of millions. A new record was established in late 2018, when Michael Bloomberg announced a commitment of $1.8 billion to Johns Hopkins University for student scholarships (Anderson 2018). Campaigns have become increasingly reliant on large gifts from a small percentage of donors. In 2013, the top 10 percent of donors provided 94 percent of the total dollars given to higher education, compared with 87 percent in 2006. The top one percent of donors provided nearly 80 percent of the dollar total, compared with 87 percent in 2006 (Hasseltine 2017).

At the same time, alumni participation rates have declined, and some observe fewer gifts in the middle levels of the gift pyramid. Increased giving to higher education is, of course, positive news. However, the increased importance of very large gifts and the shrinking of the base also raise concerns. This has led to a renewed emphasis on alumni engagement and building a pipeline of donors for the future.

CONCLUSION

As Matthew Lambert notes in the previous chapter, trends in higher education are increasing the importance of institutional advancement and require an integrated approach across the advancement disciplines. Public concern about the cost and value of a college education, the growing availability of online education, continued pressure on state education budgets, and other factors have increased the pressure on many institutions. The environment suggests that advancement will remain a central focus of higher education in the future and requires the adoption of new strategies, including those discussed in the following chapters of this book.

REFERENCES

Anderson, Nick. 2018. "Bloomberg Gives Johns Hopkins a Record $1.8 Billion for Student Financial Aid." *Washington Post,* November 18, 2018. Accessed November 18, 2018. https://www.washingtonpost.com/local/education/bloomberg-gives-johns-hopkins-a-record-18-billion-for-student-financial-aid/2018/11/18/8db256cc-eb4e-11e8-96d4-0d23f2aaad09_story.html?utm_term=.f235a71542d9.

CASE (Council for Advancement and Support of Education). n.d. "The Evolution of CASE." Accessed April 9, 2019. https://www.case.org/about-case/evolution-case.

———. 2013. "Explore the History of Alumni Relations." https://www.case.org/About_CASE/CASE_History/100AnniversaryAAS/100AnniversaryExplore.html.

Indiana University. 2016. "Council for Advancement and Support of Education Records, 1913–2002." http://www.ulib.iupui.edu/collections/philanthropy/mss002.

CAE (Council for Aid to Education). 2018. "Voluntary Support of Education 2017." Press release, February 6, 2018. https://www.case.org/Documents/Research/VSE/VSE-2017-Press-Release.pdf.

Cunningham, Sue. 2015. "Coming to Terms with Advancement." *Currents* (June). https://www.case.org/Publications_and_Products/2015/December_2015/Presidents_Perspective_Coming_to_Terms_with_Advancement.html.

Cutlip, Scott M. 1965. *Fund Raising in the United States: Its Role in America's Philanthropy.* New Brunswick, NJ: Rutgers University Press.

Halper, Jamie D., and William L. Wang. 2018. "Harvard Raises $9.1 Billion in Capital Campaign." *Harvard Crimson,* April 15, 2018. https://www.thecrimson.com/article/2018/4/15/capital-campaign-passes-9-billion/.

Hasseltine, Donald. 2017. "College Fundraising Gift Pyramid Narrows." *University Business,* November 2, 2017. https://www.universitybusiness.com/article/fundraising-gift-pyramid-narrows.

Kelly, Kathleen. S. 1998. *Effective Fund-Raising Management.* Mahwah, NJ: Lawrence Erlbaum.

Kreisel, Neil, and Vanessa L. Patterson. 2013. "How Community Colleges Can Help Themselves." *Chronicle of Higher Education,* July 8, 2013. https://www.chronicle.com/article/How-Community-Colleges-Can/140121.

Larson, Jens. 2013a. "The History of Higher Education Marketing: 1972 and A. Richard Krachenberg." U of Admissions Marketing. June 21, 2013. http://www.uofadmissionsmarketing.com/2013/06/the-history-of-higher-education.html.

———. 2013b. "The History of Higher Education Marketing: 1976 and John Maguire's Enrollment Management." U of Admissions Marketing, July 12, 2013. http://www.uofadmissionsmarketing.com/2013/07/the-history-of-higher-education.html.

McCance, McGregor. 2018. "UVA Announces Plans for $5 Billion Campaign." Press release, June 7, 2018. https://news.virginia.edu/content/uva-announces-plans-5-billion-campaign.

Pray, Francis C., ed. 1981. *Handbook for Educational Fund Raising.* San Francisco: Jossey-Bass.

Ransdell, Gary A. 1986. "Understanding Professional Roles and Program Mission." In *Handbook of Institutional Advancement,* 2nd ed., edited by A. Westley Rowland, 373–86. San Francisco: Jossey-Bass.

Reck, W. Emerson. 1976. *The Changing World of College Relations.* Washington, DC: CASE.

Richards, Michael D., and Gerald R. Sherratt. 1981. *Institutional Advancement Strategies in Hard Times*. Washington, DC: American Association for Higher Education, ERIC Clearinghouse on Higher Education.

Seltzer, Rick. 2017. "Aiming for Billions." *Inside Higher Education* (October). https://www.insidehighered.com/news/2017/10/17/colleges-and-universities-set-high-targets-latest-fund-raising-campaigns.

Worth, Michael J., ed. 1985. *Public College and University Development*. Washington, DC: CASE.

II

Foundations of Advancement

The key word in *institutional advancement* is *institutional*. In other words, the work of advancement professionals is useful and important only so long as it enables a college or university to achieve its goals and increase its impact—on students, the region and state, and fields of knowledge and in other ways. It's not primarily about the funds raised, the alumni engaged, or the messages communicated—it's all about advancing the *institution* and its mission. In this section, three authors discuss the importance of linking advancement programs to the larger context of the college or university—its goals, its constituencies, and its service to society.

As Darrow Zeidenstein explains in chapter 3, a vision for the institution's future is meaningless without the resources to implement it, but it is also not realistic to think that substantial support can be secured in a vacuum, without an inspirational vision and a plausible plan for achieving the institution's goals. For that reason, campaigns often begin with institutional strategic planning.

However, as Zeidenstein argues, a traditional strategic planning approach may not be desirable under all circumstances, and strategic planning is not a substitute for *strategy*. External stakeholders may contribute to strategic thinking, so advancement officers must play a central role in engaging those individuals and should be involved in institutional planning.

The university does not exist for itself. It exists to provide benefits to the society that supports it. As James Langley discusses in chapter 4, it is engaged in an *exchange*, consistent with the definition of *marketing*. The institution's goals are meaningless unless its value proposition can be defined and communicated. In other words, it must be clear that the institution provides a benefit to society commensurate with the resources it consumes. The process is more than just pushing out messages; it requires listening, engaging, and aligning the institution's case with donor values. Langley argues that higher education has not listened sufficiently, accounting in part for disaffection and a decline in the number of individuals providing philanthropic support.

CASE (n.d.) defines *advancement* as a "strategic, integrated method of managing relationships." The key word is *integrated*. As described in chapter 2 of this volume, in the past several decades, the advancement disciplines have become increasingly integrated in *structure*, with chief advancement officers holding responsibility for their overall operation. But, as Michael Eicher observes in chapter 5, the reality remains that "more often than not, advancement is nothing more than a collection of kindred professions, working with related audiences, using similar tools, all in service to the university's leadership but hardly classified as a fully integrated operation."

In a time when higher education faces challenges, this unfortunate reality stands in the way of achieving institutional goals. Eicher argues that integration can be achieved and discusses approaches to accomplishing that objective. He points out, "Advancement, at its best, exists to steward the relationships of its loyal and caring constituents. While the component units' metrics may be different, every advancement professional should care about making the lives of the people we serve better in meaningful ways."

REFERENCE

CASE (Council for Advancement and Support of Education). n.d. "About Advancement." Accessed March 23, 2018. http://www.case.org/About_CASE/About_Advancement.html.

THREE

Strategy as the Foundation for Advancement

Darrow Zeidenstein

The American journalist and commentator Thomas Friedman morphed a famous Thomas Edison quote to declare, "[A] vision without resources is an hallucination" (Friedman 2007). Higher-education leadership understands Friedman's point. Implementation of a vision depends on securing financial resources. This is the reason a lengthy and expensive fundraising campaign invariably follows on the heels of a college or university strategic plan. This pattern of *strategic plan → institutional goals → campaign priorities* is now established orthodoxy and considered best practice among fundraising consulting firms (Semple Bixel Associates, n.d.).

Additionally, a good strategic plan not only articulates what the institution seeks to accomplish, but it also provides the information or narrative necessary to convince key donors to support that vision with their philanthropy. University planning consultant Karen Hinton aptly notes, "In the highly competitive world of institutional advancement, any fundraising campaign is dependent on its ability to offer information about the institution that is attractive to donors" (2012, 38).

Finally, there is governance. A good strategic-planning process, in theory, has engaged an institution's faculty and has received some sort of academic imprimatur to prevent the advancement tail from wagging the university dog.

STRATEGIC PLANNING AND THE CAMPAIGN

As seemingly sound and as clearly conventional the pattern of *strategic plan → institutional goals → campaign priorities* appears, there are good reasons to believe this way of going about planning for the fundraising campaign may not always be optimal. For example, does an institution carry on with a comprehensive campaign when the strategic-planning process was widely viewed as flawed and demotivating?

From a different perspective, does a focused campaign effort, perhaps directed at student scholarships and career development, need to be enshrined in a university's strategic plan to be successful in raising funds? Does a university seeking to increase its campaign goal and extend its campaign time frame need to undertake a strategic-planning process in order to develop new and timely fundraising priorities from those developed six or more years ago?

These commonplace examples drive home the point that strategic planning is not necessarily a prerequisite to high-impact, strategic fundraising. The argument of this chapter is that the relationship between institutional strategic planning and campaign planning, however executed, is not as simple and sequential as conventional wisdom contends.

This is not to say that strategic planning is trivial or unimportant or that a fundraising campaign should be thrown together on a whim. Rather, strategic planning and campaign planning are both very important and potentially impactful on the institution, but it is the institution's context and its leaders' strategic motivations within that context that should dictate what these processes are and what the outcomes should be.

Put in different terms, institutions do not necessarily need strategic planning to develop the kind of big, strategic ideas needed to power a successful fundraising effort, be it a focused fundraising initiative or a grand, comprehensive campaign. Likewise, some elements of campaign planning—such as feasibility testing and engagement of principal-gift donors in an institution's strategic thinking—may be crucial parts of an institution's strategic process to develop big ideas.

CONTEXT IS EVERYTHING

Rand Corporation's Charles A. Goldman and Hanine Salem argue that university strategic planning is more effective when the process is *"orient-*

ed toward specific motivations [italics original]" (2015, 3). The authors go on to indicate a range of internal and external motivations, such as institutional values, competition, reduction in funding sources, and the like (Goldman and Salem 2015, 3).

Implied in this formulation is a deeper institutional *context*, a set of internal and external factors motivating or demotivating the need for the institution to undertake some sort of planning to achieve strategic goals. While motivations may drive the goals of a strategic-planning process, the context should drive the fundamental parameters of any sort of strategic visioning or planning process, including timing, scope, and implementation.

A brief hypothetical case clarifies the importance of context. Suppose public University ABC has a president who is likely to announce her retirement at the end of the academic year, but the institution also faces potentially acute cutbacks in public financial support over the coming few years. In this context the *strategic plan → institutional goals → campaign priorities* sequence is inappropriate. A long, two-year strategic-planning process that cuts across a presidential transition is imprudent. Similarly, a comprehensive campaign as an outcome will not replace base funding cuts in the short term and probably will not make much of a dent in the budget shortfall, even over the long term.

In this scenario, University ABC will be decidedly better served by forming a tiger team—a group convened under urgent circumstances to take on an important problem and develop agile and possibly innovative solutions. The tiger team for University ABC should be comprised of representatives from across the university and should undertake scenario- and budget-contingency planning to focus fundraising on a very small number of crucial priorities, such as unrestricted or budget-relieving funds, or to bolster funding for mission-critical priorities, such as faculty recruitment and retention in a time of fiscal stress.

The hypothetical case of University ABC sheds light on the salient factors that should be present to undertake the typical, long-term strategic-planning process. First and foremost, the institution needs to be in a place of stable governance so that it can afford to take the time to do long-range planning. Unrest among board fiduciaries, a period of possible presidential transition, or both are obviously not optimal times to undertake strategic planning.

Second, the institution must have its finances in reasonably good order so that immediate and urgent fiscal pressures do not impinge upon
long-term strategic planning. Finally, as the opening quote of this chapter
declares, the institution needs to be in a position to fund the plan or to
invest in revenue operations, such as advancement.

LEADERS' STRATEGIC MOTIVATIONS

In a highly cited critique of strategic planning within the scholarly litera-
ture, management professor Henry Mintzberg (1994) posits the following
important distinction between strategic planning and strategic thinking:
"Strategic planning isn't strategic thinking. One is analysis, and the other
is synthesis." Mintzberg goes on to declare that "strategic planning often
spoils strategic thinking" by conflating successful strategies as plans with
metrics and numbers rather than visions. For Mintzberg, organizational
vision making is about synthesizing information of all kinds and from all
directions to chart a new direction for the entire organization.

Such acts of strategic thinking rarely emerge from a formal planning
process, and synthesis is about rethinking and possibly inventing "new
categories, not rearranging old ones," under which an institution plans
(Mintzberg 1994).

In the context of this discussion, Mintzberg's (1994) distinction can be
framed as follows: Strategic planning for universities is fundamentally an
exercise in *incrementally* improving what they do and scaling up who
they are, whereas strategic thinking is about formulating a new direction
for the university that entails a new strategy to realize it. For example,
digital technologies offer a way for universities to rethink a range of
categories, such as "student," "alumni," "textbooks," and "campus." Rice
University recently approved a strategic plan that implicitly embraces
this notion of strategic thinking, especially with respect to how a relatively small research university can have global impact (Rice University,
n.d.).

Leaders' strategic motivations are crucial to keep in mind when trying
to figure out whether a strategic-thinking or a strategic-planning process
is the best way to move forward. Strategic motivations are the reasons an
institution's leadership is calling upon the institution to plan and do
things differently.

For example, in the earlier hypothetical example, University ABC may call for a university-wide initiative to reduce wasteful spending and achieve certain efficiency targets because its leaders anticipate declining public investment over the coming years. The strategic motivation here is to reduce spending and husband resources for the lean times ahead. In contrast, University XYZ's leaders may be seeking to expand their institution's global footprint, believing that an institution has to be great globally to be a great university. The motivational intent for University ABC is not to change who the institution is or what they fundamentally do; incremental budget savings can be wrung out of the system by a strategic-planning process that sets targets, proposes tactics, and engages enough stakeholders to make the plan work.

However, University XYZ's strategic motivation is to reimagine or rethink who it is, who its stakeholders are, and even some aspects of its business model on a new, global scale. Before University XYZ can even undertake successful strategic planning, it needs to undertake some sort of strategic-thinking process to imagine a new vision for the enterprise and a broad sense of which strategy it will pursue to get there in alignment with the strategic motivations of the leadership.

MATCHING PROCESS TO MOTIVATIONS

Much of the criticism leveled against university strategic plans may be the result of muddled or misunderstood strategic motivations. In a humorously caustic tirade on how strategic plans are an exercise in administrative power and co-optation to the disservice of faculty, Benjamin Ginsberg (2011) writes, "The interchangeability of visions . . . underscores the fact that the precise content of most colleges' strategic plans is pretty much irrelevant . . . [and] is another reflection and reinforcement of the continuing growth of administrative power." Ginsberg's criticism rings true to many in academia, especially the faculty, because university leaders often do not communicate clearly the strategic motivations driving the nature and scope of the strategic-planning process.

Moreover, the strategic-planning process itself should be contoured to match the strategic motivations. If, for example, university leadership is undertaking a planning process to formulate top priorities for an upcoming comprehensive campaign, it should declare as much and shape the planning process accordingly. A good example of this more explicit approach is Stanford's "long-range planning" process announced in April 2017. Stanford did not use the phrase *strategic planning* and explicitly stated that elements of this process would be used to drive their next campaign (Chesley 2017).

Rice University undertook a streamlined planning process focused on students and involving the president, the dean of undergraduates, key faculty, student leaders, and alumni and parent volunteer leaders. This process took place soon after the completion of a comprehensive campaign, when it was clear there was little appetite to launch a new comprehensive campaign but strategic motivation to maintain alumni and parent engagement and donor momentum. Out of this streamlined planning process emerged Rice's three-year Initiative for Students, an integrated engagement and fundraising effort without an explicit campaign-dollar goal but with annual objectives to be realized (Rice University 2018). Here, we see explicitly an alignment of the following four elements: *strategic motivations → planning process → strategy → plan execution*.

STRATEGY AND THE CHIEF ADVANCEMENT OFFICER

The previous two sections of this chapter argue that universities should not default to the conventional strategic-planning process and the orthodox comprehensive campaign model if either the institutional context or the strategic motivations of university leadership are not aligned to do so. This concluding section turns to the two key roles that the chief university advancement officer must fulfill in supporting the university's strategy development and execution.

The first role of the chief advancement officer in university strategy development is to ensure that external stakeholders are brought into the process in the appropriate way. External stakeholders, such as key donors and influential alumni, not only provide an off-campus point of view but also will be crucial at some point in funding elements of the planning effort.

Recalling Mintzberg's (1994) distinction between strategic thinking and strategic planning discussed earlier in this chapter, external stakeholders in the university enterprise would likely be a good source for unconventional or synthetic reasoning needed to push strategic thinking forward. The chief advancement officer is in the best position to assess the value of external stakeholders to the process and to work with them to ensure their engagement is a meaningful one.

In preparation for writing this chapter, I conducted a survey in August 2018 of the chief advancement officers of sixty leading institutions regarding their strategic planning and received responses from thirty-two. Only nineteen responses could be used because only cases where the chief advancement officer had been a part of the strategic-planning process at her or his institution were relevant to this discussion. While a relatively small sample, these nineteen responses represent some of the most mature and sophisticated university advancement operations in the world. Surprisingly, only about two-thirds of the respondents to the survey noted that current or potential lead donors to the campaign were involved in planning. This is surprisingly low given the importance of obtaining philanthropic revenue to support key elements of university planning.

The second key role of the chief advancement officer is to serve as an advocate for the appropriate nature and scope of institutional planning. This chapter argues that a comprehensive, multiyear, strategic-planning process may not always be the best way to bring forward the biggest and best fundraising priorities, especially if the institutional context and the strategic motivations are not aligned.

Chief advancement officers are professionals with a duty to advise university leadership on how best to develop, execute, and garner the appropriate resources for the strategic priorities and needs of the institution. As one of the (anonymous) respondents to my survey noted, the chief advancement officer needs to "ensure alignment of all stakeholder groups in developing and adopting the process that will be followed. Start with the end in mind."

It is indeed telling that only 42 percent of survey respondents agreed or strongly agreed with the statement that they "would strongly advise the leadership to follow the same process it is following/had followed" in developing its strategic plan. Yet, 95 percent of the survey respondents noted that they were "fully engaged" in the planning process. The disconnect between being fully engaged and not generally recommending the process again suggests that our engagement needs to be at the process-development level and not merely as participants.

Chief advancement officers need to influence the process for strategic thinking or strategic planning as it is being developed if they are to give their advancement teams the optimal chance to raise the right philanthropy in the right way.

CONCLUSION

The picture that emerges from this discussion is one that is both more exciting and liberating to the chief advancement officer and more broadly to all advancement staff who have a vested interest in strategic planning. Chief advancement officers need to be deeply engaged in understanding the strategic motivations of institutional leadership and supporting a process of strategy development that aligns with those motivations. This means that the chief advancement officer should not be merely the officer in charge of the fundraising but also the one who harnesses the ideas and energies of stakeholders to push institutional strategic thinking forward.

Similarly, the chief advancement officer may need to lead her or his team to develop a fundraising approach that is not the tried and true multiyear comprehensive campaign to meet the crucial needs of the institution's strategy, even if doing so is hard, may result in less overall philanthropy, and may make advancement officers and key volunteers uncomfortable at first.

At the end of the day, the chief advancement officer should be evaluated by how effectively her or his team has been in supporting the appropriate strategy process and the resulting plan's fundraising objectives, not simply by how much of an arbitrary fundraising goal has been realized.

REFERENCES

Chesley, Kate. 2017. "President, Provost Launch University-Wide Planning Process." *Stanford News*, April 4, 2017. https://news.stanford.edu/2017/04/04/president-provost-launch-university-wide-planning-process/.

Friedman, Thomas L. 2007. "Live Bad, Go Green." *New York Times*, July 8, 2007. https://www.nytimes.com/2007/07/08/opinion/08friedman.html.

Ginsberg, Benjamin. 2011. "The Strategic Plan: Neither Strategy nor Plan, but a Waste of Time." *Chronicle of Higher Education*, July 17, 2011. https://www.chronicle.com/article/The-Strategic-Plan-Neither/128227.

Goldman, Charles A., and Hanine Salem. 2015. *Getting the Most Out of University Strategic Planning: Essential Guidance for Success and Obstacles to Avoid.* Santa Monica, CA: Rand. https://www.rand.org/content/dam/rand/pubs/perspectives/PE100/PE157/RAND_PE157.pdf.

Hinton, Karen E. 2012. *A Practical Guide to Strategic Planning in Higher Education*. Ann Arbor, MI: Society for College and University Planning. https://oira.cortland.edu/webpage/planningandassessmentresources/planningresources/SCPGuideonPlanning.pdf.

Mintzberg, Henry. 1994. "The Fall and Rise of Strategic Planning." *Harvard Business Review* (January–February). https://hbr.org/1994/01/the-fall-and-rise-of-strategic-planning.

Rice University. n.d. "Overview." Accessed October 22, 2018. https://v2c2.rice.edu/overview.

———. 2018. "Initiative for Students Impact Report." http://giving.rice.edu/student-initiative.

Semple Bixel Associates. n.d. "The Role of Strategic Planning in Fundraising." Accessed October 22, 2018. http://semplebixel.com/wp-content/uploads/2012/01/the_role_of_strategic_planning_in_fundraising.pdf.

FOUR

Marketing and Communications

James M. Langley

Marketing research, as defined by the Marketing Accountability Standards Board, is designed to yield "information used to identify and define marketing opportunities and problems," then develop the "information required to address these issues" (MASB 2018). Marketing, according to the same source, uses that research to inform an array of "processes for creating, communicating, delivering, and exchanging offerings that have value for customers, clients, partners, and society at large." Strategic communications is the means by which that information is creatively and compellingly delivered to target audiences.

MARKETING CHALLENGE TO HIGHER EDUCATION

Higher education now confronts a classic marketing challenge. Regardless of whether it is recognized as such by campus leaders or not, the challenge is so pervasive that it will form and inform the context for all campus-specific marketing and communications. This challenge is the questioning of the essential value proposition of higher education by many individuals and by society at large. One of its most troubling manifestations is the growing disconnection between higher education's private-funding aspirations and the dwindling number of individual donors responding to them.

Vivid evidence of this trend can be seen in data on giving to American higher education by source over the past decade. In the data for 2017 (see table 4.1), we see the continuation of a trend. Foundations have eclipsed alumni as the largest source of support, a phenomenon that first occurred in 2002. Even if alumni giving through family foundations were excluded from these totals, the net result would be the same. Compare these numbers to overall giving for all charitable purposes in the United States by source in the same year (see table 4.2).

Higher education is attracting less support from individuals, the largest philanthropic source, and by a wide margin. Higher education is also attracting less support from what traditionally has been its most likely source of strong individual support: alumni. Both total alumni support, measured by dollars given each year, and the rate of alumni participation, or the percentage of all alumni giving to their alma mater annually, have been declining for more than two decades. Causes and symptoms of that erosion include:

- Tuition increases that outstripped the consumer price index over three decades, leaving an ever-larger percentage of alumni in debt, while the size and real earning power of the middle class is shrinking.
- More alumni concluding that the value of their education did not exceed the cost or that they have paid so much in tuition that they do not wish to give more to the institution.
- Changing philanthropic attitudes and values for generations that followed the baby boomers, resulting in their favoring grassroots causes, particularly those that offer hands-on volunteering and an outlet for their talents and passions.
- An overall decline in the percentage of Americans giving to charitable causes and purposes, albeit more recent and less pronounced than the twenty-five-year decline in alumni giving.

Table 4.1.   *CAE, 2018, p. 2*

Alumni	$11.37 billion	26.1%
Nonalumni individuals	$7.86 billion	18.0%
Corporations	$6.60 billion	15.1%
Foundations	$13.13 billion	30.1%
Other	$4.64 billion	10.6%

Table 4.2. *Giving USA, 2018*

Individuals	79%
Foundations	16%
Corporations	5%

This erosion has occurred even as the total amount given to higher education has increased. The record totals have been driven by increasingly larger gifts from fewer, older, wealthier donors. This reflects a continuation of the dollars-up/donors-down phenomenon that most institutions of higher learning have experienced in the past decade and beyond. Further, the dollars-up phenomenon has proven especially true for the twenty most elite institutions, which receive one-third of the total given to all of higher education by individuals and foundations.

While the current and projected impact of lost individual support varies according to institution, all of higher education has been and will be affected. The trend portends a further erosion of individual support in direct proportion to the mortality of baby boomers.

More responsive and adaptive marketing and communication tactics are essential to stemming this trend. Current and future efforts must be rooted in more extensive and more finely attuned market research that will allow institutions to listen better and react more adroitly to the hopes and concerns of individual donors.

In high-functioning institutions, listening and responding to constituent concerns is not relegated to market researchers who are asked to conduct the occasional survey. Instead, it is a way of being. Such institutions listen through a variety of means and work to bring the most important information to the top of the organization, where it can be turned into responsive communication and outreach.

ROLE OF MARKETING AND COMMUNICATIONS PROFESSIONALS

Marketing and communications professionals in higher education, working in close collaboration with their colleagues in development, must help create a stronger institutional ethic around the importance of structured, integrative listening, with a particular emphasis on individual alumni donors and prospects. When this is achieved, these professionals must take the lead in aggregating what has been heard and converting it into responsive messages and engagement strategies that resonate. They must be mindful of the opportunity to capture valuable information when any member of the advancement staff or overall institution interacts personally with any donor or prospect. They must also try to remediate lost or suboptimized listening opportunities that occur when:

- Gift officers qualify new prospects on the basis of hunches rather than on evidence yielded from a structured interview designed to surface, codify, and record their deepest philanthropic motivations.
- Donor or prospect contact reports are filed for the sole purpose of building individual profiles rather than being cross-referenced to track larger donor trends.
- Individual responses to telephone or electronic appeals are not aggregated and studied for what they reveal about trending donor attitudes.
- Events do not have interactive elements or, at least, follow-up processes.
- Cases for support or other collateral material are developed in splendid isolation and then sprung on unsuspecting prospects rather than by engaging donors during conceptual stages.
- Institutions launch strategic plans that have not involved or been vetted by key donor segments, such as major gift donors, loyalists who have given ten years or more, or estate givers.
- Institutions engage in all-send/no-receive communication or otherwise seek to rah-rah, browbeat, nag, guilt-trip, or lecture their prospects into philanthropic submission.

LISTENING AND COMMUNICATING IMPACT

The first order of business in marketing and communications is always to make the best use of everyday listening tools, then seek to augment or clarify that information with selective, strategic listening exercises, including:

- Focus groups
- Intimate salon events (in which a group of ten to twenty people are invited to review and contribute to the development of a new initiative)

- Requests for individual feedback to white papers describing early-stage initiatives
- Donor-satisfaction interviews or surveys
- Debriefing volunteers to see if their time and talents have been well used
- Alumni surveys
- Web-based spot polls
- Post-event surveys

The more ways institutions find to listen, the more they learn and the faster they can detect and repair any fissures with individuals or groups of donors, and the more they validate the values and generosity of their donors, thereby strengthening their affinity. The results of these and other listening exercises should then be used to inform four interrelated objectives that, if pursued in earnest, will lead to higher, broader, and more sustainable levels of private support. They are:

1. Define the institution's niche and describe in specific, distinct, and compelling ways the benefit it renders to its charges and to the larger society.
2. Offer specific portals through which alumni and other key constituents can engage with their institutions in pursuit of the former.
3. Develop cases for support that explain how and where specific levels of philanthropic investments in their institutions will generate significant, sustainable societal returns.
4. Demonstrate complete accountability to their various stakeholders and to society at large.

Defining the Institution's Niche

If the first objective is to be met, then more higher-education leaders, working with their marketing and communications teams, need to define the rationales for campaigns or even annual fundraising activities more by mission impacts to be achieved than by the dollars to be raised. With few donors giving simply because an institution is in a campaign and even fewer giving to help institutions to meet their goals, it becomes imperative for institutions to speak more clearly about where they intend to make a greater difference given their unique educational, cultural, historical, and geographical assets.

The end goal of these efforts should be the realization of specific, significant, sustainable societal impacts. With so many institutions embracing the same themes—such as green, global, and interdisciplinary—it is important to differentiate an institution's unique approach, unique capabilities, and specific goals.

Offering Specific Portals for Engagement

Meeting the first objective creates the foundation from which the second objective can be more readily met: constituent engagement. The causality between constituent engagement and giving has long been known. The more deeply involved alumni or other constituents become, the more likely they are to give and give generously. However, droves of alumni are staying away from traditional alumni events and social gatherings.

With the rise of social media, fewer look to their alma maters to connect them with friends. With more couples working longer hours, fewer alumni are interested in coming back for broad social purposes or just to have fun. In the years ahead, the most attractive and productive engagement activities will be those designed to attract civic-minded and purpose-driven alumni and others.

When individuals are afforded opportunities to lend their time and talent and to work through institutions of higher education to pursue the purposes and outcomes that resonate most deeply with their values, their treasure will naturally follow. Numerous studies show this is the key to engaging greater numbers of younger alumni, millennials in particular.

Developing Cases for Support

Achieving the third objective requires marketing and communications professionals, working in concert with fundraising colleagues, academic officers, and others, to develop targeted funding appeals designed to secure the largest levels of support from the most significant philanthropists. They are major and megadonors, whose giving often constitutes 90 to 95 percent of total giving to an institution, on both an annual basis or over the course of a campaign.

Targeted appeals are essential because these donors are and will be much less inclined to provide unrestricted support. According to *The 2016 US Trust Study of High Net Worth Philanthropy: Charitable Practices and Preferences of Wealthy Households*, "The great majority (76.8 percent) reported donating to *neither capital nor endowment campaigns*. Only 11.1 percent of high net worth individuals indicated they contributed only to a capital campaign, and 8.7 percent indicated they donated to both a capital and endowment campaign" (US Trust and the Indiana University Lilly Family School of Philanthropy 2016, 24).

Securing support from these all-important prospects, therefore, is less about making a broad case for institutional efficacy and more about microtargeted appeals that demonstrate how specific and unique institutional capabilities, if appropriately funded, will deliver measurable results to areas and fields those donors care about most. These donors will be less interested in alleviating the needs of your institution, no matter how pressing, and more inclined to leverage your strengths. They will be less likely to reward your institution for what it has done and more likely to invest in what it proposes to do.

Communications and marketing professionals must understand and help their institutions respond to these propensities. Increasingly, they will find themselves applying lessons learned from larger commercial markets, especially the need to segment their messages to appeal more strongly to niche markets.

While major and mega gifts require highly personalized approaches, it must be remembered that even loyal donors will give more when institutions listen for and respond to their most closely held values. This is true at every level of giving—including annual, major, and estate giving.

The sooner institutions can forge alignments with first-time or early-stage donors, the more they will be able to sustain their support. The more they sustain support by showing donors how their broader values and purposes are being advanced by giving through their organizations, the more donors will continue to invest and, when their means increase, to give more.

In the vast majority of instances, the bulk of an advancement operation's efforts should be directed to the retention of current donors. The reason is simple: Donors are by far the most likely sources of future support. In addition, donors who give regularly are more likely to make major gifts and arrange for bequests to the institution. Donor retention, therefore, is the best way to build a richer pipeline of major gifts, estate gifts, and blends of the two.

To protect any fundraising gains, marketing and communications professionals need to use their expertise to detect early warning signs of donor attrition. This can be done by mining donor records and tracking donor trends within key segments, including alumni by generation and gender, parents and alumni parents, loyal donors, and recently lapsed donors. In these segments, they must look for clues that might reveal where and why current support is waxing and waning and which reinforcing or corrective actions need to be taken. (In chapter 7 of this book, Daniel Frezza expands on the use of such metrics in managing the annual giving program.)

Marketing professionals need to form strong alliances with their advancement colleagues in the field to ensure that they are asking the right questions of their donors; hearing what those donors are trying to tell them; and relaying that field intelligence to some central repository, where it can be synthesized to guide the development of more effective communication strategies.

Demonstrating Complete Accountability

Realizing the fourth objective is essential to sustaining and widening circles of giving over time. Demonstrating institutional accountability goes well beyond the traditional understanding of stewardship, which has been generally seen as the need to thank donors in a timely way, provide due and proportionate donor recognition, and generate customized reports to major gift donors. Those activities are of immense importance; however, many donors feel that they are adequately thanked and recognized for their gifts, while not all of them think they are sufficiently informed as to the impact of their giving.

Many studies have demonstrated that donors would give more if they better understood the impact of their giving. Demonstrating institutional accountability, therefore, is the acceptance of an obligation to convert any and all investments, in this case private support, as effectively and economically possible, into significant and lasting results. It must be embraced, demonstrated, communicated, and personally modeled, especially by those in the highest echelons if it is to become an institutional ethic.

These are the ways by which colleges and universities can more closely match their capabilities and aspirations to current and emerging philanthropic interests. Doing so strengthens the fact and perception of institutional viability and relevance and thereby foster the building of broader and stronger communities of shared purpose. Indeed, the missed opportunities and struggles we see in the present can invariably be traced back to the inability of institutions to listen in the past, to pick up cues about changing interests and tastes or the early murmurings of discontent, and to adjust accordingly.

CONCLUSION

An institution's ability to listen in the present determines its ability to seize opportunity and avoid constituent loss in the future. Marketing and communications professionals must be the chief advocates of objective listening, the architects of effective constituent intelligence gathering, the framers of messages that correspond to what their market research has revealed, and (when necessary) the sounders of alarms when the direction of an institution starts to veer from the hopes and interests of those who are most apt to support it. In a prescient article in *Trusteeship Magazine*, Brandon Busteed of Gallup writes,

> There's a coming data revolution in higher education, but it's not the "big data" revolution that many have been hyping. This revolution will be more about the *right* data than *bigger* data. And it's not data on traditional education metrics, but rather data that have been largely — indeed, embarrassingly — missing from higher education. *This revolution will be about the voices of consumers and constituents in higher education. . . . And it will usher in a new era of rigorously tracking the expectations, experiences, emotions, and outcomes of students, alumni, staff, and faculty in the spirit of understanding how institutions of higher education are performing, and how they can improve.* (2016; italics added)

The implicit criticism in Busteed's prediction is that higher education, in the main, has not listened as attentively as it should have to its alumni and other key constituents. In saying that a revolution will come, he is really saying that a revolution must come if higher education is to correct its course and strengthen or reestablish its value in the minds of its most important constituents. When the revolution comes, it will not be across the entire landscape of higher education. It will arise from the most capably led and broadly accountable institutions. At such institutions, the most capable marketing and communications professionals will be at the vanguard of that revolution.

REFERENCES

Busteed, Brandon. 2016. "The REAL Data Revolution." *Trusteeship Magazine* (July/August). https://www.agb.org/trusteeship/2016/julyaugust/the-real-data-revolution.

CAE (Council for Aid to Education). 2018. "Voluntary Support of Education 2017." Press release, February 6, 2018. https://www.case.org/Documents/Research/VSE/VSE-2017-Press-Release.pdf.

Giving USA Foundation. 2018. *Giving USA 2018: The Annual Report on Philanthropy for the Year 2017*. Chicago: Giving USA Foundation. https://givingusa.org/tag/giving-usa-2018/.

MASB (Marketing Accountability Standards Board). 2018. *Common Language Marketing Dictionary*. http://marketing-dictionary.org/m/marketing/.

US Trust and the Indiana University Lilly Family School of Philanthropy. 2016. *The 2016 US Trust Study of High Net Worth Philanthropy: Charitable Practices and Preferences of Wealthy Households*. New York: US Trust Philanthropic Solutions and Family Office Group. https://www.ustrust.com/publish/content/application/pdf/GWMOL/USTp_ARMCGDN7_oct_2017.pdf.

FIVE

The Integrated Advancement Program

Michael C. Eicher

"You want me to do *what*?"

That was the reaction of a young development officer when his institution's government relations director asked him to approach a donor and request that he travel to the state capital, four hundred miles away, to spend the day talking with legislators about the importance of the university. "And by the way," the director continued, "it would make things much easier if we could travel on his private jet."

The idea seemed crazy. The development officer had a carefully crafted plan for this donor, and the strategy for a really big ask did not include imposing on him. Requesting his valuable time and the use of his personal airplane was surely going to take things down the wrong path.

It was easy to understand why the government relations director wanted the donor's help. Of course he would be influential with elected officials. He was a prominent citizen who had a history of giving to political causes. The problem was that this ask was not part of the development agenda. It had nothing to do with fundraising goals or the development officer's performance metrics. Besides, the donor had a relationship *with the development officer,* and this project was going to bring him into contact with many other university staff, possibly distracting him from the path to a major gift.

The alarm bells were very loud. What if the donor said, "No"? What if he said, "*No!*"? Wouldn't that make the solicitation harder or even ruin a beautifully developed, professional, tidy, and well-ordered strategy altogether? After all, wasn't the value of this individual's personal time and transportation cost already approaching a significant gift? Stonewalling seemed the only option—delaying long enough that the government relations officer would just move on to find someone else to ask some other donor to perform this service.

But time helps bring many problems into perspective. After a few days of thinking about the options and running through all the worst-case scenarios, the development officer relented and, with some trepidation, asked the donor to assist the university in this way. The response was instantaneous and enthusiastic: "Happy to help! When should we go?" The donor was flattered to be asked to do something meaningful for the university he valued. He had something important to offer and felt pleased to be appreciated for more than his financial support.

After the trip, instead of being distracted, the donor was energized and excited. Spending the day talking about the university deepened his relationship with his alma mater. He had been helpful with our legislators, and he knew it. The donor effectively advocated for the university and, in the process, moved one step closer to making a significant gift. In hindsight, the day at the state capital accelerated the plan for this individual and increased the odds that the next solicitation would be met with open arms.

The young development officer in this story is the author of this chapter, and these events happened twenty years ago. The lessons from that experience have informed an understanding of how the pieces of advancement fit together and how advancement connects with the greater university community in support of its mission.

The foundation of a fully integrated advancement model rests on three important principles: (1) shared goals that connect advancement units to each other; (2) leadership that works to integrate the assets and resources of advancement across its traditional functions and concentrates the organization on the most essential issues rather than the most urgent; and (3) broader partnerships, greater involvement of our community, and an expanded view of who contributes to advancement's success.

INTEGRATION STARTS WITH COMMON GOALS

Unfortunately, more often than not, advancement is nothing more than a collection of kindred professions, working with related audiences, using similar tools, all in service to the university's leadership but hardly classified as a fully integrated operation. Each element of an advancement team has its own proud history, its own culture, and its own distinct metrics that delineate the nature of its businesses. They exist side by side, functioning as associated but as separate administrative units with very little in common except geography. They are not operating as a team.

A team is a group of individuals working together to achieve a goal. Teams are described and measured by those goals. A sports team's goal is to win. A business team's goal may be to beat the competition to market with a new and better product. A disaster response team's goals are to save lives and reduce suffering. Without shared goals, a team is merely a group. So what is the advancement team's goal, its reason to exist? This is not a question related to how the staff is organized or who reports to whom. It is a much more fundamental question: Are we really a team?

A team knows why it exists, what its goals are, and how success is defined. More importantly, all members of the team know their roles, and they trust others to play their assigned positions. They are dependent on each other to achieve a goal that is larger than any single member could realize alone, and the very composition of the team is reliant on members' complementary strengths to address key challenges. The most accomplished teams are not filled with replicas of one another but are made up of people from different backgrounds, with varied worldviews and a range of skill sets. The more diverse the team's membership is, the more likely it is to develop creative, new solutions to challenging problems.

So what are the common purposes, goals, and objectives that bind together the components of advancement and make it a team? Every advancement program will formulate this a little differently, but it deserves careful thought and consideration because the forces that pull the advancement disciplines apart—as fundamental as language, culture, and metrics—can seem stronger than the things that tie them together. The more explicitly leaders describe shared targets and common metrics, the more valuable the team and its programs will be.

At Ohio State, one of the things that unites the advancement functions is a common concern with moving our audiences along a three-step path:

the journey from knowing about the university to caring about it to believing that together we can do important things for society and the world.

The challenge all advancement professionals share is to continue deepening relationships with our community of friends, alumni, donors, patients, current and prospective students, parents, academic colleagues, and many others. It is a venture that cuts across advancement. It is a mission that unites us in a single pursuit: the unending desire to expand the network of those whom we can count on as friends, investors, and advocates.

This simple framework for defining our collective purpose is not about transactions but about long-term, personalized relationships. It is a single-minded approach that has brought the formerly isolated advancement functions closer together and made us dramatically more effective. Defining the annual giving program as equally a fundraising strategy, an early-engagement approach, and a first-rate messaging opportunity and housing it within alumni relations rather than development has led to impressive results that buck the national trends for declining participation.

Similarly, labeling the alumni magazine as a joint responsibility of the marketing team and the alumni-relations staff and closely connecting it to the development operation led to a total overhaul of the publication. Individuals from all three areas recently worked together to rethink the purpose, frequency, look, feel, and metrics for the magazine. The results were uniformly applauded as a big step forward for Ohio State's effort to engage its expansive alumni community.

The best example of common goals and purpose is the approach we have taken to campaign planning. Campaigns are commonly thought of as the exclusive purview of the development team. By making campaign planning an effort that encompasses all of the advancement team, we have broadened the campaign's reach, set loftier goals, engaged a broader audience of volunteers and alumni, and increased our commitment to each other. Campaigns are, after all, marketing constructs, with aimed messaging, targeted audiences, and inherent urgency that drives action. They are a perfect framework for mounting a more active and productive cross-advancement approach.

In 2018, Ohio State was in the planning phase of a campaign. We used this as an opportunity to collect and share our community's stories with audiences that go well beyond the traditional donor population. It was a special moment to express who we are and why our work is important to society, as well as an opportunity to concentrate our alumni communications on our future and to develop messages that enhance our institution's reputation. Advancement units bring their unique perspectives and skills together to form a more complete, productive, and sophisticated effort. Our constituents become crucial audiences for the campaign message, whether they are donor prospects or not.

This understanding about a broader-than-fundraising view of campaigns dictates that campaign goals are far more than just numbers with dollar signs and that planning involves colleagues from all aspects of advancement. Campaign strategies are approached from marketing, engagement, alumni relations, and development perspectives, and goals are not finalized unless they are approved by the entire advancement leadership team. At the celebratory conclusion of the campaign, the entire advancement team, and frankly the entire university, should collectively shout, "We did it!" not "Way to go, Development!"

INTEGRATIVE LEADERSHIP

The key to a fully integrated advancement program is visionary and dynamic leadership that understands how the pieces of our discipline fit together seamlessly. The function of leadership should not be confused with management. Management is related to the position one holds in the organization. It is concerned with very important issues like order, reducing risk, organization, and proper administration. Leadership, on the other hand, is a mind-set, a way of approaching a task. Anyone in the organization can exercise leadership. In the advancement profession, as in many others, effective leadership is a precious commodity.

The US Department of the Army defines a leader as "anyone who by virtue of assumed role or assigned responsibility inspires and influences people to accomplish organizational goals. Leaders motivate people, both inside and outside the chain of command to pursue actions, focus thinking, and shape decisions for the greater good of the organization" (2015, 1.13).

In a fully integrated advancement program, sound management is necessary, but enlightened leadership is crucial. Leadership is about creativity, embracing risk, bold innovation, and taking accountability for decisions made. It is about being curious; finding new pathways; sharing ideas; and learning from our academic partners, volunteers, and colleagues. It is also about developing talent; helping individuals explore their potential and their career aspirations; and—perhaps most importantly—fostering the next generation of directors, executives, and vice presidents.

Successful leadership depends on the ability to prioritize issues and ask the right questions. Richard Chait, professor of education emeritus at the Harvard Graduate School of Education, is a renowned expert and author in the field of governance and leadership in colleges and universities. He argues, "What great governance does, what great leadership does, is it selects and frames the problems" (Chait 2005, 1). In essence, a leader chooses which problems to spend time on and which ones to kick down the road. Individuals may come up with very different solutions to problems depending on how they articulate the central concern.

When Chait (2005) reflects on framing a problem, he emphasizes the importance of asking the right questions. Leaders need to be methodical in asking why before addressing how, when, or where. The first is a strategic question. The others are tactical. Probing for the widest range of conceivable solutions to address a looming challenge often resets our thinking in ways that lead to better outcomes.

An approach the advancement leadership team at Ohio State has adopted is to think backward. That means imagining what outcome is desired before considering options for a solution. It is often more constructive and more efficient to focus on defining the best possible conclusion to an urgent and important difficulty before deciding what our action steps will be. Leaders in every position in the advancement organization need to be empowered and trained to ask the right questions in the right order.

A few years ago, a team of advancement staff from across the disciplines at Ohio State, including individuals with various levels of seniority, was charged with designing the campaign-closing event. They started by framing the task in a novel way. First, *event* became *experience*. This subtle but important reframing allowed them to think not just about creating a dinner or some similar evening affair but about redefining the audience to include people who were distributed around the globe.

Even more importantly, instead of beginning with typical planning questions ("Where will we have the event?" "Who will attend?" "When will it be?" "How much will it cost?"), they changed their emphasis. They started by asking "How do we want our participants to feel after the experience?" Their answer, based on a series of focus groups, was multi-faceted: proud, surprised, motivated, and eager to engage even more deeply. This insight made all the difference. It pointed them to the right issues, drove creativity, emboldened them, and in the end led to the best campaign closing anyone could imagine.

Asking the right questions and framing the problem as developing emotional connections with our constituents rather than as the planning of a special dinner completely transformed the finale. The staff learned to fixate on the important, not the urgent. They had fun, bonded with each other, and were ultimately so proud of what they accomplished that they have taken the lessons learned to every corner of the advancement organization. They became leaders in their own right and role models for dozens of other aspiring advancement leaders.

Clearly, the pace of change in advancement has increased rapidly over the last several decades. Today's leaders need to be especially nimble and particularly discerning regarding which changes present threats, which are opportunities, and which are innocuous. They are called upon daily to make important priority decisions that do not have clear right and wrong answers.

Fundamental questions to be addressed include "Should I concentrate on projects that will produce immediate results or ventures that will take years to mature?" "Should I hire another major gift officer knowing the return on that investment is likely to be fairly soon or spend additional resources building the alumni-engagement strategies, recognizing the payoff on that investment will take significantly longer to be realized?" "Should a leader emphasize building brand strategies or a data analytics team?" "Should I focus on culture or fiscal year-end results?" "Should I be more concerned with engagement or dollars?"

None of these choices represent simple binary decisions but instead are dependent on short-term versus long-term objectives that need to be carefully considered and balanced. I am an advocate for metrics-driven cultures, however these values repeatedly drive us to make decisions that favor immediate and urgent objectives, leaving long-term growth for someone else to handle. The profession requires leaders who can balance these needs if we are to perform at the highest levels.

INTEGRATION WITHIN AND ACROSS THE UNIVERSITY

The elements of advancement are interdependent. Each one's achievements hinge on the accomplishments of the others. Fundraising cannot attain its full potential unless alumni engagement and the university's branding and marketing functions are also strong and vibrant. The same can be said from the perspective of any of the other units. Advancement is able to flourish only when each of its functions understands, supports, and relies on the others.

The great thing about working in our field is that it brings us into contact with just about every aspect of the university. The university depends on us. The flip side is that our productivity is dependent on the great work of others. It is limiting to think of advancement, even a fully integrated operation, as a self-contained whole.

Framing the integrated advancement office as only the work of the disciplines of marketing, communications, alumni relations, development, and advancement services invites others to believe that advancement is a delegated, independent responsibility, concentrated within the confines of a specific staff team. In reality, advancement is linked to every aspect of the university in one way or another. It is also influenced by every facet of the university's operation.

Advancement should be the concern of the governing board, president or chancellor, academic and administrative leadership, faculty, alumni, volunteers, donors, and friends. The entire university community needs to be engaged. The highest-performing integrated advancement shops take pains to outline their scope of work and boundaries in an inclusive way. There is very little anyone in advancement can do alone.

The trick is to express the work of advancement as the duty of many individuals without defining the work so broadly as to lose accountability and the core responsibility for the work. It is possible to devise ways for many people to be involved and still have a highly metrics-driven and accountable advancement team, but it takes great effort to clearly define everyone's role in such a way as to assign responsibility without giving up control.

Shortly after I arrived to be senior vice president for advancement at Ohio State, Dr. Justin Fincher was hired to be chief of staff. He was young but smart and knowledgeable well beyond his years. The advancement functions had only recently been merged, so the whole concept of an integrated program, while strongly endorsed by the university's leadership, was not well developed. Our charge was to build a high-functioning, fully integrated program that lived up to its lofty aspirations and incredible potential.

Justin had a rather simple mandate: Figure out how to get stuff done. The senior vice president would need to be out in the community and would need to spend time filling vacant positions. Meanwhile, Justin's job was to learn the strengths of the team in order to get a sense of who was doing what and whether things were organized for optimum performance. He was good at his job, and the advancement team soon learned to trust him and readily sought his advice.

He proceeded in a way that showed instinctive understanding about advancement and its place in the university: He set out to find the staff in other units whose job, like his, was to get stuff done. He went to the Office of the President, Legal Affairs, Student Affairs, Academic Affairs, Facilities and Planning, and a half-dozen other departments looking for the individuals we would need if advancement was going to be fully successful. In other words, he tracked down that most precious of resources, the other "doers" in the university. Through this process, he built strong relationships and a network, such that anytime we had an issue, he was one phone call away from the person in the other office who could address it.

Justin intuitively realized that the advancement program's growth was 100 percent dependent on partnerships with units that the advancement leadership did not supervise. He understood that the advancement office could not rely just on what it controlled but would need to activate personal relationships and influence to broaden its reach.

In fact, advancement's ability to thrive goes beyond the boundaries of the university. The Ohio State University's prosperity is dependent on and related directly to the fortunes of Columbus, the state of Ohio, and the region. It is related to the achievements of such organizations as the Columbus Foundation, Jobs Columbus, and Columbus 20/20, all important groups focused on strengthening the community. Each one of these organizations is tied to the realization of our brand, our growth, our alumni, and the trust and confidence the community has in our labors, as well as their willingness to invest in us. To view advancement integration as anything narrower is to adopt a competitive and self-defeating stance with those most capable of influencing our mutual achievements.

The university–community relationship is fully reciprocal. Just as we benefit from our communities' strength and well-being, we also help advance the social, economic, and cultural vitality of our communities. Universities are a valuable and integral part of civic life, and the community sets the stage for the realization of advancement's full potential.

CONCLUSION

Advancement at its best exists to steward the relationships of its loyal and caring constituents. While the component units' metrics may be different, every advancement professional should care about making the lives of the people we serve better in meaningful ways.

Since its early roots, which are discussed in chapter 2 of this volume, advancement has developed into a highly professional and essential component of the higher-education landscape. Our teams are larger than ever before and filled with individuals with better skills and more specific expertise. Boards, academic leaders, and the public take great pride in the success of the advancement function, knowing full well the university's dependence on its alumni, friends, and investors for its financial and reputational success. Our goals are the university's goals, but as such, they are a constantly moving target.

Just as asking the donor more than twenty years ago to participate more broadly in the life of the university turned out to be a rewarding and mutually beneficial strategy, advancement leaders must understand the importance of goals that transcend the traditional internal boundaries of advancement. As leaders, we must stay focused despite complex and competing demands, and above all, we must deliver meaningful results for both our current constituents and for those who follow. We must all embrace the concepts of full integration within and beyond the university because, when we do, our institutions thrive and advance.

REFERENCES

Chait, Richard P. 2005. "Governance as Leadership: An Interview with Richard P. Chait." By Barry S. Bader. *Great Boards* (Summer): 1–2. https://www.aisgw.org/wp-content/uploads/2015/10/Chait-Interview.pdf.

US Department of the Army. 2015. *FM 6-22 Leadership Development*. 22nd ed. Vol. 6. Washington, DC: Department of the Army. http://www.milsci.ucsb.edu/sites/secure.lsit.ucsb.edu.mili.d7/files/sitefiles/fm6_22.pdf.

III

Raising Funds from Individuals

The four chapters in this section address the important questions raised in the introduction of this book: "What is working now?" "Where are we going?" and "What will the future of advancement look like?" The authors of these chapters approach those questions with regard to programs that raise funds from individuals, including alumni, parents, and other constituencies.

In chapter 6, Armin Afsahi expands on concepts introduced by James Langley in chapter 4. In a time when some people have become skeptical about the value of higher education and its institutions and when they face many options for their investment of time and resources, we can no longer assume their loyalty. Community must be built and nurtured based on shared values and common interests.

One result of the failure to build community may be declining rates of alumni participation in annual giving, which Daniel Frezza addresses in chapter 7. These two trends are interconnected. Effective annual-giving programs not only raise money but also help to develop long-lasting relationships between individuals and our colleges and universities. Those relationships are, in turn, essential to increased giving.

As discussed in chapter 2, campaigns have become increasingly reliant on large gifts from a small percentage of donors. That points to the importance of major and principal gifts, which Ronald Schiller discusses in chapter 8. Schiller emphasizes that major and principal gifts arise from a partnership between the donor and the institution based on belief and confidence and that many donors today are focused on impact. He also emphasizes how a principal gift is distinguished from a major gift by more than the dollar amount.

The growing importance of planned giving reflects both the maturing of the donor base and the growing financial sophistication of many individuals. In chapter 9, Jeff Comfort describes the process of a planned gift, summarizes some of the basic tools available to practitioners, and identifies current trends, including the growing importance of blended gifts. Comfort concludes that the practice of planned giving, similar to other advancement disciplines, combines science and art.

In discussing the art of planned giving, Comfort agrees with Schiller's conclusion in the preceding chapter and with other authors in this volume: It is about identifying the values and goals that motivate individuals to give and the ways in which our institutions' priorities advance *their* visions of the future.

SIX

Engaging Individuals and Building Community

Armin Afsahi

Advancement is a rewarding profession. As advancement professionals, we have the unique opportunity to lead a versatile, twenty-first-century advancement enterprise that represents the excellence and nobility of the educational institutions we serve. We represent institutions with missions that transform lives, serve communities, and fulfill the fundamental promise of education.

As advancement professionals, we work tirelessly every day to secure resources and build communities in order to advance our missions and create opportunities for individuals to realize the benefits of education and research. Working in advancement also is a privilege. With this privilege comes responsibility. Today, we are being called upon to embrace our work with greater precision, accountability, and creativity.

The purpose of our work has remained consistent. However, we must change how we work and how the value we create benefits students, alumni, families, and friends. We can no longer rest on our laurels; expect that, if we build it, they shall come; and rely on tradition and history to galvanize communities to support and advance our missions.

Because communities and individuals behave and express their expectations in dramatically different ways, we must rethink how we approach our work in this new economy and in a rapidly changing global community. Attention is sparse, competition is fierce, and our constituents will be much less forgiving if we are underwhelming or underserving them.

NEW REALITIES

For centuries, students have left our hallowed halls as graduates and continued to be proud, loyal, and ever faithful in support of their alma mater. That is often not the case now. What changed? Quite a lot, but three distinct shifts in particular have fundamentally altered the trajectory of engagement. First, we have seen most Americans (including many of our alumni and donors) become markedly and increasingly suspicious of established institutions. We also have seen our society shift from limited options for engagement to an unprecedented abundance of opportunities. Finally, we have witnessed our entire world transformed by innovation.

Prior to these changes, the basic principles of advancement work had been largely constant for decades. We had the luxury of operating in a comfortable environment, with no threat to our vitality, no challenge to our validity, and no question of our viability. We hired and promoted individuals based on the same skill and competency framework. We existed in a bubble, but these three forces—suspicion, an abundance of options, and innovation—have created driving and restraining forces never witnessed before.

Now we must embrace a new normal if we are to remain relevant. In order to embrace our new reality, we should first seek to understand the forces that have brought us to this point.

SUSPICION OF INSTITUTIONS

The last several decades have been filled with monumental failures and disappointments, all of which have shaped a sense of uncertainty and suspicion in our society. The two most recent severe economic recessions have reshaped the attitudes of younger generations regarding consumerism, stability, faith, association, and loyalty.

There have been numerous reports and examinations of how failures of our churches, financial institutions, politics, and even university leadership have affected attitudes. These failures are compounded by disruptions in centuries-old brands and an increased demand by a fickle consumer base that expects everything yesterday.

Imagine for a moment that you have been a loyal iPhone user since Apple first introduced the product in 2007. Inundated by the overcrowded marketplace of cell phone choices, you unwaveringly commit to the Apple iPhone. You do so because Apple has made you a promise. You are loyal to the full suite of Apple products, but imagine what would happen if the product became mediocre and unreliable and generally disappointed you? You are likely to walk away and try a new platform. The same happens when one considers institutional affinity and loyalty. If a brand fails to deliver on its promise or does not consistently keep that promise, the consequence is severe.

With unprecedented levels of skepticism and ambiguity, securing and retaining loyalty is one of our greatest challenges. What are the fundamental promises we have made to our students, and how well have we consistently delivered on those promises?

Higher education has been playing a low-stakes game in this arena. After all, alumni of our institutions will be alumni forever—they cannot return their educations or exchange their degrees. But they can certainly devalue their experience with our institutions; lose interest in affiliating; and easily find alternative forms of enrichment, community engagement, and lifelong learning. Too many of our former customers are disappointed, disengaged, or disinterested because we have taken their loyalty for granted and failed to deliver on our promises.

In a consumer market, failing to deliver on your company's promise is the surest way to go out of business. Yet, higher education historically has been complacent and resistant to transformation. There is only one way to reverse this tendency toward suspicion and disappointment, and that is not to *expect* the philanthropy of our community members but rather to *earn* and keep it.

The stakes have never been higher. Indeed, education as a whole and higher education in particular—committed to inclusive access, opportunity, and efficacy—may well represent one of the most important forces for good in our time. Universities should be revered for what they create and what they provide to the local and global communities they serve. But we have to do more to earn the trust of those communities, and we have to work harder to deserve their loyalty.

Our alumni may not be able to exchange their degrees, but they can easily choose to support other organizations aligned with their values, beliefs, and interests and in which they feel trust.

AN ABUNDANCE OF OPTIONS

At the same time that this deep sense of suspicion began to draw supporters away from our institutions, most Americans' worldviews began to shift rapidly from a scarcity of opportunities for engagement to an overwhelming abundance of opportunities to engage. For many decades, universities have been the only link for alumni who wished to reach back to their friends and college communities. The university was the best source of information and knowledge and also the most readily available conduit for making a philanthropic impact. Our alumni engaged with us because we packaged up things they needed or wanted and because they perceived us to be best positioned to provide these things.

Now, with the advent and rapid acceleration of technology and access, our alumni stay connected to their college communities through social media. They also can form new communities around work, life, family, and global interests. They have unprecedented access to knowledge in the age of information, and they support causes they care about through more than 1.5 million charitable organizations registered in the United States alone (NCCS 2018).

When our supporters have such tremendous access to communities, causes, and information, we can no longer expect them to rely on universities to fulfill their needs for affiliation, appreciation, and impact. In order to remain competitive in an economy of such information abundance, we must deliver truly meaningful and delightful experiences and opportunities that create formative memories. Beyond that, we must make sure those experiences are uniquely and inextricably associated with our institutions.

It simply is not enough to throw a great party so that old friends can reconnect. We must demand more of ourselves because our students, alumni, families, and donors are absolutely demanding more of us or, worse, they are seeking it elsewhere. If they choose to invest their time, money, and ambassadorship in our universities, it is not out of loyalty or obligation, and it is not for lack of options. If they choose to support us, it is because we have delivered an experience, an opportunity, or a chance to make a difference that either no one else can provide or no one can provide as well.

HUMAN INGENUITY AND INNOVATION

We live in an era when innovation and creativity are creating a constant influx of intoxicating (and at times irritating) experiences. Nearly every twentieth-century industry has experienced the range of reinvention to extinction. The main driver for this is the innovation fueled by human ingenuity.

Human beings are evolving, and the importance of tapping into those significant human developments in our work has never been more important. Human ingenuity drives the choices we make as individuals, including our collective sense of community. To fully understand the implications of this, we must first consider how the very definition of *community* has fundamentally changed and, consequently, the parameters of community membership.

Communities have historically been defined by fairly obvious constraints. The shared demographic, psychographic, social, and affinity characteristics of each group defined its membership. Those communities operated separately and homogeneously, united by shared characteristics. When we think about the reality of human identity, though, it is clear that none of us is entirely defined by homogeneous characteristics. We are far more sophisticated, complex, and complicated than that.

We are each a unique combination of multiple, evolving, integrated attributes and interests that merge together at a specific time in a specific set of circumstances and that change constantly as those circumstances evolve. Although basic human needs to interact, relate, matter, and belong may remain the same, the norms and values that shape community and culture have evolved.

As we look back at historical concepts of our university communities, we see that those communities have historically been anchored by the institution, surrounded by concentric circles of people who share a single institutionally defined attribute. That may include residential cohorts, Greek life, athletics, or academic-affinity circles. Consequently, for decades, we have designed programs and services to nurture them.

When we look forward, however, we see that our communities cannot be sustained with this model. We must look beyond what we consider the one or two defining characteristics of our individual alumni and seek instead to understand their interests, passions, personal and family dynamics, and professional ambitions. With this knowledge, we can provide services that are truly relevant and meaningful to those individuals and benefit from the multiplier effect of gaining access to their vast, rich networks, as well. This work must remain as agile and creative as the world around us.

Human ingenuity equips us to see the world through multiple, varied, sometimes competing lenses to understand what motivates each of us to take action. Our greatest challenge in generating support for higher education is to find ways to scale this powerful competency to see the full range of complex individuals in our communities and leverage that knowledge to inspire their philanthropy.

NEW IMPERATIVES FOR A NEW PARADIGM

If you accept increased suspicion, an abundance of options for engagement, and complex innovation resulting from human ingenuity as drivers in a paradigm shift we are experiencing, then a new set of modalities is needed to design and deliver meaningful programming. The following are imperatives to guide you in creating an organizational ethos that builds an engaged community around the mission of your institution—a community that generates clear, healthy, and sustained returns in the form of sincere ambassadorship, deep engagement, and dedicated philanthropy.

Imperative 1: Understand and Curate Your Institution's Culture and Values

Great organizations have clarity around culture and values and how they connect and unify their employees as a team. CEOs often refer to this powerful sense of shared values as their "true north." What is yours? What are the norms, rituals, behaviors, and beliefs that shape your institution? And how do you constantly reinforce them across your organization? If you are uncertain of the answer to any of those questions or if the answer is not something you agree with and embody yourself, then it is time for a culture audit. Thoughtfully, honestly, and deeply understanding your organizational culture is the first crucial step toward being able to fully harness its power.

Start by learning the baseline of where your team is today. What are the positive aspects of how your team members interact with each other, and what values seem to be shared and upheld across functional and organizational lines? What are some of the dynamics that seem challenging? Are the existing norms and behaviors generally positive, or do you need to build a new code to unify and guide your team moving forward?

Once you have audited the existing culture, you must immediately shift toward reinforcing the desirable values and behaviors you have identified. Then, you must continue to reinforce them. And continue. And continue. One employee, one decision, or one action often erodes culture, sometimes irreversibly.

The good news is that culture is also fortified by repetition. Consider how you can consistently integrate messages that continue to define your culture, how your actions as a leader faithfully reflect the values of your team, and how your goals inherently align with your institution's culture and ethos. Once you have done the hard work of building your organization's culture, the only way to protect and strengthen it is to live it personally and to reiterate it frequently.

Additional efforts you can undertake to facilitate this include:

1. Consult with your faculty in sociology and cultural anthropology to determine feasibility of conducting a formal study of culture, values, shared experiences, and norms—perhaps engaging your graduate students.
2. Tap into your alumni-founded or alumni-operated companies with exemplary practices in culture and identity. Request a site visit, or engage in a short-term study of strategies, tactics, and best practices.

Imperative 2: Embrace Students, Their Spirit, Their Genius, and Their Doing

Everything we do must, without exception, begin and end with serving our students. But sometimes we neglect to see that they are also remarkably adept and well positioned to serve our institutions. There is an abundant nature of goodness that exists among the exceptional young people we serve, yet most institutions do not acknowledge—let alone leverage—their inclination to be involved, influential, and philanthropic. Students self-select into a variety of groups based on their multiple, dynamic identities, and they naturally exhibit the types of behaviors we work hard to elicit after they graduate.

Whether it is through Greek organizations, athletics, recreation, interest clubs, or other groups, students have consistently proven they are capable of building communities with deep affinity. They have also demonstrated their willingness to give of their own time and treasure, as well as influence the philanthropy of others when they consider the cause and organization worthy. Rather than allowing this engagement to be segmented and fractured across dozens of groups on our campuses, universities should seek to understand and celebrate the collective impact our students make in local and global communities. Student philanthropy programs have become important.

One approach is to develop and activate a student foundation, with trustees selected from among your most actively involved students. A student foundation can be a way to activate the nature of goodness ingrained in our student communities while also fostering leadership, engagement, and philanthropy among our future alumni. They can serve as a powerful multiplier of values, habits, and behaviors that will endure long after graduation. Additional efforts you can undertake to facilitate this include:

1. Craft a communication that acknowledges and celebrates your students' contributions to the public good, either through volunteerism or service, and share it broadly on behalf of the president or chancellor.
2. Host an annual signature event to highlight students' community engagement, and recognize innovation and impact.
3. Test-drive the design and launch of a student foundation dedicated primarily to cultivating the philanthropic spirit among students.
4. Consistently engage with students who are doing extraordinary work and elevating the university's brand and value.

Imperative 3: Know Your Talent Quotient

If we acknowledge that our paradigm has shifted and that the environment in which we operate has changed, then how we accomplish our goals needs to be fundamentally different. The information revolution has created market conditions for transformations in work, worker productivity, and talent development. It is hard to point to a set of creative talent initiatives in advancement beyond training, recruitment, and onboarding initiatives. It stands to reason that the knowledge, skills, and abilities required to do advancement work must be reexamined.

Most of our organizations have continued to hire from the same pools of professionals, from tactical event planners to outgoing gift officers, with little or no regard for how those professionals match up with the unique needs of an agile and rapidly evolving industry. Advancement leaders must honestly assess the individuals we employ in our organizations and ascertain the talent, knowledge, and skill we need to fulfill our twenty-first-century programs and services. Our talent strategies can no longer be about filling vacant positions but rather about being extremely diligent in reshaping our competency matrix to reflect the outcomes for which we are accountable.

Once you have identified the skills and acumen your program requires, you can establish specific strategies to hire for those attributes or to cultivate them from within your team. If you hope to inspire philanthropy in an age of suspicion and doubt, then you cannot model your development team on a sales force.

Likeability is no substitute for a deep understanding of the mission and the funding opportunities that support it, so your fundraising professionals must possess a strong sense of curiosity and the proficiency to translate information to diverse audiences. Likewise, if you strive to make a lasting impression on your constituents in an environment of abundant options, your events-management professionals must function as executive producers who can clearly envision and deliver a unique, heartfelt experience from start to finish.

Finally, if your strategy reflects the deep complexity of human ingenuity, then engagement professionals must be savvy strategists with a keen understanding of innovative marketing approaches (segmentations, persona development) and designs of unique value propositions. Our success in navigating and succeeding in this new model is dependent on our ability to stop using outdated approaches to acquiring, cultivating, and activating talent in our profession.

Additional efforts you can undertake to facilitate this include:

1. Examine your current job descriptions and recruitment announcements. Ask yourself if you would apply for the role if you were not

a member of the advancement profession. Adjust all communications appropriately.

2. Hire a talent consultant from the private sector (e.g., consumer goods, professional services, financial industry) to assess your talent, knowledge, and skill matrix.

3. Cultivate talent from admissions, student life, and academic units who have a direct responsibility to serve communities (e.g., hospital system, social work, law school).

Imperative 4: Define a Unique, Lasting Value Proposition

For students, the university is a universe in and of itself, filled with ideas, knowledge, connections, and opportunities to explore. During that time, students have the proclivity and the freedom to be fully immersed in that contained universe.

One mistake we often make in advancement is to assume and act as though we are still the students' universe after they graduate. Trying to be everything to everyone is a sure way to fail because we are but one component of the multifaceted, exciting, dynamic lives our alumni lead. Our challenge, then, is to remain relevant in their lives in order to maintain a share of their affinity and attention in a market and a world that competes fiercely for it.

If the value proposition of higher education generally is to prepare our students to lead purposeful lives as engaged and knowledgeable citizens, then it is our obligation to support their success and achievement long after graduation. Repeated surveys confirm that the primary reason students attend college is the expectation of being better prepared for their careers. If we do not hold ourselves accountable and support our students' long-term successes, then we will not deliver on our value proposition. That will continue to foster suspicion and apathy among our alumni.

One of the most plausible ways to deliver on this promise to our students is to fully commit ourselves to the successes and achievements of our students and alumni. An exciting movement in higher education is the integration of career services with advancement. A strong partnership with student services is crucial to the success of our career platform, but the team responsible for providing this service must be incentivized to achieve long-term results. The group best positioned to do so is the one responsible for maintaining lifelong connections with students after they become alumni. Though the organizational dynamics may prove to be complicated and painful, universities should immediately move toward a model that integrates career services with advancement in order to fulfill the distinct value proposition that is our lifelong promise to our graduates.

Additional efforts you can undertake to facilitate this include:

1. Examine universities that have aligned career development and advancement functions to determine a possible roadmap for your university.
2. Conduct focus groups with your engaged and disengaged alumni, parents, and students to test your value proposition.
3. Build capacity within your team to facilitate this effort with consistency and authenticity.

Imperative 5: Elevate Your Expectations

Despite sweeping changes in almost every other industry in the modern economy, advancement has held tightly to the status quo. We continue to seek the guidance and approval of "experts," knowing their expertise often is no more robust than our own. We double down on expensive business practices with limited—and diminishing—returns. We outsource to third parties who have no interest or stake in our achievement and purpose. We do all the same things, and yet, we genuinely expect to see different results.

As you assess your programs, consider whether they achieve your purposes and whether they do so in a viable, sustainable, and practical way. Traditional annual-giving programs are a great example of how many of us have failed to objectively evaluate our work and take action accordingly. If we can clearly define our mission and purpose and have built a strong culture dedicated to serving it, then everything we do, every experience we deliver, and every program we implement must be dedicated to achieving that end.

We must be strategic and economical in accomplishing our goals. It is our right as advancement leaders to expect more from ourselves and from our teams, and it is our obligation to make the hard decisions that lead us to exceed those higher expectations.

CONCLUSION

If you accept that our world has been fundamentally changed in the ways that this chapter discusses and if you take the time to address the new imperatives described, then you will have the opportunity to lead a versatile, twenty-first-century advancement enterprise that represents the excellence and nobility of the educational institutions we serve.

REFERENCE

NCCS (National Center for Charitable Statistics). 2018. "Quick Facts About Nonprofits." https://nccs.urban.org/data-statistics/quick-facts-about-nonprofits.

SEVEN

Annual Giving

Daniel H. Frezza

A stepping stone is useful as something that helps one make progress toward a specified goal. Or there may be a group of stones that enable one to cross a small body of water—beginning, continuing, or ending a journey. Annual giving at one point in time was considered the stepping stone for higher-education fundraising, just the beginning step in building a comprehensive program—or a career in advancement.

Today, institutions invest in annual giving at levels that would have been unimaginable just a decade ago. The reason for this is an increased understanding of what has always been true: annual giving is a stepping stone that leads to more effective higher-education fundraising programs.

THE CURRENT LANDSCAPE

The annual-giving industry today has emerged from its shackled "annual fund" days. Just a decade or two ago, the vast majority of these programs would focus entirely on one annual fund that was fueled mainly by one population—alumni. The leading programs today have evolved from a focus on the annual fund to annual giving, encompassing everything to which donors may give annually. The days of one unrestricted annual fund are almost entirely gone, as are the donor populations that supported them.

Alumni donors supported those funds for decades, and while alumni still comprise the highest percentage of annual donors, the landscape is evolving. Over the past two decades, other groups have grown in importance in annual giving, including parents, faculty and staff, friends—even students—in addition to alumni. Today's donors are attracted to more restricted and tangible areas of fundraising.

The donor who gives annually has an immediate and regular impact on the mission or cause. The donor who gives annually to unrestricted areas provides the opportunity for the institution to develop, shape, and plan its mission and programs. This creates the first philosophical junction that every annual-giving professional will at one point find herself facing: Are we a program that is focused on raising unrestricted dollars or increasing donor populations and participation rates? The answer should be both, but we need to understand which is the leading priority.

In 2016, the total of charitable gifts from American individuals, estates, foundations, and corporations was estimated to be $390.05 billion. That represents a total increase of 2.7 percent in current dollars from the total provided in 2015 (Giving USA Foundation 2017). Higher education received roughly 11 percent of that total, $43.6 billion (CAE 2018). These numbers have soared over the years, while at the same time alumni participation rates have declined. A smaller minority of the donor population is contributing more and at a faster pace. This is the prime reason many programs have decided to ignore participation rates or goals for increased numbers of donors over the past two decades. Since 1990, alumni participation rates nationally have declined from above 18 percent to below 10 percent in 2017 (CASE 2018, 12).

REVERSING THE TREND

The reasons for declining participation rates have been well documented. But some programs have begun to successfully buck this trend. How have they done so? This section discusses just some of the ways, as entire works have been dedicated to annual giving and all of its contemporary methods.

Rather than cover the how-to of direct mail, phonathon programs, reunion-class giving, and days of giving, this section covers three functional areas that all leading programs today have embraced and that fuel all aspects of annual giving. They are (1) a core focus on metrics that matter, (2) a dedicated approach to laying the foundation for the next generation of donors, and (3) fully embracing new technology.

METRICS THAT MATTER

The use of analytics has emerged as a necessity for modern annual-giving programs. No longer is a one-dimensional report showcasing donors and dollars year over year sufficient to guide a successful program. Even adding a second dimension (retention rates, reactivation rates, or acquisition growth) will only do so much. Programs that are finding success in today's environment are looking at a complex array of metrics, and that is certainly making the difference.

The Magic Number

Whether through an outside vendor or through internal analytics, the ability to read your program's internal algorithm is important. Call this the magic number. Every program has one, and it is important to know what it is. Each program might define it differently or categorize it in another way, but it is important nonetheless.

The magic number has to do with retention rates and donor habits. We know retention rates are crucial to maintaining a strong program and growing alumni participation, donor growth, or both. Retention rates are also important in growing the size of a donor's average gift. In addition, it can take up to seven to ten years of giving for some donors to finally commit to a major gift.

There are many factors that can increase the likelihood of retaining a donor. The magic number identifies the average donor habit or profile that exists for donors at or above your institution's retention rate. In order to be analytically sound, you will want to find two or three correlative data points. The most common will be consecutive years giving, gift level, and gift frequency. When you look at each of these factors, at some point you will identify the trends and see where retention drastically changes in favor of your program.

For a hypothetical example, suppose a donor with two consecutive years of giving might renew at 55 percent, while a donor with four years might renew at 65 percent. Donors contributing twenty-five dollars might renew at 40 percent, while donors at the seventy-five-dollar level might renew at 65 percent. Donors contributing one gift in a single fiscal year might renew at 55 percent, while donors contributing two gifts might renew at 70 percent. If your institution's overall retention rate is below 65 percent, then you can gather that donors who either give more consecutively, at higher levels, or at a higher frequency are driving your retention rate success.

New Donor Activity

Well-managed programs are keenly aware of their new donor activity and how to measure for success. For this purpose, a *new donor* is defined as an individual making their first cash gift to either a specific area or the institution as a whole. The first step is obviously to secure this new donor, but it is what institutions do next that makes a difference.

In 2017, the median overall retention rate for 222 public and private universities taking part in a survey stood at 60.4 percent. The same rate for new donors from the same report stood at just 24.4 percent (Blackbaud 2018, 10). This shows a striking difference between a program's overall retention rate and the rate at which the newest donors renew. Even leading annual-giving programs still commonly experience new donor retention rates dropping below their overall rates, although the gap between the two is surprisingly smaller. Growing participation rates or donor totals requires a careful balance of acquisition and retention.

In sales, it costs more to attract a new customer than to simply retain one. Annual giving is no different, and the programs that recognize this statistic are the ones beginning to turn the tide. Careful stewardship of these groups requires creativity and investment.

First-time-donor packets are a prime example and affirm the importance of both demonstrating appreciation and valuing the relationship. Programs that go one step further are extending this approach with their consecutive-year-giving societies. Recognizing and celebrating consistent giving demonstrates appreciation and showcases authentic value.

It is important to understand that you will never renew all donors at 100 percent and that many will eventually lapse. A new-donor-reactivation plan is as important as a new-donor-retention plan. Experience has proven that, the longer a donor remains lapsed, the less likely that donor is to renew. If a long-lapsed donor does renew, then they typically behave more like a new donor, and hence the process begins again.

The important time frame to consider is the one-to-five-year range. Annual-giving programs should try to reach lapsed donors before surpassing the fifth year; that is especially true for donors who lapsed after making their first gifts. It is essential to look at the channels through which these donors first contributed. That may suggest the best strategy for reactivating a lapsed donor.

Consecutive-Year Givers

As mentioned previously, this important metric is at the core of the magic number. Leading annual-giving programs today have either created or increased their investment in new giving societies that measure, recognize, and leverage this important segment of their donor base. This is because of the impact they have on donor pipelines. Donors with five or more years of consecutive giving are renewing at much higher rates than others.

Programs that are focused heavily on undergraduate-alumni participation rates are emphasizing this metric in working with students and recent graduates. For example, William & Mary structured its program so that the first milestone occurs at the fifth consecutive year. This allows William & Mary to recognize recent alumni in the first year after graduation if they contributed in each of their four years as undergraduate students.

Opportunities to leverage this type of giving society do not end at the recent-graduate level. Programs built through analytics should look to build or strategically alter their milestone or threshold occasions. Retention rates change drastically the longer a donor stays consecutive. Unfortunate circumstances do exist where programs see consecutive donors lapsing. At times these may show as trends. It is desirable to build milestone or threshold levels to combat lapsing and support "good behavior" among all donors.

LAYING THE FOUNDATION FOR THE FUTURE

Taking a long-term view, building the tradition of philanthropy requires focusing on current students as well as recent alumni. Let's look at some of the innovative approaches that are being taken with these two groups.

Approaches to Student Philanthropy

Over the past five years, the percentage of new donors who are students or graduating seniors has increased for both public and private universities. Private universities are significantly more reliant on students to drive their new-donor growth than public universities, with a percentage of new donors at 55 percent compared to 15 percent (Blackbaud 2018, 8). The larger national public universities tend to have lower percentages due to large alumni populations and undergraduate-student class sizes.

Whether a university is trying to grow alumni participation or the number of donors, student philanthropy is crucial. Each year the denominator of total alumni grows; increases in class sizes are the number one reason. Alumni make up the overwhelming majority of a university's donors. Students today are the alumni of tomorrow, and the programs that choose to ignore them are losing ground by the year.

This emphasis on students is a national best practice and trend. For example, the Massachusetts Institute of Technology (MIT) has implemented an underclass-giving competition, engaging students with hands-on philanthropy. The program began in 2006 and is still considered one of the industry's trendsetters. The program encourages students to think of big ideas or projects and spend a week advocating for funding from classmates. Due to this program, MIT sees more than 50 percent of their students give back annually, including freshmen, sophomores, and juniors (MIT, n.d.).

William & Mary built a similar initiative labeled Impact Week, which seeks submissions from students for funding needs. Three projects are selected, and a week of fundraising commences. Students vote for the project that they deem most worthy through their own individual gifts. A challenge donor is used to partially or fully fund all projects.

Both initiatives, MIT's and William & Mary's, harness two important factors within student philanthropy: engagement and impact. The idea of engaged philanthropy is important for all donor groups; however, it is particularly important for students. Both MIT and William & Mary were able to create advocates by turning student volunteers into fundraisers on behalf of projects for which they were either responsible or passionate. This type of program should include education as well as solicitation. Regardless of the vehicle for the message, the important goal is to highlight the impact private support provides to a current student experience.

Senior-class giving has long been a staple for most annual-giving programs. However, it typically existed as the sole effort and is somewhat of an outdated student-philanthropy approach. With this traditional approach, students spend more than three years ignoring philanthropy before finally being engaged. This lack of engagement affects retention rates for these donors.

Student-philanthropy programs today are starting earlier so that, by the time a student emerges as a senior, they've been engaged with philanthropy for more than three years. Statistically, this increases the likelihood that they will continue to give, increasing retention rates and driving donor numbers and participation rates higher. (Kestrel Linder and Felicity Meu discuss additional points about student giving in chapter 12 of this book.)

Young Alumni

Young-alumni engagement in philanthropy is crucial. Increasing young-alumni participation or donor numbers is difficult, though it is made easier with the use of a robust student culture. The idea of engaged philanthropy that we try to create for students should also be carried over to young alumni.

In a 2017 survey conducted by Ruffalo Noel Levitz, 81 percent of institutions solicited young alumni within one year of graduation (5). Programs at the University of Chicago, Northwestern University, the University of Pennsylvania, and William & Mary, among others, have put resources and creativity into creating engaged philanthropy and are seeing gains in young-alumni participation rates, as a result.

Many different channels work with young alumni, including phonathons and crowdfunding. Phonathons are still a useful tool with younger donors and have again become viable because mobile phone numbers have stabilized. However, it should not be a surprise to see that giving days, crowdfunding, and peer-to-peer fundraising lead the way for new-donor acquisition and engagement for young alumni. More than 70 percent of respondents to one survey selected one of those three methods as their most effective with young-alumni donors (Ruffalo Noel Levitz 2017, 7).

Days of giving and crowdfunding help to create engaged philanthropy because they do indeed allow for donors to become involved in the process. However, they also present challenges. Retention rates from days of giving vary from program to program. Some institutions experience a higher retention rate from their giving day than in their overall programs; others have the opposite result. One problem is that a giving day usually occurs once a year, which makes it difficult to determine whether a donor returns as a result. The same is true of crowdfunding because projects change annually. While both approaches afford great opportunity for engagement, neither offers great consistency.

Event-based fundraising and stewardship may be useful with young alumni. Some programs have witnessed moderate success by going to the market rather than expecting the market to come to them, that is, by holding regional events. Many programs hold events that are just for young alumni donors, using a give-at-the-door approach. These are more than simply donor parties; they are engagement opportunities, as well. They present the opportunity to experience and witness the impact of philanthropy while also enjoying fellowship at the same time.

POSITIONING NEW TECHNOLOGY

Fundraising in higher education has evolved rapidly due in large part to new technology. We are only about fifteen years removed from printed alumni directories, and there are people leading annual-giving programs today who remember starting as phonathon callers!

Technology has enabled much greater reach and is more cost effective than many traditional methods. Annual-giving programs today do still use traditional direct-response methods, such as direct mail, although they are evaluated through more detailed metrics with support from modern algorithms. They still are useful to reach certain segments of donor prospects. But many programs today have added new technology to either complement or even replace traditional methods.

E-mail

E-mail has long been expected to eventually surpass direct mail as the leading channel for giving. The percentage of gifts made online increased sharply from 2013 to 2017, from 16.9 percent to 31.1 percent at private institutions and from 8.6 percent to 18.6 percent at public institutions (Blackbaud 2018, 14). But that giving does not necessarily result from e-mail solicitations directly. It simply reflects the fact that individuals prefer to make gifts and payments online; they may be responding to solicitations through other channels.

Web marketing, specifically content marketing online, has exploded in the private sector in recent years. While higher-education fundraising has been slow to capitalize on this trend, some institutions are now testing e-mail nurture campaigns. With this approach, the program reacts differently to each target market based on the actions of the recipients. Reacting to what your donors are telling you through their behavior and building a more individualized campaign around their activity positions you better for success. Within the private sector, this strategy increases open rates and offers a more strategic and effective approach than one that casts too wide of a net.

Volunteer Management

Volunteers can be an incredibly powerful resource, though they also require plenty of care. If mismanaged, a volunteer program can actually do more harm than good. Leading private institutions have a long history of doing this well and have applied new technology to managing their programs in recent years.

Historically, institutions either built their own in-house volunteer-management system or purchased a noncustomizable canned program from a national vendor. Programs with fewer resources simply managed this process through spreadsheets and file-sharing software. Those methods required a number of staff positions to manage a sizable volunteer base.

Within the last decade, technological advances have provided tools that are mobile friendly and volunteer centric. This has helped to provide an approach that is both volunteer centric *and* staff centric. The new technology makes it possible to manage the volunteer base with half the staff as in the past or, alternatively, for the current staff to manage twice the number of volunteers.

Online portals now enable a single staff member to provide a variable-driven script to hundreds of volunteers with relative ease and make it easier for volunteers to send a variable-driven e-mail to hundreds of their classmates with the same level of ease. Volunteers can provide contact reports, which help increase data integrity, accuracy, and coordination with other advancement staff, and the institution can gain more consistency in both message and timing.

Social Media

One of the newest channels for annual-giving programs is social media. Each program must approach its goals differently based on structure and staffing. Whether you choose to leverage this solely as a part of a microcampaign, such as giving days or crowdfunding, or you incorporate it as a major channel for solicitation, the most important aspect is ownership or access to the major social channels for the institution. If those do not exist, then the time creating channels and attracting viewers can be daunting.

Programs that have found success through social media have both accessed institutional accounts and created fundraising-specific accounts. On your institution's page, you will need to share space and time with other partners, whereas you can control 100 percent of your own space on a page you create.

The more successful programs meet their donors where they are. Understanding the preferred platform—the one your donors most often access—allows you to segment and become more strategic with shared and created content. It is important to understand that social media is mostly about engagement. Gifts will occur; however, reaching donors to show impact or communicate about an upcoming campaign is also an important objective. Similar to e-mail, the volume of gifts may seem low, but the communication reach is worth the investment.

One use of social media that has emerged in recent years is pixel-based and segment-based advertising. This provides the ability to explicitly target your population with content-specific advertisements and can complement a digital microcampaign very well. Two approaches have been viewed as unique and effective.

The first approach involves boosting your presence at crucial periods. For example, if your university wins a national championship, receives an award, or finds itself in the news (for something positive!), the ability to react is important. Institutions that immediately put out a solicitation-driven advertisement during these periods are increasing their chances for engagement and visibility.

The second approach is more comfortable for most annual-giving professionals—data-driven segmentation. We now have the ability to use data to identify donors and target populations through social media. For example, imagine if nondonors in reunion classes were notified of their upcoming reunion by providing a link that brings them to their reunion-class page, which includes a class-gift link. These should be soft or subtle asks that merely drive the right audience in the intended direction.

Social media is a risky venture. Simply using it invites your constituents to engage with you. Be prepared to receive the positive and the negative. Be ready to engage and foster relationships. Targeted social media can also be risky, as you will need to recognize the limits of your base. Social media is a safe space for many and is becoming more similar to a digital backyard. Making a large splash right away might be deemed obtrusive. Ease into the relationship, establish rapport, and meet your constituents where they are.

CONCLUSION

Annual giving is entering an exciting period. Whether it is considered a stepping stone or cornerstone, it certainly is leading to something greater and long-lasting. We are in a new era for the visibility of annual giving, in which most programs scarcely resemble what they once were.

Today's programs are marketing machines that reach farther than any other outlet at a university. Annual-giving programs contact more constituents than any other arm of the institution. They are responsible for the past, current, and future through engagement, philanthropy, and stewardship.

Deeply rooted in analytics, a modern annual-giving program can provide a return on investment in ways that once were not anticipated. They fill in the gaps with essential data points and help to qualify potential donors, supporting other fundraising efforts. They have grown to become important brand and message carriers. They provide educational opportunities at the student level and afford opportunities for major gifts through challenge-driven causes. Giving days and crowdfunding have become visible illustrations of philanthropy at work and a reminder of how fun it can be. Incorporating these three essential areas into a program's approach at any level will improve overall numbers.

Annual-giving programs are earning investments from their institutions that just a short while ago would have been unfathomable. These investments are wise and will be of long-term value to the institutions.

REFERENCES

Blackbaud. 2018. *2017 donorCentrics Annual Report on Higher Education Alumni Giving: Summary of Annual Giving Key Performance Indicators.* Charleston, SC: Blackbaud. https://institute.blackbaud.com/wp-content/uploads/2018/05/2017-donorCentrics-Annual-Report-HE-Alumni-Giving.pdf.

CAE (Council for Aid to Education). 2018. "Colleges and Universities Raised $43.6 Billion in 2017." Press release, February 6, 2018. https://cae.org/images/uploads/pdf/VSE-2017-Press-Release.pdf.

CASE (Council for Advancement and Support of Education). 2018. *Voluntary Support of Education 2017.* Washington, DC: CASE.

Giving USA Foundation. 2017. "Giving USA 2017: Total Charitable Donations Rise to New High of $390.05 Billion." Press release, June 12, 2017. https://givingusa.org/tag/giving-usa-2017/.

MIT (Massachusetts Institute of Technology). n.d. "Underclassmen Giving Competition." Giving to MIT. Accessed October 19, 2018. https://giving.mit.edu/ugc/index.html.

Ruffalo Noel Levitz. 2017. *Advancement Leaders Speak 2017: Digital Tactics and Young Alumni Engagement Strategies Reported by Today's Fundraisers.* Cedar Rapids, IA: Ruffalo Noel Levitz. http://learn.ruffalonl.com/rs/395-EOG-977/images/ALS_Digital%20And%20Millennial%20Engagement_1.0.pdf.

EIGHT

Major and Principal Gifts

Ronald J. Schiller

Major- and principal-gift fundraising is always changing. The ways money is earned and inherited, the means for giving away money, the composition of the nonprofit landscape, and the overall economic environment, among other factors, are constantly in flux. The pool of potential major donors is increasingly diverse. At the same time, the long-held view that 80 percent of fundraising revenue comes from 20 percent of donors has been replaced by a 95–5 or even a 98–2 rule, with most of the dollars coming from a very small percentage of donors.

But one aspect of major- and principal-gift fundraising remains constant: The most satisfied and successful givers and fundraisers recognize that fundraising at these levels is not about the transaction but about the partnership. It is about finding ways for generous individuals and families and the nonprofit organizations they support to pool resources to accomplish something neither could without the other—something that has an impact on society and that is important to both.

A quick note to define *major* and *principal*. Though the scale of these gifts varies by institution—from the thousands into the millions of dollars—most organizations define *major* and *principal gifts* as those that are made occasionally rather than regularly and usually over and above regular gifts, such as annual-fund gifts. The occasion may be a campaign or other special fundraising effort or may be timed to a special event on the part of the donor, such as the sale of a company, an inheritance, the creation of an estate plan, or even a birthday or anniversary.

Major and principal gifts are often pledged and paid over several years and often involve assets other than cash. Above all, for the purposes of this chapter, they are at a sufficiently high level for the institution to give them customized attention, usually with a staff member assigned to assist the organization in managing the giving relationship between the institution and a specific set of individuals in a so-called major gift prospect portfolio.

Corporations and foundations also make major gifts, and many ideas in this chapter apply to these institutional donors. They are covered in greater depth in chapter 11 of this book. Fundraisers that focus on individual donors have much to learn from their colleagues in foundation relations when it comes to listening to donor objectives and developing proposals based on shared objectives and shared interests in measurable impact. But most institutions, in using the terms *major gifts* and *principal gifts*, are referring to programs focused on individuals, families, and family foundations.

In the United States, philanthropic growth remains strong. According to Giving USA's 2018 report on philanthropy for 2017, Americans gave more than $410 billion to charity, the first time philanthropy surpassed the $400 billion mark. That's up from $307 billion ten years earlier, a growth rate significantly higher than inflation (Giving USA Foundation 2018).

Furthermore, the vast majority of those in a prospective donor pool with the wealth capacity to make major and principal gifts are also philanthropic. The *2018 US Trust Study of High Net Worth Philanthropy*, conducted in partnership with the Indiana University Lilly Family School of Philanthropy, cites the Lilly School's finding that 56 percent of the general US population makes charitable gifts, but "as in past years, the overwhelming majority of American high net worth households reported making charitable donations." Ninety percent of high net worth households gave, with average giving of $29,269 per household in 2017 (US Trust and Indiana University Lilly Family School of Philanthropy 2018).

At the same time, there is significant untapped potential. Thirty years ago, people consistently expressed their belief that philanthropic capacity and intent surpassed philanthropic expression—that people with whom they worked could and wished to give more. Despite continued growth in the nonprofit sector and despite growth in giving well beyond inflation, many people across the field of advancement believe that the same holds true today.

A recent Fidelity Charitable report, based on a 2016 survey conducted among 3,254 adults in the United States who donated and claimed itemized charitable gift deductions in 2015, concluded that "most donors (95 percent) would give more under the right circumstances" and "addressing donor concerns about charitable impact and financial planning have the greatest potential to influence the amount donors give overall" (Fidelity Charitable 2017). Eighty-one percent of these donors expressed concerns about nonprofit transparency and understanding the impact of their giving (Fidelity Charitable 2017).

Donors always have wanted their giving to have impact; no one wants to waste an earned or inherited dollar. Major- and principal-gift fundraisers with a deep appreciation for the importance of a partnership stance are the best positioned to unlock this additional, untapped potential.

PHILANTHROPIC PARTNERSHIP

The book *Belief and Confidence: Donors Talk about Successful Philanthropic Partnership* (Schiller 2016) includes quotes from many leading philanthropists, describing aspects of the most productive fundraising programs *from the perspectives of these donors*. The most important findings from the work reported in that book are:

- Donors give their largest gifts to organizations that embrace them as partners.
- Everyone in a nonprofit organization has the power to contribute to increased levels of belief and confidence that in turn drive increased fundraising results; everyone likewise has some capacity to damage levels of belief and confidence in the organization.
- Donors with high levels of belief and confidence who are embraced as partners often make major and principal gifts without even being asked—most reported that their largest gifts were overwhelmingly, if not exclusively, self-solicited.

Dennis Keller states, "Most of our gifts have been self-investigated and self-initiated" (quoted in Schiller 2016, xvii). He continues, "The best way, that has the happiest reverberations for philanthropists and organizations, is to encourage deep engagement through which philanthropists figure out what they want to do based on their core beliefs and informed desires to help" (Schiller 2016, xvii). According to major- and principal-gift donors, being engaged and embraced as partners is important in decisions about major gifts; it is almost always essential when it comes to decisions about their largest gifts.

There are two ways of viewing fundraising. Many (perhaps most) people view it as the process of *moving money from someone who has it to an organization that needs it.* In contrast, those who have had great success in major-gift fundraising view it as *enabling generous donors and capable organizations to pool resources to achieve something that is important to both.* People who hold the first view see fundraisers first and foremost as solicitors. They are often scared of fundraising, think they are not good at it, do their best to avoid it, make donors uncomfortable, raise much less than they otherwise could for their organizations, burn out in fundraising jobs or volunteer roles, or any combination of these. Those who hold the latter view see fundraisers first and foremost as facilitators of generosity in a context of philanthropic partnership. They gain the trust of donors, experience the appreciation and joy of donors who make meaningful and satisfying gifts, help both donors and organizations realize shared objectives for meaningful impact on society, and think they have some of the best jobs in the world. Even more importantly, the donors who work with them give more and give more often.

Facilitating a philanthropic partnership takes more time and effort on the part of fundraising professionals, not less. If performance metrics reward expediency over long-term outcomes, those in the best positions to facilitate philanthropic partnership instead move forward with plans and proposals, waiting until the end of the process to engage potential donors. This type of fundraising can work; indeed, it produces fundraising revenue all the time. But donors are much less invested in outcomes and thus inevitably make smaller gifts than they are capable of making.

Successful major- and principal-gift fundraisers are active listeners. Their personal passions are aligned with an organization's mission. They have a kind and generous spirit, and they are both resilient (fundraisers will hear "no" many times!) and humble (successful fundraisers recognize that gifts are never the result of only one person's work). Above all, they are authentic in all interactions. In other words, "fundraisers must be prepared to represent an organization professionally, knowledgeably, and passionately. They must be equally prepared to learn the values, hopes, dreams, and motivations of donors" (Schiller 2018, 62).

Sophisticated major-gift donors look for authentic commitment to partnership and will avoid fundraisers who are merely after the quick win. Philanthropist Leonard Lauder says,

> Once you know what you want to do, don't just say "yes" to the first person who knocks on your door. Think, think, think. Ask yourself, "Are they looking to solve a great problem or to keep themselves employed? Will they help you change people's lives, or will you just be one of many keeping the organization or the development department alive? Will the organization survive without you?" It's hard to know all the right questions, but start by asking yourself these, and many more questions will follow. Eventually, you'll find the answers that give you the confidence you've found the right organizations and the right leaders—the right partners to help you get done what you most want to do. (Schiller 2016, 75)

Some fear that embracing donors as philanthropic partners leads to donors exerting inappropriate influence on strategic decisions. However, this is rare. When it happens, it is almost always because a donor has not been given sufficient information and access to understand how their giving objectives do and do not align with an institution's objectives so that they can make good giving decisions.

When we say "no" to a donor, it should almost always be because we believe the donor's gift will not succeed—that they will not be proud of the result. Fundraisers can say "no, period" when their organizations do not want the restrictions donors want to impose on gifts, but it is generally better to say instead something like "I know what the organization is trying to accomplish, and I know what you are aiming to accomplish with your philanthropy, and I'd like to explain to you why this gift will not be successful in our organization at this moment in time." That kind of "no" requires knowledge of organizational objectives and capacity, as well as knowledge of donor objectives; it is not possible unless fundraisers have acquired both types of knowledge.

When donors see themselves as partners and when they are treated as partners, they also give more than their financial resources. As Jerold Panas (1984) found when he was writing *Mega Gifts*, there is a high correlation between involvement as a volunteer (board member or otherwise) and major giving. For example, philanthropic couples who were inter-

viewed in one study typically served on four or more boards and reported that their largest gifts went to the organizations where they were
serving (Schiller 2016). Provided an organization has adequate opportunity for meaningful engagement, this is good news for major- and principal-gift fundraisers, in that high-net-worth donors volunteer at twice the
rate of the general US population (US Trust and Indiana University Lilly
Family School of Philanthropy 2018). But this also presents a challenge;
some donors do not want to serve on boards, and others are not suited to
board service. Furthermore, boards cannot function effectively with hundreds of members. As demands for philanthropy grow, so must opportunities for deep engagement.

Although planned giving is discussed in more detail by Jeff Comfort
in chapter 9 of this book, one point is especially relevant in the context of
this chapter: *Most major gifts are planned, and most planned gifts are major.*
Today's major- and principal-gift fundraisers must take into account the
Fidelity Charitable (2017) finding cited earlier in this chapter—that the
vast majority of donors would like to give more and that financial planning along with impact are the principal concerns holding them back.

IMPACT

The top reasons for giving of high-net-worth individuals in the United
States, per the US Trust 2018 report, are "their belief in the mission of the
organization" and "their belief that their gift can make a difference." Just
17 percent of wealthy donors said they were always motivated to give by
tax benefits, a percentage consistent with earlier studies.

Eighty six percent of individuals in the US Trust 2018 study have
confidence in nonprofit organizations to solve societal or global problems. Less than half have confidence in the federal executive or legislative
branches. Furthermore, 74 percent draw on their personal values when
determining which nonprofit organizations to support, underscoring the
importance of partnership as discussed earlier in this chapter. Yet only 42
percent of wealthy donors believe their giving is having the impact they
intended. Most reported that they do not know the impact (US Trust and
Indiana University Lilly Family School of Philanthropy 2018).

As expressed in a previous work, "A valuable and often-heard saying
in the world of philanthropy is that donors don't give major gifts to
organizations that *have* needs, but rather to organizations that *meet* needs.

Leading philanthropists go further to say that need is the wrong emphasis altogether; instead, opportunity is what motivates both sides in a philanthropic partnership" (Schiller 2016, xviii). When philanthropists see and understand opportunity for impact, they will give more and more readily. Often, they will give before they are asked.

Donors with a clear sense of their desired impact will also move beyond organizations with which they have an existing affiliation in order to find the best partner to meet needs. In fact, "it is not uncommon for a philanthropist to begin with an idea, *even without an organizational partner in mind*, and then to find the best partner or partners to implement the idea. Especially in these cases, philanthropists' intentions are to give to society *through* the organization as much as to make a gift *to* the organization" (Schiller 2016, xviii).

Donors who do not see impact and those who lack confidence in an organization's ability to shape and deliver on shared objectives will put money in temporary gift accounts, such as donor-advised funds. For donors still focused on building their businesses and their wealth, donor-advised funds allow them to defer allocation of gifts until they have time to focus on finding and working with the right nonprofit partners. Most fundraisers agree, however, that recent dramatic growth in donor-advised funds is also due to insufficient confidence on the part of donors when it comes to nonprofit transparency and impact, as confirmed in the Fidelity Charitable report (2017) cited earlier in this chapter.

Successful major- and principal-gift fundraisers focus on impact rather than organizational need, and multiple studies make clear that much greater success in fundraising is possible with yet more attention to impact. Impact provides an excellent lens through which to reexamine all the stages of major and principal-gift fundraising: identification, cultivation, solicitation, and stewardship.

IMPACT IN ALL PHASES OF THE FUNDRAISING CYCLE

Identification begins with wealth screening and assessment of affiliation; is the potential donor a loyal graduate, a happy parent, a grateful patient, or a past donor? The impact lens requires examination of potential for philanthropic partnership. Has the potential donor given to organizations with a similar mission? Do her family's philanthropic priorities align with any of the objectives of the organization? Does he know about the impact we have had in areas that are important to him and his family? Fundraisers working with these potential donors must ask not only about passion for the organization but also about overall philanthropic objectives.

Universities routinely leave money on the table by engaging alumni only as graduates of one department rather than as representatives of generous families with potentially wide-ranging philanthropic interests. An article on Harvard's recent campaign notes that most of the largest gifts in the campaign supported more than one school and that the "campaign committees of eight schools had at least one co-chair who was not an alumnus of that school and was not married to one" (Joslyn and Sandoval 2018).

As the Harvard data suggests, educational institutions interested in true philanthropic partnership open themselves to every possible way of engaging the current philanthropic objectives of donors, using prior affiliation (such as the department from which someone graduated forty years ago) only as a starting point, not a restricting factor. They also see major-gift officers assigned to a specific unit not as *owners* of prospective donors who graduated from that unit but as contributors to the overall advancement team's and donor base's knowledge about that particular unit. That knowledge, combined with knowledge from team members with other special expertise (such as planned giving), enables donors to understand the full range of impact possible in their philanthropic relationship with the overall institution.

In cultivation and solicitation, a focus on impact requires that fundraisers communicate about the impact of a donor's past gifts, the impact of philanthropy on the organization's ability to fulfill its mission, and the impact of the organization's work on society. The *organization's need* must not be the focus of discussion but rather the *objective* shared by the donor and the organization.

Leading fundraisers challenge organizational leaders to answer the question, Why? We want more endowment for student financial aid. Why? Because we want to reduce student-loan debt. Why? Because we want to remove financial obstacles for the best and brightest students. Why? Because the best solutions come from having the best minds and the greatest diversity of perspectives at the table.

We want more money for graduate fellowships. Why? Because that enables us to attract and retain the best faculty members. Why? Because additional faculty members and graduate fellows in this department will allow us to do more and better research. Why? Because we will accelerate our work in genetic research that will contribute to breakthroughs in understanding and curing Alzheimer's.

In cultivation and solicitation, a focus on impact also requires attention to measurable outcomes. Philanthropist Jeanette Lerman-Neubauer says, "We prefer partners whose strategic vision is aligned with our philanthropic objectives and whose leaders are committed to data analysis that measures progress against a specific plan" (quoted in Schiller 2016, 23). "Find a partner who ascribes to your vision and values, who brings the most innovative ideas to the discussion, and who can carry it through," she continues. "The right leader wants the right donor partner and vice versa. Then measure, or you won't know if you've arrived" (Schiller 2016, 76–77).

Finally, a focus on impact requires a deeper commitment to stewardship. Donors want to be thanked, and organizational representatives can't say "Thank you" enough. Some donors also want to be recognized publicly. But all major- and principal-gift donors want to know that their gift had impact. *The most important way to thank and recognize donors is to ensure that their gifts have the impact they desire and the impact they were promised.*

MEETING DONORS AS THEY PREFER

Key findings of the 2018 US Trust study include:

- "Giving is being shaped by a diverse donor universe of different ages, ethnic backgrounds and gender identities."
- "Women are at the forefront of philanthropic engagement and impact." (US Trust and Indiana University Lilly Family School of Philanthropy 2018, 7)

These realities are explored in detail in part V of this book and have significant implications for major- and principal-gift fundraising. Another excellent resource is Kathleen Loehr's book *Gender Matters: A Guide to Growing Women's Philanthropy* (2018). Every aspect of fundraising, from identification to cultivation to solicitation to stewardship, must be reexamined in light of an ever-evolving and diverse world of philanthropy to ensure that donors have an opportunity to engage in ways that lead to the most mutually beneficial philanthropic partnerships.

While one-size-fits-all strategies for major- and principal-gift fundraising have never been effective, the importance of meeting top donors as they prefer, with customized cultivation and solicitation strategies, is greater than ever. It is also more complex, challenging, and interesting than ever.

BELIEF AND CONFIDENCE

Major- and principal-gift donors and those who facilitate their giving believe in the power and importance of giving, they believe in the missions of the organizations they serve, and they share the visions of the leaders with whom they partner. Belief allows donors and leaders to dream great dreams about transforming organizations and improving quality of life. But vision without strategy is wishful thinking.

Belief without confidence—confidence borne of due diligence and grounded in trust—can lead to unsuccessful and disappointing giving experiences. As Harold J. "Si" Seymour wrote in his highly influential book *Designs for Fund-Raising*, "Giving is prompted emotionally and then rationalized. The heart has to prompt the mind to go where logic points the way" (1966, 29). Belief provides the emotional spark, and confidence provides the rational structure. Belief and confidence are both required and on multiple levels.

Interviews with leading fundraisers and top philanthropists revealed sixteen types of belief and confidence that are typically strong in top-performing major- and principal-gift fundraising programs (Schiller 2016). Those beliefs and confidences among donors include:

1. Belief in the importance of giving
2. Confidence in personal financial circumstances—present and future
3. Confidence in other personal circumstances
4. Belief in mission
5. Confidence in leaders
6. Belief in vision and confidence in strategy
7. Confidence in organizational financial planning and stability—present and future

Those beliefs and confidences among organizational leaders include:

1. Confidence in the capacity to raise additional funds
2. Belief that the organization is worthy of philanthropic investment
3. Belief and confidence in each other's leadership, vision, strategy, and planning
4. Confidence in the chief development officer and development program
5. Confidence in capacity to meet fundraising goals
6. Belief in philanthropic partnership

Those beliefs and confidences among fundraising staff members and volunteers include:

1. Belief in mission
2. Confidence in leaders, plans, and goals
3. Belief that individual contributions make a difference

Weakness in any one area can weaken a philanthropic partnership and lead to reduced or delayed giving. Strength in some areas can be leveraged to create strength in others, and strength in many areas leads to an upward spiral in confidence that builds on and sustains itself. Organizations and donors together form winning teams, and others want to join the team. Organizations with winning fundraising teams raise more, not because they need money, but because they and their donor partners have greater impact, achieve shared objectives, and dream yet bigger dreams.

PRINCIPAL GIFTS

With mega gifts in the hundreds of millions or even billions of dollars making headlines, many organizations think of principal gifts as the domain of only the largest, wealthiest institutions. But there is a definition of principal gifts that is applicable to every institution. Prospective principal-gift donors are those with the capacity and potential desire to make an organization one of the primary beneficiaries of their generosity and whose wealth capacity, combined with the inclination toward engaging in philanthropic partnerships, will enable them to make the organization's largest gifts (Schiller 2018).

While a major-gifts program will typically address the five percent of donors who give 95 percent of dollars, a focused and disciplined principal-gifts program allows an organization to increase the size of its ten largest gifts and raise the belief and confidence of donors at all levels. Principal gifts are not merely major gifts with more zeroes; they are the expression of philanthropic partnership at the highest levels from donors who, together with administrative and board leaders, drive transformational growth in an organization's impact on society.

Ensuring that an organization's largest gifts are as large as possible requires special focus, discipline, and approaches to shaping culture, identifying potential donors, developing shared objectives, creating big ideas, composing relationship-building teams, and structuring engagement.

DRIVING PERFORMANCE

Thanks to technology and to more rigorous measurement of some of the factors involved in identifying, cultivating, soliciting, and stewarding major- and principal-gift donors, the fundraising profession has increased the capacity of volunteer and staff fundraisers to raise more and larger gifts. We know more about the assets of donors and potential donors, we can make better decisions about the assignment of major-gift officer portfolios, and we know more about average behaviors when it comes to numbers and types of so-called moves required before solicitation. With all that improvement, however, eight out of ten donors express concern about nonprofit transparency and understanding the impact of their giving, and 95 percent say they would give more under the right circumstances (Fidelity Charitable 2017).

Metrics related to quantity are a powerful tool but cannot and must not replace measurement of the quality of donor engagement and evaluation of the quality of the donor–organization partnership. The more an organization is viewed as a priority in a donor's giving, the less applicable many quantitative metrics become.

For example, the standard practice of assigning a rating based on a percentage of known wealth may be useful early in the process of narrowing a large number of potential donors to a manageable portfolio, but this rating should not be mistaken for a predictor of what a highly engaged philanthropic partner might ultimately give. Someone with an initial rating of $1 million might well give $10 million, whereas someone with an initial rating of $5 million might love the organization and still give $10,000 when their family's priority for philanthropy lies elsewhere. Overadherence to wealth-capacity ratings routinely leads to undersolicitation as well as oversolicitation.

When gift officers are measured by little more than a dashboard, they will perform to the dashboard. Even against their better judgment, with the wrong incentives, they will ask for a smaller gift this year rather than build a partnership that would yield a much larger gift next year. They will schedule five visits instead of devoting that same amount of time to in-depth discussion with a donor's peer who is ideally placed to raise that donor's sights to much higher levels. Instead of following up on the more complex work of helping donors figure out how to give more than they thought they could give, they settle for the quicker gift of cash or appreciated stock. Activity is important, but it should not be confused with outcomes when measuring the quantitative aspects of major-gift work.

David Lively's book *Managing Major Gift Fundraisers* (2017) gives useful guidance for creating dashboards—or "placemats"—that drive the best overall outcomes. He makes a strong case for reducing portfolio size while incentivizing fundraisers, based primarily on the number of major gifts secured. This advice takes into account the reality that, while major gifts without meaningful relationships will be smaller and less frequent, relationships that do not involve regular major giving will not advance the institution's work.

As already discussed in this chapter and by other authors in this book, changing demographics require active-listening skills, a capacity to meet donors as they prefer, a natural curiosity about what donors are trying to accomplish both for and beyond any specific institution, and authenticity in all interactions. Improvement in these skills and results of their application rarely appear in any major-gift-officer performance metrics.

With technological advances and tremendous improvement in quantitative metrics, the fundraising profession is better equipped than ever to support and drive excellent fundraising performance. But it is also more vulnerable than ever to overreliance on simplistic measurement that can short-circuit the development of deep and lasting philanthropic partnerships.

It is easy to agree that facilitating philanthropy, as opposed to parting wealthy people from their money, is more joyful *and* more productive for both donors and organizations. It is not so simple to ensure that metrics and ultimately incentives are aligned with this approach and simultaneously drive fundraising revenue. Without both quantitative and qualitative metrics and without proper balance of these, fundraising results will be suboptimal. Organizational leaders will continue to wonder why peers are raising more, and the philanthropic intent of the organization's donors will continue to far surpass their expression of that intent.

By contrast, when major- and principal-gift fundraisers authentically help generous people make gifts with impact and gifts that the donors find satisfying, the happiness they give the donors will spill over. The fundraisers themselves will gain much more satisfaction than any promotion or raise can ever provide. Hiring managers who know how to incentivize deep and lasting donor engagement and commitment will attract and retain the best fundraisers and drive the most sustainable growth in fundraising.

CONCLUSION

In 1993, Michael J. Worth edited the book *Educational Fund Raising: Principles and Practice*, sponsored by the American Council on Education. The chapter on major gifts was written by my principal fundraising mentor from Cornell, David R. Dunlop. In his chapter on major gifts, Dave highlights the importance of developing each prospective major-gift donor's "awareness, understanding, caring, involvement, and commitment to the institution and to the purpose for which their gift is sought" (Dunlop 1993, 116). He also notes, "When people first encounter an institution, they view its people and projects in the third person, in terms of 'they,' 'them,' and 'those.' Before they can become prospects for significant giving, that perspective must change to the first person: They must speak, think, and feel in terms of 'we,' 'us,' and 'our'" (102).

Much has changed in the nearly thirty years since that book was written. Advancement programs have grown dramatically in size and complexity, and technology and data have allowed for much more sophisticated portfolio assignment and management. Donors also have much more access to information and data to guide their giving decisions. The opportunities for impact on society—for both nonprofit institutions and for the donors who partner with them—change as the world around us changes. And the gender, race, ethnicity, and age composition of the donor base evolves along with changes in the demographics of the population at large, the constituencies served by individual institutions, and the distribution of wealth.

Yet the fundamentals of major- and principal-gift fundraising remain the same. Ultimately, the role of fundraiser is to facilitate generosity—to build philanthropic partnerships in which donors and the institutions they support accomplish something together that neither could without the other. Attention to wealth capacity, portfolio size, visits, proposals, numbers of solicitations, and dollars raised in any given fiscal year is important.

But ultimate success is measured by the depth of awareness, understanding, caring, involvement, and commitment achieved and by the inevitable expressions of that depth of commitment on the part of generous people. This occurs when donors "speak, think, and feel" (Dunlop 1993) in the first person and when they choose the institution as one of the primary vehicles through which their major giving has a significant and meaningful impact on society.

REFERENCES

Dunlop, David R. 1993. "Major Gift Programs." In *Educational Fund Raising: Principles and Practice*, edited by Michael J. Worth, 97–116. Phoenix: American Council on Education, Oryx Press.

Fidelity Charitable. 2017. *Overcoming Barriers to Giving*. Boston: Fidelity Charitable. https://www.fidelitycharitable.org/docs/overcoming-barriers-to-giving.pdf.

Giving USA Foundation. 2018. *Giving USA 2018: The Annual Report on Philanthropy for the Year 2017*. Chicago: Giving USA Foundation. https://givingusa.org/tag/giving-usa-2018/.

Joslyn, Heather, and Timothy Sandoval. 2018. "The Art of the Giant Campaign." *Chronicle of Philanthropy*, October 30, 2018. https://www.philanthropy.com/article/How-HarvardMichigan-Made/244923.

Lively, David. 2017. *Managing Major Gift Fundraisers: A Contrarian's Guide*. Washington, DC: Council for Advancement and Support of Education.

Loehr, Kathleen. 2018. *Gender Matters: A Guide to Growing Women's Philanthropy*. Washington, DC: Council for Advancement and Support of Education.

Panas, Jerold. 1984. *Mega Gifts: Who Gives Them, Who Gets Them*. Chicago: Pluribus Press.

Schiller, Ronald J. 2016. *Belief and Confidence: Donors Talk about Successful Philanthropic Partnership*. Washington, DC: Council for Advancement and Support of Education.

———. 2018. *Raising Your Organization's Largest Gifts: A Principal Gifts Handbook*. Washington, DC: Council for Advancement and Support of Education.

Seymour, Harold J. 1966. *Designs for Fund-Raising: Principles, Patterns, Techniques*. New York: McGraw-Hill.

US Trust and Indiana University Lilly Family School of Philanthropy. 2018. *The 2018 US Trust Study of High Net Worth Philanthropy: Charitable Practices and Preferences of Wealthy Households*. New York: US Trust Philanthropic Solutions and Family Group. https://www.ustrust.com/articles/2018-us-trust-study-of-high-net-worth-philanthropy.html.

Worth, Michael J., ed. 1993. *Educational Fund Raising: Principles and Practice*. Phoenix: American Council on Education, Oryx Press.

NINE

Planned Giving

Jeff Comfort

Gift planning always begins with the donor and the goals of the gift. In typical planned-giving training, the trainers often strongly encourage planned-giving professionals to carry either a laptop computer or flip chart depicting various gift scenarios. They suggest that visual representation is the best way to tell the story and market planned-giving products. However, the practice of planned giving, including interactions with donors, teaches that it is *never* about our story. It is not about trying to make our points, and it is not about our technical plans. The most important thing is the donors' stories; listening to them is the best marketing tool we have. It is all about them. This chapter is premised on that perspective.

Planned giving is a major source of revenue in higher-education fundraising today, and collaboration between planned giving and major-gift programs is essential. Ways of fostering that collaboration are explored in a later section. But again, despite the technical points that are discussed, the emphasis should always be on the donor and his or her philanthropic intent rather than our role as fundraisers.

BASIC DEFINITIONS

What is a planned gift? There are many definitions of *planned giving*, almost all of which focus on its technical aspects. Some may choose to define it as any gift that requires the assistance of a professional staff person or financial advisor. However, such a definition focuses on the staff side of the process. A more appropriate definition is focused on the donor. From this perspective, planned giving is the answer to a would-be donor's objection that he or she "would like to do more for your institution, but . . ." More broadly, it is the process of planning gifts in light of:

- Someone's dreams for making a difference
- Their personal and family values
- Their financial resources and objectives
- Current and future planning opportunities

Virtually every development office has a major-gifts program, the goals and practices of which are well understood throughout the institution. Planned-giving programs have tended to have more of an aura of mystery, with their operations shrouded in the technical aspects and complexities of gift planning.

The case for planned giving is clear. Mature planned-giving programs may generate 20 to 40 percent of total annual institutional fundraising revenues. Planned-giving programs are usually more cost-effective than annual giving, major giving, special events, and other programs. Any single planned gift is typically anywhere from ten to one thousand times larger than any one of the donor's lifetime outright gifts.

THE PROCESS OF PLANNED GIVING

Completing a planned gift usually involves deciding on the right gift plan, funded with the best asset and moved on the donor's time frame. It also *always* involves donative intent on the part of the donor. Figure 9.1 depicts the process.

The donor's consideration of a gift can start at any point around the circle. For example, say that a donor has a highly appreciated asset and wants to avoid incurring a capital gains tax when selling it. The conversation then may move to the gift plan, addressing such questions as, Does the donor want an income for giving the property, or does the donor want the largest tax deduction and to see his gift impact on the charity immediately? As for timing, this can refer to when the gift is made or when the gift funds may actually be received by the charity. Often, this is years or decades in the future.

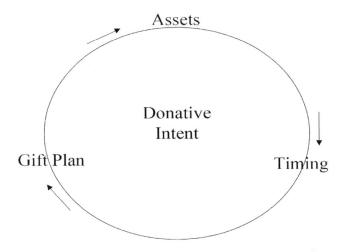

Figure 9.1. Process of a Planned Gift

Figure 9.1 features donative intent in the center of the process. If donative intent is not there at least to some degree, then the gift will probably not occur. Every gift plan has the word *gift* in the name of the plan for good reason. There is never a situation in which the donor actually comes out financially ahead, especially if the time value of money is included in the consideration. If a donor does not have donative intent, then it would be best to recommend that he or she work with a for-profit entity, which can help them with their quest for the best financial outcome for themselves.

GIFT PLANS

This section provides a brief look at some of the common gift plans is use today. Most planned gifts fall into one or more of three categories: (1) outright gift (usually of complex assets), (2) life-income gifts, or (3) bequests (gifts at death).

Outright Gifts

The most common form of outright gift is a cash donation. However, it is almost always to a donor's advantage to give gifts of appreciated property instead of cash, particularly for large gifts. This allows the donor to receive a tax deduction for the full market value of the gift and avoid all capital gains tax. Most gifts of appreciated property are gifts of stocks or real estate, though other property, such as artwork or other tangible property, may sometimes be appropriate.

Outright planned gifts are generally for prospects who can afford to make the gift you are proposing but are looking for the most tax-efficient way to give. Rule of thumb: Itemizing major gifts will save about a third of the value of a cash gift in reduced taxes or about half of the value if the gift is made with highly appreciated property.

Life-Income Gifts

The various life-income gift plans all involve a person making a gift but retaining an income interest from the gift for themselves or others for life or for a set term of years. While the various plans have different features, they all offer the following benefits: a substantial ultimate charitable gift; a current income tax deduction for a portion of the gift (based on federal tax law, usually 30 percent to 50 percent); and lifetime income for one or more recipients (usually the donor and spouse, though it may go to anyone). Income from the gifted asset often is greatly increased and capital gains tax is avoided if the gift is made with appreciated property.

These plans include charitable remainder trusts (CRTs), which may pay variable or fixed income, and gift annuities, which pay a fixed income. Which approach the donor may prefer depends on age, as well as other considerations.

Bequests

Bequests are the easiest way to make a large gift and the largest single source of planned gifts. The most bequest income to institutions comes from estates of persons with moderate wealth. Bequests can be tax-wise ways to give. In addition, retirement-plan beneficiary designations can be a source of gifts and include a tremendous pool of wealth available to many donors today.

In addition to the types of gifts summarized here, there are a variety of other types of planned gifts that may be attractive to donors in certain circumstances, including charitable lead trusts (CLTs) and the retained life estate. Again, there are many excellent sources of detailed information available to any reader who wants more specifics on how any of the gifts mentioned here can be designed.

CONSIDERING THE DONOR'S ASSETS

While donors can give only what they have, they often have more to give than they think they do—or at least more than they care to tell us. Donors always think first of their cash or income when we ask them for gifts, even very large gifts. Most outright major gifts come from a donor's income or from cash or cash equivalents. Almost all planned gifts are made with assets. Most wealthy donors hold a very high percent of their wealth in assets other than cash, such as stocks, bonds, and real estate. Helping a donor move the gift consideration from their income or cash to assets they own can allow them to contemplate a much more significant gift. This is how planned giving often adds one, two, or three zeros to the gift conversation.

How do you help a donor think about assets as opposed to income or cash? It can be as simple as saying, "You know, most donors make their gifts from their income or cash; however, many donors have found tremendous additional benefits by making gifts of assets, particularly appreciated assets. Is this something where you may want additional information?"

Explaining your role as a planned giving officer and, in a sense, asking permission to ask about assets and plans usually leads to a highly productive conversation. It might go something like this: "Mr. Donor, my job is to help donors plan their gifts in a way that best fits their overall financial and estate plans. The more information you can share with me about this, the better I may be able to recommend gift ideas for you to consider with your advisors. Of course, you and your advisors know more than I ever could or should know about your assets and plans. Would you be open to sharing with me some information about your plans and the assets you hold?"

In this scenario, the planned giving officer has asked permission for the conversation and positioned himself or herself alongside the donor's advisors. It is not uncommon for the conversation that follows to reveal a lot about what assets the donor holds and what his or her financial and estate plans and aspirations are.

THE IMPORTANCE OF TIMING

Outright major gifts are often made based on the timing of the institution's near-term funding priorities or a campaign. Planned gifts are almost always made based on the donor's time frame. Most major gifts support immediate projects. Most planned gifts are not realized for years or decades into the future, so from a donor's standpoint, what's the rush?

It is often life events that drive a planned gift to closure. At any given time, a planned-giving officer may have prospects in his or her portfolio who have been considering their gifts for several years. Someone might ask, "Why do you still have that donor in your portfolio? It looks like it has been years. Is this donor really a prospect?" A good response would be, "When the donor is ready, the gift will appear." Many of the largest planned gifts are years and years in discussion before documents are signed, so it is important to stay in touch with these longtime prospects.

Most planned gifts require the donor to meet with an attorney. This often requires making and documenting complex decisions, facing mortality, and a big expense. Donors with no estate plans or wildly outdated estate plans are in good company! Then, sometimes suddenly, circumstances change. A loved one passes away, a serious health condition surfaces, a new grandchild arrives, or the donor simply retires and a life event drives the donor to estate planning. The time may be right to revisit the gift conversation.

Timing should also be considered for the ultimate designation of a planned gift. As discussed earlier, it rarely makes sense to speak with a donor about a bequest to support a capital project like a new building. The dean's priorities are certainly important for outright major-gift discussions but are not often a good fit for a planned gift that will most likely be realized many deans hence. For these and other reasons, planned gifts are usually designated for an endowment to support a program that can be expected to be a priority for generations to come.

FOSTERING COLLABORATION BETWEEN MAJOR GIFTS AND PLANNED GIVING

As mentioned previously, professional staff working in planned giving and major gifts are the two titans of the fundraising world today. They account for the largest gifts and a majority of total gifts at virtually every charity in the United States. They are the foundation of every successful capital campaign. Yet in most charitable organizations, they lack coordination, functioning independently at best and, at worst, in outright competition. Why is this?

In my opinion, the answer is often found in gift-crediting policies. Particularly with the advent of metrics, gift-crediting policies can drive a wedge between planned and major gifts. Many of the highest-capacity planned-gift prospects are managed in the portfolios of major-gift officers, yet it is the planned-giving officers who have the experience and expertise to help complete a planned gift with these prospects.

To facilitate collaboration, it is essential that gift-crediting policies allow for joint credit for both the major- and the planned-gift officers when a planned gift is completed. Ideally, this would be joint *full* credit for each officer. The highest-performing planned-gift programs all model absolute trust and collaboration between the planned- and major-gift programs.

COUNTING PLANNED GIFTS

Another essential for collaboration between the major- and planned-gift staff is counting policies that include planned gifts. Development officers are incentivized through metrics, performance appraisals, and merit compensation to work on gifts that are closed and counted. Although some may disagree, it can be argued that counting policies that report irrevocable and revocable gifts at face value motivate and produce many more planned gifts.

Some further explanation of counting revocable planned gifts is in order here. As mentioned previously, these are most often simple bequests in a living donor's will or trust and are often referred to as bequest expectancies. Over the past century, far and away the most common planned gift has been a simple bequest. However, planned-giving staff members spend the majority of their time on more complicated gifts, like a charitable remainder trust, because these take more planning than a simple bequest.

Most of the time that the planned-giving staff dedicates is, therefore, associated with gift sources other than bequest gifts, despite the fact that bequests and bequest expectancies are by far the single largest source of planned-giving revenue. Recent national surveys show that, for most institutions, even those with highly sophisticated and well-staffed planned-giving programs, bequests and bequest expectancies provide a very high percentage of their planned-gift revenue.

The most cited counting policies are the Council for Advancement and Support of Education Reporting Standards. These policies provide for counting certain bequest expectancies at face value toward a *campaign goal*, with documentation, and recommend adopting a minimum age requirement. The CASE standards suggest counting revocable gifts, such as bequests, at full face value in campaigns for donors age seventy or above. Those guidelines also recommend establishing separate goals for outright and deferred gifts and reporting the totals separately (CASE 2009, 87). The majority of higher education development programs do count bequest expectancies toward their campaign goals.

Some oppose this practice for various reasons. The funds have not yet been received, so how can we put bequest expectancies on our books? But we should not confuse the Generally Accepted Accounting Principles (GAAP), used in the institution's financial accounting, with development or campaign counting and reporting standards. Bequest expectancies are *not* put on financial statements. If they are included on campaign progress reports, however, then these two sets of books will reconcile when and if the gifts arrive.

Another concern is how to recognize a donor's $1 million outright gift alongside another donor's $1 million bequest expectancy. Aren't these apples and oranges? Technically yes, and they are also both beautiful gift commitments. Two donors generally do not worry about how their respective gifts are recognized, so long as they are.

Recognition aside, it certainly is worth discussing the reliability of counting revocable gifts, given that the donor may change his estate plans in the future. This concern is primarily raised with regard to commitments that may not be realized until far into the distant future. However, major-gift donors making a five-year pledge can change their minds, too, although such commitments have a very low default rate. Similarly, only a small number of bequest-expectancy donors change their charitable estate commitments, and many who do actually increase their charitable-gift provision. Also, a donor whose bequest expectancy has been publicly recognized and well stewarded is much less likely to take away the estate gift.

Our purpose is to advance the mission of the charity. As we seek to encourage donors to make gifts, the largest gifts possible, we should be mindful that, for some, this may include a planned gift as opposed to an outright gift. In this context, largest means the gift with the most value, in terms of both present and future value, not simply the largest present face value. Again, bringing the concept of gift planning to the conversation can and often does add at least one or more zeros to the gift.

When you read someone's will, what you often find are gifts to family members and loved ones. When a donor includes a gift for a charity in a will, they have elevated that institution to the status of family. It's often also a statement of the donor's lifetime values. Shouldn't we recognize and celebrate these donors for their philanthropic commitment?

BLENDED GIFTS: PUTTING MAJOR AND PLANNED GIFTS TOGETHER

One of the arguments for counting bequests relates to the growing importance of blended gifts. Robert Sharpe coined the phrase *blended gifts* in 1995 when discussing generational changes in giving (Sharpe Group 2016). Sharpe's outlook was prescient.

Baby boomers are now in their peak giving years, and blended gifts have accordingly become a hot topic in development. Blended gifts generally refer to working with a donor on a current outright gift and also on a planned gift, such as a bequest expectancy. From a development standpoint, this usually requires collaboration between major- and planned-gifts staff. From the institution's standpoint, it usually results in much larger combined gift commitments. Most donors do not see this as two separate gifts but rather simply as fulfillment of their overall philanthropic interests.

Working on blended gifts is really just an extension of moving typical principal-gift-fundraising practices down the donor pyramid to major and planned gifts. An inside look at most principal gifts frequently reveals a basket of commitments. That is, these principal gifts often include some outright and some planned-gift commitments that are combined in the publicly announced total gift. A holistic approach to these donors' philanthropic interests may result in a blended gift, meaning additional funds for the charity and happier donors, as well.

A word of caution on blended gifts: Some see this practice as making a dual ask. This can be a disastrous approach, as it requires the donor to make two simultaneous significant gift decisions, which can result in no gift being made. A blended-gift approach that is likely to be more comfortable for the donor is a sequential ask.

A sequential ask entails soliciting a donor for an outright gift commitment and then, after good stewardship over time, asking the donor to consider endowing the same program through a bequest. Alternatively, it may entail a donor committing to an endowment through a bequest later and, again after good stewardship over time, being asked if they would like to enjoy seeing their ultimately endowed program in action through the immediate impact of an outright gift now.

PLANNED GIVING: THE SCIENCE AND THE ART

There are abundant resources on the technical aspects of planned giving: intricate plans; elaborate tax deductions; convoluted tax rulings; and, of course, the all-encompassing Internal Revenue Code. This may be considered the science of planned giving and is often a crucial element at some point in the process of finalizing a planned gift. Our planned-giving community abounds with highly skilled technicians. But the highest-performing planned-giving programs understand the value of the art of planned giving as well. The art of planned giving is infinitely more complex than the science.

The complexity of the art of planned giving results from the need to delve deep into the psychology of donors. The impetus for each donor to consider any planned gift may be found in the culmination of each unique individual's lifetime experiences and events.

A not-uncommon approach to planned-gift fundraising is to market or ask a donor about a particular gift plan. For instance, we might ask, "Would you be interested in a gift plan that could provide you with an income for life and a big tax deduction? Then you should consider a gift annuity." This product or package-sale approach can result in a good number of closed planned gifts.

But planned gifts solicited through the sale approach tend to be smaller in size for the institution and less than fully satisfying for the donor than those resulting from a more holistic approach of discovery, delving into the philanthropic motivations of the donor. A better approach is to spend more time listening to the donor, allowing that individual the opportunity to share their passions.

One of our most powerful tools in a donor visit is the pregnant pause. Ask a deep question, and then make sure the donor talks next, even if it takes what seems like forever. Here is a question that can be quite effective in helping a donor move forward in their gift planning, especially if the process seems to have stalled: "What would your parents think of your making this gift?" Of course, like a good lawyer in a courtroom, you will want to know the answer before you ask this question.

Often in the early stages of getting to know a donor considering a planned gift, it may be useful to ask "Where did you learn your philanthropy?" or "Did your parents support their favorite charities?" It is pretty common for donors to reply that they learned to give early in life and that their parents did indeed make charitable gifts. Usually the planned gift in consideration is much larger than the gifts they recall their parents making. Such donors often reply that their parents would be amazed or very proud of the gift. This can be a very powerful motivator in moving the gift forward.

Another effective question in a first or early meeting with donors considering a planned gift is "What would you like this relationship to look like going forward?" This can be extremely instructive on planning for the process. Sometimes, the donor may answer along the lines of "Aw shucks, I don't need any special attention." Take that with a grain of salt, and listen for clues that the donor may really enjoy meeting with the dean or some other form of recognition.

CONCLUSION

It is appropriate to conclude this chapter on a theme similar to how it began, in the words of one of the well-known figures in the field, Robert F. Sharpe Jr., who offers this powerful perspective on planned giving:

> In my experience there are two types of fundraisers. There are those who believe donors want to give and set about to help them do what they would like to do with respect for them as a complex human being. Many donors would like to make gifts larger than they are making but just don't think they can do it because of natural factors in play in their lives. Fortunately we have many tools to help them.
>
> Then there are the fundraisers who believe that most donors don't really want to give and they have to figure out how to get them to do something they really don't want to do. They see the donors as "targets" and the process as linear, starting with research and ending with

a successful ask and a closed gift. All the recognition, all the tax benefits, all the peer pressure and "all the king's men" may get them to give
once but often not again.

Both methods can lead to success, though the former approach
leads to the greatest results over time in my experience. The people
who grasp and internalize the fact that they must understand who their
donors are, why they want to give, and are able to then help them
figure out what is best to give, when to give, and how [will be the most
successful].

While you may "close" gifts in some cases, it is more satisfying to
do what you do at a birthday party when friends bring you gifts. You
don't "close" those gifts, you "open" them and you often get more than
you ever imagined or hoped for. (Sharpe 2014)

REFERENCES

CASE (Council for Advancement and Support of Education). 2009. *CASE Reporting Standards and Management Guidelines*. 4th ed. New York: CASE. https://www.case. org/Samples_Research_and_Tools/CASE_Reporting_Standards_and_ Management_Guidelines.html.
Sharpe, Robert F., Jr. 2014. E-mail to author, May 10, 2014.
Sharpe Group. 2016. "The Emergence of Blended Gifts." *Sharpe Group Blog*, April 27, 2016. https://sharpenet.com/uncategorized/the-emergence-of-blended-gifts/.

IV

Campaigns and Project Fundraising

Comprehensive campaigns are among the most visible fundraising strategies implemented by colleges and universities, and as discussed in chapter 2, campaign goals have increased dramatically in both private and public institutions in recent decades.

In chapter 10, Fritz Schroeder provides an overview of the principles involved in planning and managing comprehensive campaigns. As he notes, campaigns not only are vehicles for raising substantial funds but also serve as "wonderful opportunities for storytelling and moments to amplify the aspirations of an institution's particular direction and trajectory." Campaigns thus require the involvement of communications, marketing, and alumni-engagement professionals, as well as development officers. They are, indeed, efforts to *advance* the university in more ways than financially.

The current environment presents challenges to campaigns, which Schroeder considers. He concludes, "Despite headwinds, the comprehensive campaign is likely to continue as an important fundraising strategy for most colleges and universities. . . . But it will be essential to adapt the historic model to reflect the new forces affecting higher education today and in the future."

Specific objectives are one defining characteristic of campaigns, which are not primarily efforts to raise unrestricted funds. That is also the case with programs that seek support from corporations and foundations, which are generally not promising sources of general institutional support. In chapter 11, Shaun Brenton and Jenny Bickford discuss current trends and directions in foundation and corporate giving.

Like all of the authors in this book, Brenton and Bickford observe significant change that is bringing new challenges to higher-education institutions. And like others, they conclude that, despite a changing environment, there are opportunities for colleges and universities that adapt new strategies and respond to the needs and priorities of their donors.

TEN

The Art and Science of Comprehensive Campaigns

Fritz W. Schroeder

As discussed in chapter 2 of this book, the modern concept of fundraising campaigns in higher education began in the early twentieth century. Yet this concept did not develop in a vacuum; antecedents date back to the 1600s in America and include fundraising by church-affiliated institutions, whose presidents embarked on extended trips to secure gifts from the congregations to support defined projects (Thelin 2004, 62).

History also has chronicled numerous targeted efforts by groups of wealthy donors intent on achieving specific higher-education goals, such as the Women's Medical School Fund Committee, spearheaded by Mary Elizabeth Garrett and a circle of close friends, to raise the money for the Johns Hopkins Medical School in 1890 (JHUSOM, n.d.). In 1919, Harvard University was the first higher-education institution to employ professional fundraisers to manage an endowment-fund drive. Alumnus John Price Jones (1877–1964) led the campaign, which raised $14.2 million in less than a year. He went on to establish his own fundraising firm, among the first of its kind (National Philathropic Trust, n.d.).

Johns Hopkins University, where I am vice president for development and alumni relations, was founded by the individual philanthropy of the Baltimore merchant and railroad investor for whom the university is named. As early as the 1920s, the university conducted specific fundraising campaigns tied to the construction of a series of academic and student housing facilities. Over the past three decades, Johns Hopkins has launched and concluded three multibillion-dollar campaigns; the most recent, Rising to the Challenge, was completed in 2018 with $6 billion raised.

CHARACTERISTICS OF CAMPAIGNS

Fundraising campaigns have shared common characteristics for more than a century. Although many things have changed, these characteristics still mark contemporary campaigns:

- A defined monetary goal
- A clear articulation of purposes (e.g., scholarships, capital projects) and an increased sense of urgency that is different from the typical fundraising cycle
- A specific time frame (traditionally six to eight years in length)
- Specific priorities to be addressed by the campaign
- A unique marketing strategy that usually involves a name or a theme (for example, "Rising to the Challenge: The Campaign for Johns Hopkins")

These campaigns have positioned higher-education institutions to increase the investment in strategic priorities with the results that are produced by fundraising and alumni- and donor-engagement efforts.

KEY ELEMENTS OF SUCCESS

Diving more deeply into the modern era of campaign efforts, it is clear that there are several key elements that drive success:

- Comprehensive academic planning
- Defined time frame, goals, and sequence of activities
- Increased investment in fundraising and engagement
- Volunteer leadership and support
- Coordinated communications and marketing
- Increased donor stewardship and impact reporting
- Integrated alumni and constituent engagement and programming

Comprehensive Academic Planning

Although self-evident, this point bears repetition and emphasis: The fundraising agenda for any institution *must serve* the academic agenda and mission of the institution. Therefore, the first step in a comprehensive campaign is the academic planning process. In its simplest terms, the process should ask *academic leadership* to consider the following questions: What are the key priorities and directions for each school or unit involved in the campaign in the coming five to ten years? What resources will be required to address these priorities? How does philanthropy fit into this mix of resources? Does the market or constituency respond to the ideas? Are they compelling? What other resources will be required for us to be successful? How will success and progress be measured at the five-year or ten-year mark?

During the academic planning process, which can and should take months and perhaps a full year prior to the initiation of the campaign itself, the development staff should remain actively engaged. Development staff have the responsibility to facilitate planning efforts through discussions, retreats, goal templates, and other tools; to reflect on the priorities identified and serve as a temporary spokesperson for the donor community during the initial stages of the process; to organize, curate, and create themes around the ideas and priorities in a way that enables reflection and refinement; and to maintain open and transparent lines of communication with academic leaders during and after the process. This process should produce both an organized, comprehensive view of campaign priorities and clearly articulated goals that are coherent, relevant, and translatable to the donor community.

Defined Time Frame, Goals, and Sequence of Activities

Following the academic planning process, the burden of work returns to the development team for the next stage: scaling the aspirations of the campaign priorities against the capacity and reality of the institution's efforts. It is not an exaggeration to say that every initial list of priorities created by an institution in the first planning stage far exceeds the donor capacity, staff, budget, and historical fundraising levels of the organization.

At this stage, the development team should engage in a thorough process to evaluate the priorities identified and compare them to potential donor capacity (both in terms of the individual numbers of donors and the expected scale of their giving) and to possible donor interest in key priorities.

As Johns Hopkins planned its most recent campaign, senior development staff spent two full days reviewing the priorities and trying to identify potential donors and gifts from both existing donor lists and dream lists of individuals or organizations whom these priorities might attract. At the end of this exercise, there were several chart pages with very few names on them—a tangible and visual sign of the need to be realistic about the potential of those priorities in the coming campaign.

Traditionally, campaign planning at this stage has included a feasibility study, in which bulk surveys are deployed and individual and group interviews are conducted (often by outside consultants) to test the potential priorities with real donors. Feasibility studies have allowed institutions to have meaningful data to inform goals and priorities. Recently, however, the role of the feasibility study has changed. Often, schools will conduct their own listening tours, with volunteers hosting small gatherings of ten to fifteen people. The president, provost, dean, or campaign chair attends and gives a pitch for the upcoming campaign, allowing the academic leaders a chance to rehearse key messages in advance of the public stage.

After initially testing priorities and goals, the next step is to model the aspirational goal against these tests and assemble the campaign time frame and key milestones. This can be done in a variety of ways, but the goal is to determine how much money might be raised in what period of time. This often uses a blend of methods, for example:

- Determine a historically typical amount of annual dollars raised, multiplied by the expected number of years, perhaps with a 20 percent increase to acknowledge the momentum of a campaign.
- Identify the pool of specific, potential donors for leadership gifts (usually $1 million and higher) and assign a likelihood rating to each (percent chance of completion), projecting that perhaps 60 to 70 percent of these gifts will be received. Add a standard run rate of annual gift activity below $1 million.
- Using the aspirational campaign goal, create a straight-line projection that begins with a starting point and increases consistently to reach the end goal. For example, if a six-year campaign goal is $100 million and typical annual fundraising activity is $15 million, the

goal for year 1 might be $18 million and would increase by 5 percent each subsequent year, to reach $100 million by the end of year 5.

It is extremely important to recognize that no fundraising campaign has been launched in higher education or elsewhere with a goal and a set of annual projections toward that goal that have exactly matched the reality of the results. In addition, no set of projections has ever been supported by the certainty of knowing who the ultimate donors will be and the amount of their gifts. Some of campaign goal setting and projections is a leap of faith, based on the momentum and excitement that the campaign will provide to the staff, the leadership, and the donor community.

The final component of this stage is building the time frame for the campaign. This process has changed very little over the decades and includes these basic phases:

1. The quiet phase: Following the completion of planning but before formal announcement of the campaign, initial gifts are secured, messages are tested and refined, and models for the campaign are built. This phase allows for an early assessment of the effectiveness of the campaign message and the gift projections. Typically, between 30 and 50 percent of the campaign's initial goal is secured in this prelaunch phase, helping to ensure that the campaign is on a path toward success when it becomes more public.

2. The public launch: Many institutions choose to hold launch events on a grand scale at events with hundreds or thousands in attendance. In other cases, the public launch takes the form of a series of smaller but equally meaningful regional events. Either way, the public launch is accompanied by strategic work with the marketing and communications teams to determine the external messages and communications strategy to support the announcement.

3. The public phase: A period of multiple years where the full apparatus of the campaign is in force—marketing, events, engagement activities, solicitations, celebrations, and more. The key during this phase is sustained energy, activity, and messaging.

4. The final year: As the concluding year of the campaign draws near, activity and messaging take into account the approaching end of the effort. In this phase, fundraisers often try to engage those elusive donors who have not yet had the inclination to participate.

Also, in many cases, donors who gave earlier in the campaign are asked for a second (or even a third!) gift.

Note that even identifying the final year can be elusive. As the campaign moves into the final years, it may be that some original goals have been met, while the momentum may still be tremendous. It is tempting to add a year or two and another increment to the goal to ride the wave of the success. Seven-year campaigns become eight-plus. Goals of $100 million become $150 million. The key is to be very honest about why an institution wants to extend the campaign and build that into the strategy.

5. The campaign close: Serving as a bookend event to the public launch, this moment seeks to celebrate the entirety of the campaign, to thank those who participated, and to reflect on what the campaign has accomplished for the institution. One of the important balancing acts during this last phase is to acknowledge the dollars raised while making sure that the amount does not become the main story. The emphasis should be on the extraordinary impact that level of philanthropy has on the institution's students, faculty, teaching, and research efforts. *The story of the campaign closing is about impact and outcomes, not numbers and goals.*

In summary, the life of a campaign might be something like that depicted in figure 10.1.

Increased Investment in Fundraising and Engagement

Campaigns always have been developed with at least a modest assumption of increased budget support for the development and alumni-engagement efforts. Beginning with the more episodic campaigns (every decade or so) that were standard for many institutions in the 1950–1990 era, development offices would to ramp up for a campaign by adding front-line fundraising staff, engagement and events staff, and stewardship support.

In the modern era of campaigns, the majority of institutions view the fundraising campaign as a mechanism to raise the sustainable level of fundraising during and following the campaign years and therefore do not engage in the downsizing that signaled the end of earlier campaign models. So it stands to reason that the budget increases that might accompany a campaign's launch will eventually become a standard element of the ongoing investment in the program.

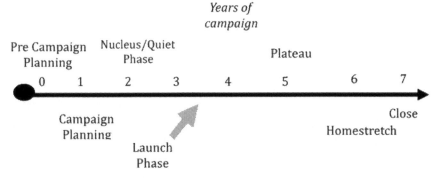

Figure 10.1.   Life of the Campaign

If the campaign is an expression of an institution's desire to raise more private support, then such growth does not happen simply by working harder. It has to be positioned by the leaders of the campaign as a strategic investment to increase the productivity of the program. So, where does that case for investment develop? Through a thorough review of the program and the creation of key growth opportunities, following this set of guidelines as an example:

1. Conduct a simple but candid assessment, perhaps using SOAR (Strengths, Opportunities, Aspirations, Results) or another analytical tool. What works with the development and alumni program, and what does not? Where are the opportunities for growth, and where are the threats to long-term success?

2. Determine the aspirations of the campaign. How will success be defined, not just in terms of total dollars, but also in terms of alumni engagement and other areas?

3. Match these aspirations against the current capacity of the organization. This is not a complicated process, but it should highlight where there is not sufficient capacity to deliver, either in fundraising revenue or engagement strategies and programming.

4. Determine the nature and the amount of investment needed. To make the case effectively, these calculations need to be rigorous and as detailed as possible. In addition, make sure that these calculations also include a look at what the program can *stop* doing.

5. Develop opportunities to report back on investment and return on it over the course of the campaign. That makes it possible to review

requests for increases in the budget in a transparent and responsible way. Doing this will make it clear to institutional leadership
that there is accountability for the investment.

Where can we find the resources to invest in the campaign? While the
unique and varied ways that institutions fund advancement offices make
it very difficult to suggest a standard funding strategy for campaigns,
there are general approaches worth a review. A number of institutions
use a central funding mechanism that would allow a dean, provost, or
chief financial officer to simply increase the formula or the source of
funds to allow for growth in a campaign budget.

As a second strategy, many organizations place assessments or taxes
on incoming gift dollars to generate the needed increase in development
budgets. Different institutional cultures greatly influence whether or how
this strategy is employed. Gift tax levels range widely but are generally
from 4 to 20 percent. The decision to implement a gift assessment is an
incredibly individual choice for the institution, and one standard should
be universal: *Gift assessments must be transparent and disclosed to the donor.*

A twist on the gift assessment is the concept of scraping a very small
percentage from endowment earnings. The key to this strategy is not
interfering with the corpus of the donor's gift nor decreasing the payout
given to the intended program within the university. Instead, the scrape
is applied to a small band of the earnings above the payout that consti-
tute the return that is reinvested into principal to grow against future
inflation.

Volunteer Leadership and Support

The nature of comprehensive campaigns requires that we validate
institutional aspirations with a voice beyond the paid staff. The leadership and legitimacy provided by volunteers to a campaign is crucial. A
campaign chair or cochairs allow the voice of the donor and volunteer to
lead the campaign publicly. The impact of volunteer leadership in a campaign is profound and, given the multiyear time frame, a remarkable
expression of support by the individuals who accept the invitation.

In most campaigns, the role of campaign chair is a pivotal position—
one that is selected to be both aspirational (in terms of their own philanthropy) and inspiring (in terms of their passion and commitment for the
campaign and the institutional story). Traditionally, campaign chairs are

members of the board of trustees, and their participation acts as a signal of leadership and commitment from the very top of the organization.

In addition to the chair or cochairs, many campaigns assemble a group that may be known as the campaign cabinet or campaign council. This group provides a broader army of volunteers who represent the various corners and cultures of the institution. A campaign cabinet might include dozens of volunteers representing the schools, the alumni association, specific regions or geographical areas, specific affinity groups (athletics, student affairs, or the Greek system), and other affiliations that are important to institutional culture. As with any group that an institution assembles, it is crucial that the cabinet reflects the diversity of constituencies in terms of race and ethnicity, age and gender, geography, and connection to the institution.

Many larger institutions form a tiered volunteer structure, whereby members of the cabinet might be local campaign chairs for a school or a group within the university. In this case, the role of the individual volunteer is to lead the campaign for their local unit and represent that unit on the larger cabinet in terms of reporting and information sharing.

Regardless of the specific role, one element of volunteerism is crucial: These individuals should be aspirational models for their peers. This is particularly true if we engage them in the process of donor cultivation, solicitation, and stewardship. The age-old truism of peers responding best to peers certainly still applies today.

Coordinated Communications and Marketing

Campaigns provide institutions with wonderful opportunities for storytelling and moments to amplify the aspirations of an institution's particular direction and trajectory, as well as the role of philanthropic and volunteer partners. As such, it is important that the marketing and communications teams are close partners in the development of the campaign story from the beginning.

Creating the campaign message requires a blending of the existing set of narratives about the institution and the aspirations for where the campaign resources will carry it in the future. These messages should include a campaign name or slogan that is unique and specific to the institution. A brief and concise descriptor provides a consistent platform from which our collateral material, events, and stories all draw and celebrate.

The goals of a campaign should be organized into a set of themes that simplifies the story and allows for its easy repetition throughout the campaign. It is much simpler for a volunteer (or a staff member, for that matter) to say "This campaign is about three things: student support, research, and patient care" than to list the multitude of individual goals in a seven-year campaign. The important thing to remember is that the themes should carry the large majority of the campaign goals and are useful in telling the story.

Campaign messages are best served when there is a group of stories that animates the message. Three examples are: (1) the compelling tale of a graduate student attending the university because of a donated fellowship, (2) a faculty member whose research is accelerated because of a gift from a patient family, and (3) a student-athlete who has access to career coaching to complement their rigorous training on the field.

One of the challenges in today's communications efforts for campaigns, or for institutions in general, is how these messages are translated across the various media available. Traditional campaigns (of only a decade ago) might have included a case statement, which was a publication that served as the written, comprehensive guide to the campaign. Through the popularity of social media, YouTube, and other platforms, campaign communications have undergone a transformation.

The collateral material used in campaigns has changed, as well. Publications are much shorter, more of the moment, and flexible. The power of retelling campaign stories on social media networks is as strong as in any printed material. All of this underscores the first statement of this section—the partnership with the communications and marketing teams and their expertise is crucial in making sure that campaign messages are delivered effectively and reach the right audiences.

Increased Donor Stewardship and Impact Reporting

As the campaign evolves, the development and alumni-relations teams will have more donors to manage and more gifts to steward. This can put pressure on the donor-relations team to respond to everyone and to be highly creative. Make sure that the staff is prepared or that you will be able to access needed resources as time goes by in the campaign. Effective stewardship during a campaign requires the difficult balance of mass communication with personalization. It is important to inform all scholarship donors about their funds but also to make that information meaningful to each individual recipient.

It was once acceptable to send generic thank-you letters and reports that stated the market value of a donor's endowed fund and called it a day. Now, the focus is on impact reporting, which benefactors desire and deserve. We must illustrate how much their gifts are making a difference. Johns Hopkins uses experiences—lab tours, lunch with endowed professorship recipients, and a "Live the Mission" day shadowing a doctor at the children's hospital—to really connect with and engage donors. If these experiences are done well, then the donor feels very good about their philanthropy and might even consider giving more in the future.

Stewardship also is a good use of the president's and other campus leaders' time. Every gift officer should allocate a part of their work plan (20 percent) to donor stewardship. Their best prospects will enjoy getting a sneak peek into the inner workings of the organization with key stakeholders. Involving your campus partners in stewardship and donor relations also is an easy first step to take in the cycle of philanthropy. With time they might even grow more comfortable with soliciting a donor!

Integrated Alumni and Constituent Engagement and Programming

Historically, campaigns focused on raising an astounding amount of funding for a defined set of institutional priorities. Their success was measured in dollars raised and priorities completed. Yet today's evolved campaigns also are setting sights on the long-term health of the institution and the important, equal objective of alumni and constituent engagement. As discussed in other chapters of this book, an engaged community is crucial to the future of an institution. Comprehensive campaigns are, by definition, fundraising exercises focused on a relatively near-term revenue goal. Often, an unintended consequence of this focus is the lack of attention on longer-term efforts, including alumni engagement and investment.

Engagement obviously needs to extend to alumni and the alumni association. At Johns Hopkins, the development team has ensured that certain topics of the campaign are highlighted within the program of specific alumni events. It is equally important to engage alumni association leadership or officers so that they embrace the campaign and ensure that it is discussed at all association meetings—whether a meeting of officers, the executive team, or the entire council. Equally important is setting a goal of 100 percent participation from the association leadership at all times.

Campaign goals, a mission, and a purpose should always be shared with the entire student body. The Johns Hopkins Office of Alumni Relations has created several opportunities for students: One such effort is the Step Up program. Step Up is a student-led effort under the leadership of the alumni student ambassadors to celebrate the many ways that philanthropy enriches the student experience and to recognize those people who step up to sustain the legacy of philanthropy established by Mr. Johns Hopkins himself. It is a movement to thank alumni and friends who support the student body. Other programs include reunion ambassadors, managed by the central alumni relations office, and the senior class gift.

University volunteers, no matter what role they hold, need to be educated and armed with campaign information so that they are an ongoing link to all members of the institution's broader community. They should be able at any time to discuss where the institution is with regard to the campaign's goals and purpose—not only the overall goals but also goals specific to their schools.

While alumni and student engagement is a crucial component to any campaign, it is worth noting that colleges and universities have other constituents to approach for philanthropic support. That includes parents (particularly for undergraduate students) and others, depending on the nature of the institution. For academic medical centers, grateful-patient fundraising is often an essential part of a campaign. For example, at Johns Hopkins University, medical fundraising can be as much as half of the total goal in a given year. A campaign might not be as important or motivating to the grateful patient who is solely focused on supporting their doctor, disease, or both. Medicine donors also can make gifts in a shorter time frame than alumni if they want to have an immediate impact. But participating in the campaign is attractive to some donors, and it is a good exercise for an institution's school of medicine to participate in determining priorities and goal setting.

HEADWINDS IN THE INDUSTRY

What existing trends are influencing the way campaigns might be shaped in the future? Despite the enormous success of the campaign model, it is worth pausing to consider how a model that has remained largely unchanged for decades is ripe for reinvention. There are headwinds that are affecting campaigns. These are largely of our own making, but they also represent the changing landscape of higher education. The purpose of this discussion is not to dissuade anyone from believing that campaigns are a crucial and perennial tool in advancement efforts but rather to make sure that campaign planning in the future reflects important new trends, including:

1. The time frame of the campaign: Early models of campaigning tended to be five-year efforts, but now an increasing number of institutions launch and complete campaigns that extend eight, nine, or ten years and beyond. Does this matter? Perhaps not, but it does seem like it challenges the case for urgency and focus. Columbia University recently launched a $5 billion campaign that will run five years, clearly bucking the trend of extended campaigns. While the cynic might respond "Columbia *can* do that. . . . Not everyone can," it is worthwhile to understand that strategy and its potential benefits.

   Another trend that could drive a shift to shorter campaigns is the decreasing length of college presidents' tenures. In 2016, the average tenure of a college president in their current job was six and a half years, down from seven years in 2011 (Seltzer 2017).

2. The competing forces of our desire to be unique and authentic and the increasing similarity of campaign themes and priorities: Such words as *advancing, boldly, ambitions, securing, thriving,* and *seeking* are often part of campaign names, which can result in clichéd names. The campaign priorities that are identified also are often generic.

   How are we remaining unique and authentic when every institution seeks to support access through financial aid or fuel interdisciplinary research through signature initiatives? Does it matter that we are unique or original, or does the case stand up to scrutiny, even if it does sound incredibly similar to the institution down the road?

3. The growing size of campaign goals and the overall climate of concern about higher-education costs: In conversations that range from media to the halls of the US Congress to neighborhood cookouts, the question of why higher education costs so much—and the

efforts to address this cost pressure—are very real and very power-ful.

Campaigns are meant to amplify and focus opportunities for engagement, and the intersection of "college costs too much" and "we need your philanthropic dollars to remain great" is a challenging pressure point. Our colleges and universities are compelled to explain costs and value in a moment when national confidence in educational institutions has waned, as described in a Pew Charitable Trust study conducted in 2017 (Fingerhut 2017). Advancement is not immune to this challenge. Our case for support moving forward needs to account for and, frankly, strengthen the value proposition of higher education.

4. Fatigue: The concept of donor fatigue has been in our fundraising vocabulary for many decades. Every time we launch a new campaign and promote a new set of priorities, someone in the trustee board room or the academic planning discussion will ask, "When do our donors run out of steam?"

   The reality is that it is hard to find any evidence of this happening. Year-over-year performance in most programs continues to grow, while national trends continue to show steady annual increases in total philanthropic giving to education, with the exception only of the 2008 recession. Having said that, we all have donors in our individual programs who quite transparently tell us, "I'm going to wait to make this big gift for another year because I know you'll be launching a campaign soon." While that may not necessarily signal donor fatigue, it does demonstrate that the rapid relaunch is having an effect on how donors think of their giving patterns.

CONCLUSION

Despite headwinds, the comprehensive campaign is likely to continue as an important fundraising strategy for most colleges and universities. It has proven to be an effective strategy for raising funds, engaging constituents, and communicating the institution's methods. Many of the campaign principles established more than a century ago are still relevant. But it will be essential to adapt the historic model to reflect the new forces affecting higher education today and in the future.

REFERENCES

Fingerhut, Hannah. 2017. "Republicans Skeptical of Colleges' Impact on U.S., but Most See Benefits for Workforce Preparation." Pew Research Center. July 20, 2017. http://www.pewresearch.org/fact-tank/2017/07/20/republicans-skeptical-of-colleges-impact-on-u-s-but-most-see-benefits-for-workforce-preparation.

JHUSOM (Johns Hopkins University School of Medicine). n.d. "The Women's Medical School Fund Campaign." Alan Mason Chesney Medical Archives of The Johns Hopkins Medical Institutions. Accessed September 17, 2018. http://www.medicalarchives.jhmi.edu/garrett/womensfund.htm.

National Philanthropic Trust. n.d. "Harvard First Uses Professional Fundraisers." Accessed September 17, 2018. http://www.historyofgiving.org/1890-1930/1919-harvard-first-uses-professional-fundraisers/.

Seltzer, Rick. 2017. "The Slowly Diversifying Presidency." *Inside Higher Ed*, June 20, 2017. https://www.insidehighered.com/news/2017/06/20/college-presidents-diversifying-slowly-and-growing-older-study-finds.

Thelin, John R. 2004. *A History of American Higher Education*. Baltimore: Johns Hopkins University Press.

ELEVEN

Trends and Directions in Corporate and Foundation Support

Shaun Brenton and Jenny Bickford

Budgetary constraints at the state and federal levels are pressuring universities to increase philanthropic revenue from every available source. Since the onset of the Great Recession, state spending on public colleges and universities remains at historic lows. During the 2016 academic year, public colleges and universities in most states for the first time received the majority of their revenue from tuition rather than government appropriations (Brownstein 2018). Compounding the problem, particularly for research institutions, for the first time in the post–World War II era, the federal government no longer funds the majority of the basic research conducted in the United States (Mervis 2017).

Faced with shrinking funding streams from the public sector, universities are looking increasingly to corporations and foundations to plug the gaps. At the same time, the corporate and foundation philanthropy landscape has become more competitive in recent years. Foundations are limiting funding to projects with a defined scope and high potential for large-scale social impact and prioritizing institutions with whom they have previously worked. Corporations are building deeper partnerships with fewer organizations and supporting projects that contribute to business goals.

Despite this increasingly competitive climate, fundraising teams who understand the current trends and adapt accordingly can seize potentially transformative opportunities to engage with and maximize giving from corporations and foundations. This chapter explores those key trends and provides insights into how to maximize the potential for corporate- and foundation-relations growth.

TRENDS IN FOUNDATION PHILANTHROPY

Over the past several decades, there has been tremendous growth in the foundation sector, both in the number of foundations as well as the assets they hold. This growth has contributed to the pervasive and persistent misperception that foundation funding is plentiful and easy to obtain— often viewed as "low-hanging fruit."

This could not be further from the truth. Foundations are *mission-driven* organizations that identify focus areas, develop goals and strategies for achieving impact, and often craft highly detailed funding guidelines. They hire topical experts as program officers who often identify solutions as well as organizations that can implement those solutions. It's not enough to simply have good ideas; competitive ideas must be positioned to move the needle in significant and innovative ways on issues of importance to the funder.

In addition to the growth in the foundation sector, including new philanthropic organizations founded by wealthy individuals, there are other factors that contribute to enduring myths about foundation funding. The most prevalent is inaccurate or outdated information passed along from faculty and staff colleagues. Frequently, individuals outside, and often inside, the advancement office do not understand the complexities and variables that affect foundation funding. Many of us have university colleagues who, at some point in their careers, received funding from a foundation. In many cases, however, prior experiences are no longer relevant to current funding norms. These prior encounters often fuel unrealistic expectations and, because they are based on personal experience, can be very difficult to refute.

According to the Foundation Center, the number of foundations in the United States grew from 65,000 in 2002 to 86,000 in 2015, and foundation assets grew from $432 billion to $890 billion over that period (Foundation Center 2018). While this growth, particularly in assets, is remarkable, there are several important countervailing factors.

First, the number of nonprofit organizations, many of them grant-seeking organizations, also has increased. The number of organizations registered with the IRS grew from 1.38 million in 2003 to 1.41 million in 2013 (McKeever 2015). Further, nearly two-thirds of foundations have assets of less than $1 million and therefore make annual grants totaling less than $50,000 (McGlaughon 2014).

The good news is that foundation giving has also grown steadily, from just over $30 billion in 2002 to nearly $63 billion in 2015 (Foundation Center 2018). But any foundation fundraiser will tell you that it's become more, not less, challenging to obtain foundation funding. One explanation for this is that foundations have become more strategic and prescribed in recent years, as they search for greater *impact* from the grants they make.

A 2017 report prepared by Rockefeller Philanthropy Advisors (RPA), *Achieving Success in Postsecondary Education: Trends in Philanthropy*, notes that what was once a genuine partnership between foundations and higher-education institutions has shifted to more prescriptive grant making. Foundation guidelines have become more specific in tying funding programs to the organization's overall goals.

Through interviews with top higher-education funders, RPA found that foundations are now far more likely to identify their own solutions and then identify organizations that will adopt these models. The report notes, however, that local and regional foundations are often less prescriptive and may be more likely to fund innovative programs at local campuses (RPA 2017). Therefore, those of us who are foundation-relations officers should help to facilitate conversations with regional funders, which are frequently focused on identifying local solutions to the community's issues.

This move to greater proactivity can be traced to the strategic-philanthropy movement, an approach espoused by Paul Brest and Hal Harvey in the 1990s. Strategic philanthropy sought to move beyond traditional charitable giving to a more goal-oriented approach to identifying interest areas and evidence-based approaches to identifying solutions, where donors articulate and seek to achieve clearly defined goals, develop evidence-based strategies for achieving those goals, and monitor progress (Brest 2015).

In the past few years, this search for greater impact has resulted in so-called big bets. Although there is no one standard definition of what constitutes a big bet, they are generally gifts of $10 million or more designed to bring about lasting and significant social change. According to Bridgespan Group, there were fifty-eight such gifts in 2015 alone; in 2000, there were just nineteen (Dolan 2016).

The most visible big bet was 100&Change launched by the John D. and Catherine T. MacArthur Foundation in 2016. The 100&Change initiative offered a $100 million grant to "fund a single proposal that promises real and measurable progress in solving a critical problem of our time" (MacArthur Foundation 2016). Unlike strategic philanthropy, the framers were completely agnostic as to the problem and the solution. Rather, they asked the community to identify both. The competition received 1,904 submissions, with approximately 20 percent submitted by universities. Of the top two hundred submissions, eighty-three were from higher-education institutions (MacArthur Foundation 2016).

Although universities fared well overall, there were some significant differences between the projects proposed by higher education and those by nonprofit and nongovernmental organizations. First, it should come as no surprise that the proposals from universities were very well written and presented. Where the university proposals fell short was that they proposed projects that were too research-oriented and that lacked adequate plans for implementation. Frequently, this was due to a lack of meaningful partnerships with other organizations working on the ground that could help translate the research to impact.

Conversely, projects originating from nonprofit organizations were focused on implementation, but often they were not based on rigorous evidence. They also found that many of the nonprofit applicants with good ideas were not in a position to receive and manage such a large infusion of funds (Conrad 2018). This is interesting, given that one of the rationales behind big bets is to liberate nonprofits from the endless cycle of grant seeking that takes them away from their core mission.

This discrepancy between the solutions proposed by higher education and those proposed by nonprofits is not surprising. Research is a key part of what faculty and universities *do*, and research output in many fields is a journal article or a book. Nonprofits are frequently underresourced, making it difficult to access or conduct the necessary studies to determine program efficacy.

Through 100&Change, MacArthur recognized a need to connect these two groups, so it has partnered with the Foundation Center to create the

100&Change Solutions Bank, a searchable database of submitted proposals. One potential use of the Solutions Bank is to connect universities
with the practitioner community to translate research into implementable
solutions.

100&Change has sparked universities to think bigger and to consider
how their good ideas can make it to the field. In an article for *Nonprofit
Quarterly*, Cecilia Conrad (2017) points to several examples, including
Arizona State University, for which

> *100&Change* served as the impetus for new teams and partnerships to
> form and for existing teams to reach further and reimagine how an idea
> can scale and be transformative. At the University of Massachusetts
> Boston, the competition was the catalyst to think bigger and more bold-
> ly about its scope of impact. The university encouraged teams that
> submitted proposals to develop, deepen, refine, and create proposals
> collectively, with community partners.

In an article entitled "The Future of Higher Education Is Social Impact,"
Adam Garmoran (2018), president of the W. T. Grant Foundation, suggests that it's time for academic researchers in the social sciences to emu-
late their engineering and medical colleagues and translate their work to
practice. A Grant Foundation study revealed that a leading factor in
whether social science research is used in policy or practice is whether
the researchers have relationships with potential users or intermediaries
who can connect them to practitioners (Dumont 2015).

Garmoran (2018) points out that "universities do not typically reward
faculty for the time and effort needed to build and nurture these relationships, but doing so would be transformative." He believes that one way
to do so is through modified promotion and tenure policies. While academic policies are clearly outside of our purview as development professionals, we should encourage and support faculty in developing partnerships. Whenever possible, foundation-relations professionals should educate development and academic leadership about the importance of such
collaborations to securing foundation support.

As mentioned earlier, the foundation sector has grown exponentially
in the past fifteen years, as have the fortunes of the extremely wealthy. In
the past decade, vast sums have been pledged to philanthropy through
the Giving Pledge, which 183 wealthy individuals have signed. Young
technology entrepreneurs have entered the world of philanthropy, often
in splashy, public ways, many seeking to disrupt philanthropy. A leading

example of this "disruptive philanthropy" (Reiser 2017) is the use of vehicles other than private foundations to facilitate philanthropic goals. In recent years, donor-advised funds (DAFs) and LLCs have become common alternatives to private foundations. Both of these vehicles offer donors greater flexibility in combination with less accountability and transparency. David Callahan (2017) from Inside Philanthropy refers to these vehicles as "shadow giving systems" and fears that this lack of transparency gives these wealthy individuals too much power at a time of increasing inequality.

DAFs have been in existence since the 1930s but recently have become more well known and utilized by the wealthy. DAFs share features with private foundations but differ in significant ways. Most notable among these differences is that there is no obligation once a DAF is established that it make charitable contributions—*ever*—unlike private foundations, which must pay out 5 percent of assets each year.

According to the National Philanthropic Trust, six of the top ten biggest recipients of charitable giving in the United States in 2017 were DAFs. Donations to DAFs grew by 66 percent in the past five years, compared to 15 percent for all individual giving nationwide (National Philanthropic Trust 2018). Unlike private foundations, DAFs can continue to reinvest their funds indefinitely, without ever distributing them to charity, although some financial-services firms, such as Fidelity and Charles Schwab, do have annual payout requirements as a matter of the firm's policy (Collins, Flannery, and Hoxie 2018).

Although less common than DAFs, philanthropic LLCs are also growing in popularity. Most recently, Mark Zuckerberg and Priscilla Chan opted to create an LLC rather than a private foundation. While the Chan Zuckerberg Initiative (CZI) has received the most attention, they are not the first to use the philanthropic LLC. Lauren Powell Jobs, Steve Ballmer, and Pierre Omidyar use LLCs, which offer tremendous flexibility, allowing donors to make donations to nonprofit organizations, invest in for-profit firms, and fund political advocacy.

David Callahan (2017) writes, "From the start, CZI has sought to pull several major levers of change: It makes grants to 501(c)(3) groups. . . . It also invests in for-profit social enterprises. Finally, CZI is able to contribute to 501(c)(4)s and has created a fund, Chan Zuckerberg Advocacy, for that purpose." Callahan acknowledges the appeal to donors of these new vehicles, but their growing use worries him. In an article for HistPhil,

Callahan (2018) writes, "The world of philanthropy is becoming less transparent, and that's not a good thing."

Philosophical and policy arguments aside, the lack of transparency inherent in DAFs and LLCs makes our jobs as foundation-relations professionals more difficult. Grants databases have been a boon for accessing information about a foundation's past giving history. Without access to information about these entities' funding, it is difficult to assess whether there might be opportunities for our institutions to partner with these organizations.

TRENDS IN CORPORATE PHILANTHROPY

On the whole, trends in the corporate sector are less conspicuous than in the foundation giving space. Corporations by nature are more opaque. Giving data and meaningful (actionable) information regarding funding interests, especially for privately held companies, is harder to decipher, if you can find it at all. What we do know is that, according to *Giving USA 2018*, giving (including in-kind contributions) by corporations has averaged 5 percent of all annual contributions since 1996. Of that 5 percent, corporations have allocated an average of 12 percent of their total contributions to higher education during the last ten years (Giving USA Foundation 2018). It's important for development professionals working in the corporate-funding arena to recognize how relatively little corporations contribute as compared to other constituencies.

There has been relatively little fluctuation in how much corporations give year to year or how much they commit to institutions of higher education. Swings that do occur are most often triggered by business performance (for better or worse); market volatility (e.g., the financial devastation wrought by the Great Recession); and natural disasters, which are growing in number and severity.

The influence of disaster philanthropy on corporate giving drove the increased giving totals seen in 2017. Giving by corporations increased by 8 percent in 2017, totaling $20.77 billion (an increase of 5.7 percent, adjusted for inflation). Contributing to this increase was $405 million for relief related to natural and manmade disasters that occurred in 2017 (Wolley 2018, 164).

In addition to fairly constant cumulative giving totals, corporations continue to partner with universities, as they have for generations, for a host of reasons: to recruit students, to access intellectual capital, to research and develop new technologies, to burnish and grow their brand, to cultivate future customers (our students), and to improve community relations. Consistencies notwithstanding, corporations, like foundations, are shifting toward more strategic partnerships. Their giving strategies no longer favor widespread grants to numerous nonprofits. Instead, today's corporate-giving programs are closely aligned with business strategies and defined by deep engagements with a shrinking number of partner organizations.

The president of the Freeport-McMoRan Foundation, Tracy Bame, states, "The most significant trend in corporate philanthropy today is that companies are increasingly linking their giving strategy to their business focus and leveraging their own expertise and institutional knowledge to address both social issues and business needs." She goes on to say, "Corporations have started to look at how to use their philanthropy to make systems change, aligned with their business, not only locally but also regionally, nationally and even internationally, often joining forces with other businesses to collectively solve difficult and complex social challenges" (Bame 2018).

A recent report by the Education Advisory Board (EAB) states that 66 percent of corporate foundations are working with a fixed number of preselected, partner organizations in a small number of focus areas. Never before has the bottom line been more central to the case for corporate support. As an example, in 2017 the Walmart Foundation replaced its State Giving Program, which long served as an essential source of funding for which small nonprofits across the country were eligible to submit requests for up to $250,000 during annual giving cycles. According to responses in the frequently-asked-questions section of Walmart Foundation's web page, the State Giving Program was flawed because it "was not designed to prioritize outcomes or achieve focused objectives due to short-term investments and the inability of program officers to be deeply involved in shaping investments and partnering with grantees" (Walmart Foundation 2018). In its place, Walmart Foundation launched the Spark Communities Program.

The new funding program provides multiyear grants starting at $500,000 to 501(c)(3) organizations in select communities across the United States. Requests for applications are by invitation only. Walmart promotes the Spark Communities Program as an opportunity to work deeply with community leaders in chosen communities to develop locally relevant and highly impactful solutions over a three-year time frame. The program is expected to operate in five to seven communities at the outset, with additional cities added in future years.

The Spark Communities Program dovetails with Walmart Foundation's National Giving Program, which partners strategically with such organizations as Feeding America and the American Red Cross that operate on a national scale to address social issues strongly aligned with their focus. During 2017, in its inaugural year, the Spark Communities Program awarded seven grants to five recipients in Texas and the District of Columbia in response to natural disasters. The grants totaled $27,499,998. By contrast, Walmart's State Giving Program made 1,647 grants to 932 recipients in 2016, including institutions of higher education, dispersed throughout all fifty states. Funding in 2016 amounted to more than $116 million (Walmart Foundation 2018).

State Farm, the largest US home and auto insurer, provides another good example. At one time, State Farm had hundreds of operating facilities across the country, giving significantly in each of the communities where it had an operating presence. In an effort to gain efficiencies, improve processes, and concentrate employees, State Farm began consolidating its operating facilities in 2014 into three hub locations in Arizona, Georgia, and Texas. As a result of this new business model, State Farm's engagement with higher education now focuses on priority colleges and universities located near the three new hubs and its headquarters in Bloomington, Illinois.

The depth and breadth of State Farm's engagement with its priority schools is exemplified by the public–private partnership between Georgia State University and State Farm that was announced in April 2017. To launch the partnership, State Farm committed $20 million to support Georgia State's Learning, Income and Family Transformation (LIFT) program and to help minority and low-income students pursue postsecondary education.

Alignment of mission is crucial to the realization and success of the partnership between Georgia State and State Farm. "Georgia State and State Farm have the common goal of helping to solve issues important to metro-Atlanta," said State Farm chairman, president, and CEO Michael Tipsord, "and helping students graduate is key to Atlanta's future. Working together creates a stronger workforce and better environment for everyone" (Georgia State University 2017).

The trend in corporate giving toward building deeper partnerships with fewer organizations and supporting projects that contribute to business goals is the result of several forces, including a tight labor market and societal challenges. When asked about the benefits of giving to education, 70 percent of companies responded that "training future workforce" and "improving community relations" were the most important benefits to companies (Kou 2016, 162).

The aging workforce, what some call the "silver tsunami," and low unemployment rate, compounded by a growing skills gap, has left corporations scrambling to replace seasoned employees of the baby boom generation, who are retiring at a pace of 10,000 per day (Metcalf 2017). Competition for employees with specialized skills, high performers, and effective leaders is ratcheting up as the global war for talent escalates.

In order to attract today's most skilled workers, companies must position themselves as agents of positive change because younger generations want to work for companies that are making a difference. According to a recent report, "Millennials don't just work for a paycheck—they want a purpose. For millennials, work must have meaning. They want to work for organizations with a mission and purpose" (Gallup 2016).

The challenge to attract a skilled and talented workforce provides one of the greatest incentives for corporations to engage with universities. As seen in the example of the Georgia State and State Farm partnership, institutions of higher education that work directly with corporations to create a diverse pipeline of well-educated students are more likely to see significant giving from their corporate partners. "More corporate funders are looking to support education-focused programs that provide access or equity to underserved or under-represented groups," says Kaye Morgan-Curtis (2018), principal consultant for the Changemakers Commission and the former manager of corporate giving for Newell Brands and Citigroup. "This is especially true when trending news raises the issue of the absence or decline of a particular race or gender in specific industries, like technology."

In addition to supplying talent, university partnerships can help corporations build a positive charitable brand and avoid reputational risk through high-impact community involvement. Corporations that find themselves on the "wrong" side of public debates playing out in the twenty-four-hour news cycle and on social media platforms on hot-button topics—such as climate change, LGBTQ rights, or free speech—have a lot to lose financially. An important way to mitigate reputational risk is for corporations to partner with universities and other nonprofits to solve crucial problems facing the communities where they operate. "Corporations want to avoid reputational risk and have become more aware of the power of the public and its expectation that big business will willingly return something to the communities that support it," says Morgan-Curtis (2018). In short, companies want to be seen as doing good in their communities and the world.

Institutions of higher education are positioned to play a key role in that effort, if they offer funding opportunities that are tied to corporate giving and business interests and include measurable impact that points to a significant return on social investment. Today's corporate partners are tracking and quantifying results and want to know how lives or a community have been changed for the better as a result of their gifts.

SEIZE SUCCESS

In spite of—and, in some cases, because of—the trends toward more prescribed and focused giving by both foundations and corporations, the current climate offers tremendous opportunity for universities that are willing and able to adapt to the new normal and partner with organizational funders to try to solve some of the many seemingly intractable problems facing our world today. The following tips will help ensure success in today's corporate and foundation fundraising climate:

- Know your funder. Alignment between the grantee and grantor has never been more important. Develop and maintain in-depth profiles of your top prospects; if possible, meet funder representatives to listen intently and learn about their funding interests; introduce select and compelling funding and engagement opportunities that align with funders' missions and, in the case of corporations, which correlate directly to their business interests.
- Curate and catalog high-impact funding opportunities. Canvas your university for nationally distinctive funding and engagement opportunities that aim to provide broad and measurable impact.
- Develop competitive intelligence. Remain informed regarding major philanthropic priorities (e.g., MacArthur's 100&Change) and

past and present funding programs and awards. Thoroughly examine the entire ecosystem surrounding a focus area or problem, including the nonprofit and for-profit stakeholders, beneficiaries, academic competitors, and emerging technologies. Assess your institution's competencies and know (realistically) how you stack up. Focus your fundraising efforts on the select areas where your institution is genuinely competitive.

- Advance collaborations with outside entities that provide direct services at scale. Although corporate- and foundation-fundraising professionals are not able to negotiate affiliation agreements on behalf of the universities they represent, they should be empowered to suggest that faculty explore external partnerships as a way to create competitive advantage. Fundraising teams should also be aware of (and leverage) the partnerships, such as vendor relationships, that are being forged across the university for purposes other than development.

- Employ the "Heilmeier Catechism," a set of questions developed by George Heilmeier, a legendary director of Defense Advanced Research Projects Agency (DARPA) during the 1970s, to test and validate funding opportunities. These questions, which explore the project's innovation and potential impact, can mitigate the tendency to be dazzled by "brilliant" concepts that are not in fact ready for prime time (DARPA, n.d.).

CONCLUSION

Faced with pressure on revenues from other sources, universities are looking increasingly to corporations and foundations to plug the gaps. But the corporate and foundation philanthropy landscape has become more competitive in recent years, with both sources becoming more focused and selective. That reality will require that fundraising teams understand the current trends and adapt their strategies accordingly. If they are able to do so, they can seize opportunities to engage with and maximize giving from corporations and foundations.

REFERENCES

Bame, Tracy. 2018. E-mail to Shaun Brenton, August 13, 2018.

Brest, Paul. 2015. "Strategic Philanthropy and Its Discontents." *Stanford Social Innovation Review*, April 27, 2015. https://ssir.org/up_for_debate/article/strategic_philanthropy_and_its_discontents.

Brownstein, Ronald. 2018. "American Higher Education Hits a Dangerous Milestone." *Atlantic*, May 3, 2018. https://www.theatlantic.com/politics/archive/2018/05/american-higher-education-hits-a-dangerous-milestone/559457/.

Callahan, David. 2017. "Into Battle: The Chan Zuckerberg Initiative Steps Up Its Advocacy Giving." Inside Philanthropy, September 19, 2017. https://www.insidephilanthropy.com/home/2017/9/19/into-battle-the-chan-zuckerberg-initiative-steps-up-its-advocacy-giving-in-a-big-way.

———. 2018. "The Price of Privacy: What's Wrong with the New Shadow Giving System." HistPhil, August 1, 2018. https://histphil.org/2018/08/01/the-price-of-privacy-whats-wrong-with-the-new-shadow-giving-system/.

Collins, Chuck, Helen Flannery, and Josh Hoxie. 2018. *Warehousing Wealth: Donor-Advised Charity Funds Sequestering Billions in the Face of Growing Inequality*. Washington, DC: Institute for Policy Studies. https://ips-dc.org/wp-content/uploads/2018/07/Warehousing-Wealth-IPS-Report-1.pdf.

Conrad, Cecilia. 2017. "Giving Away $100 Million: A Peek behind the Curtain at MacArthur Foundation." *Nonprofit Quarterly*, September 26, 2017. https://nonprofitquarterly.org/2017/09/26/giving-away-100-million-difficult-choices-important-learnings/.

———. 2018. Phone interview with Jenny Bickford, August 15, 2018.

DARPA (Defense Advanced Research Projects Agency). n.d. "The Heilmeier Catechism." Accessed October 15, 2018. https://www.darpa.mil/work-with-us/heilmeier-catechism.

Dolan, Kerry. 2016. "Big Bet Philanthropy: How More Givers Are Spending Big and Taking Risks to Solve Society's Problems." *Forbes*, November 30, 2016. https://www.forbes.com/sites/kerryadolan/2016/11/30/big-bet-philanthropy-solving-social-problems/#546a3e8f79c5.

Dumont, Kim. 2015. "Realizing the Potential of Research in Child Welfare." In *William T. Grant Foundation Annual Report 2013*, 20–27. New York: William T. Grant Foundation. http://wtgrantfoundation.org/library/uploads/2015/09/Realizing-the-Potential-of-Research-Evidence-in-Child-Welfare.pdf.

Foundation Center. 2018. "Foundation Stats." http://data.foundationcenter.org/#/foundations/all/nationwide/total/bar:num_foundations/2015.

Gallup. 2016 *How Millennials Want to Work and Live*. Washington, DC: Gallup. https://www.gallup.com/workplace/238073/millennials-work-live.aspx.

Garmoran, Adam. 2018. "The Future of Higher Education Is Social Impact." *Stanford Social Innovation Review*, May 18, 2018. https://ssir.org/articles/entry/the_future_of_higher_education_is_social_impact.

Georgia State University. 2017. "Georgia State University and State Farm Announce Public–Private Partnership." Campus News, April 18, 2017. https://news.gsu.edu/2017/04/18/georgia-state-state-farm-partnership/.

Giving USA Foundation. 2018. *Giving USA 2018: The Annual Report on Philanthropy for the Year 2017*. Chicago: Giving USA Foundation. https://givingusa.org/tag/giving-usa-2018/.

Kou, Xiaonan. 2016. "Giving by Corporations." In *The Annual Report on Philanthropy for the Year 2015*, 162. Chicago: Giving USA Foundation.

MacArthur Foundation (John D. and Catherine T. MacArthur Foundation). 2018. "100&Change." www.macfound.org/programs/100change.

McGlaughon, King. 2014. "Think You Know Private Foundations? Think Again." *Stanford Social Innovation Review*, January 2, 2014. https://ssir.org/articles/entry/think_you_know_private_foundations_think_again.

McKeever, Brice S. 2015. *The Nonprofit Sector in Brief 2015*. Washington, DC: Urban Institute. https://www.urban.org/sites/default/files/publication/72536/2000497-The-Nonprofit-Sector-in-Brief-2015-Public-Charities-Giving-and-Volunteering.pdf.

Mervis, Jeffrey. 2017. "Data Check: US Government Share of Basic Research Funding Falls Below 50%." *Science*, March 9, 2017. http://www.sciencemag.org/news/2017/03/data-check-us-government-share-basic-research-funding-falls-below-50.

Metcalf, Maureen. 2017. "Boomers Are Retiring Rapidly: Are Successors Prepared?" *Forbes*, June 28, 2017. https://www.forbes.com/sites/forbescoachescouncil/2017/06/28/boomers-are-retiring-rapidly-are-successors-prepared/#3c3d46024472.

Morgan-Curtis, Kaye. 2018. E-mail to Shaun Brenton, August 9, 2018.

National Philanthropic Trust. 2018. *2018 Donor Advised Fund Report*. Jenkintown, PA: National Philanthropic Trust. https://www.nptrust.org/daf-report/introduction.html.

Reiser, Dana. 2017. "Disruptive Philanthropy: Zuckerberg, the Limited Liability Company, and the Millionaire Next Door." Brooklyn Law School, Legal Studies Paper No. 536. https://ssrn.com/abstract=3049021.

RPA (Rockefeller Philanthropy Advisors). 2017. *Achieving Success in Postsecondary Education: Trends in Philanthropy*. Report no. 2. New York: Rockefeller Philanthropy Advisors and the TIAA Institute. https://www.rockpa.org/wp-content/uploads/2017/06/ROCKPA-HigherEd-Report2-Web-Final.pdf.

Walmart Foundation. 2018. "Apply for Grants, Spark Communities Program." http://giving.walmart.com/walmart-foundation/community-grant-program.

Wolley, Marshawn. 2018. "Giving by Corporations." In *The Annual Report on Philanthropy for the Year 2018*, 164. Chicago: Giving USA Foundation.

V

Engaging Diverse Constituencies

Preceding chapters in this book have emphasized the significance of changing demographics in American society. In addition, as discussed in chapter 2, advancement is no longer confined to the United States; advancement professionals must maintain an international perspective. The four chapters in this part of the book explore dimensions of these changes and provide examples of new strategies that are working.

In chapter 12, Kestrel Linder and Felicity Meu address the declining rate of alumni participation, especially among younger generations of alumni. Colleges and universities are in competition for the attention of these alumni. The competitors are not just other higher-education institutions but also include multiple opportunities for meaningful experience—which are plentiful, thanks to advancing communications technology.

Linder and Meu identify nine characteristics that affect the behavior of millennials and postmillennials and offer strategies for engaging them, along with examples from institutions that have built successful programs. Not surprisingly, many of their points echo those of several other authors, including the need for advancement professionals to listen to their donors. Success in engaging new donors is crucial to the future. As Linder and Meu remind us, "The next generation of donors is waiting."

Andrea Pactor and Debra Mesch begin chapter 13 with two important reminders: "Women are more than 50 percent of the population." And, "Women are driving philanthropy today." These realities are requiring colleges and universities to understand and address women as donors with programs based on the findings of research. Scholars at the Lilly Family School of Philanthropy at Indiana University, Pactor and Mesch provide an overview of that research and its implications for advancement practice. They then offer examples of successful programs that reflect a contemporary approach.

Like Pactor and Mesch, Rachel Vassel opens chapter 14 with a statement of a fact: "The US Census predicts that American minority groups will be the majority population by 2044, with Latino Americans and African Americans becoming the top two ethnic groups in the country." Given this reality, universities must develop targeted programs to address the interests of currently underrepresented communities while also working to engage members of diverse groups in the overall life of the institution. She offers examples of creative programs and describes how technology helps to support such initiatives.

Although advancement has become an important component of higher-education management in many nations, this book reflects primarily the perspective of North American colleges and universities. But as Ivan Adames explains in chapter 15, philanthropy has become a worldwide activity, and US higher education is seeing a growing level of giving from international alumni and donors. Adames provides a roadmap for developing greater international reach, with examples of programs that have been successful. He concludes with unambiguous advice: "If you have been considering launching an international advancement program, get out there and do it!"

TWELVE

Engaging New Generations

Kestrel A. Linder and Felicity Meu

Two milestones in the mid- to late 2010s underscored a demographic transition that had been affecting young-alumni-engagement and donor-acquisition strategies since the early 2000s. In 2016, millennials—those born between 1981 and 1996—became the largest generation in the US labor force (Fry 2018). In 2018, the youngest members of the postmillennial generation (a.k.a., Generation Z) began graduating from college. These generations' coming of age has been a significant challenge for advancement offices.

A widespread decline in alumni participation has been driven in part by declining rates of alumni participation from recent graduates, especially at institutions that are graduating progressively larger classes. Few institutions have escaped these trends, giving rise to concerns about a potential lost generation of future major donors. Indeed, lessons from prior generations suggest that, if millennials and postmillennials do not develop a habit of giving in their twenties and thirties, then they are unlikely to begin giving later in life.

These generations' coming of age also represents a significant opportunity—and there is reason to be optimistic. People born after 1980 are the beneficiaries of the largest transfer of wealth in human history, measured in the tens of trillions of dollars. Their purchasing power, which already stands in the hundreds of billions of dollars, will steadily increase as more and more of them enter their peak earning years. Furthermore, early indicators suggest they may be the most philanthropic generation yet; according to numerous surveys and studies, somewhere between 80 and 90 percent of millennials give to charitable organizations each year (Notte 2018).

In sum, people born after 1980 are the future of philanthropy, and this future has arrived. Members of this generation consistently list education among the issues they care about most. So, why do so few of them make charitable gifts to their alma maters? How can we change that and ensure that they direct a meaningful portion of their philanthropy toward education in the years and decades ahead?

THE WORLD WE LIVE IN

Designing effective strategies to acquire and retain donors born after 1980 requires an appreciation for the world in which these prospective donors grew up and how different this world is from the world in which earlier generations grew up. Many people born after 1980 do not know a time without personal computers or mobile phones; the IBM personal computer was released in 1981, and the first commercially available handheld mobile phone was released in 1983.

Even the oldest millennials will struggle to remember a time without the internet; they were nine years old when the World Wide Web went live. Millennials and postmillennials grew up shopping on Amazon (launched in 1994) and searching on Google (1998), and by the time they started going to college, they were listening to music on iPods (2001) and connecting with friends on Facebook (2004).

In short, this generation grew up online, on social media, and on mobile devices. They are digital natives, and their preferences, behaviors, and expectations have been intimately shaped by the digital technology that always has surrounded them. They are accustomed to using this technology to get what they want, when they want it, where they want it, how they want it, from whom they want it.

When they want to buy something, they go to Amazon and check out in seconds. When they want to listen to music or watch a movie, they stream it on Spotify or Netflix. When they want to consume content or learn something new, they watch a video on YouTube. When they want to communicate, they use social media and text messages. When they want to support a cause, they take cues from their friends and head to crowdfunding platforms like GoFundMe. Few own checkbooks, and some have never addressed or mailed an envelope. Many do not carry cash and instead rely on mobile wallets like Apple Pay to carry out day-to-day transactions.

THE COMPETITION

Many colleges and universities have been slow to adapt to this reality and to meet and engage millennials and postmillennials in ways that they enjoy, are accustomed to, and will want to repeat. One cause for this is insufficient benchmarking—not against other educational institutions (which most do quite well), but against the competition. The competition is *not* other colleges and universities. The competition is the companies and digital technologies that alumni engage with every day. The competition also is other nonprofits.

One of the great benefits of modern digital technology is that it has made it easier and less expensive for nonprofits to reach potential supporters. This has produced an increasingly crowded marketplace for philanthropy. Generally speaking, other nonprofits have been faster to adapt to and adopt new technology—and as a result they often are winning the battle for prospective donors' time, attention, and financial support.

Studying these competitors and the *experiences* they provide is a crucial exercise, which advancement offices should conduct on a routine basis. When designing strategies aimed at driving more young alumni to give more often, we must understand what this audience is doing regularly—and why: Why do they spend four hours per day on mobile devices and two hours on social media? Why do they say that Amazon, Gmail, and Facebook are their most essential apps and the ones that would be most difficult to go without? Why is YouTube one of their most frequented destinations? (Lipsman 2017). To cultivate giving as a habit, we must first understand how and why other prevalent behaviors are formed.

NINE CHARACTERISTICS

Our research has identified nine characteristics of millennials and postmillennials that drive much of their behavior. Although the characteristics apply to virtually all people born after 1980, some are not unique to this demographic but also are applicable to Generation X, baby boomers, and even the silent generation. This is particularly true of the first five characteristics, which largely are outgrowths of digital technology and its influence. Indeed, those born *before* 1980 have embraced much of the same technology as their younger siblings, children, and grandchildren, and as a result, their behavior, preferences, and expectations have been similarly affected by this technology. This means that strategies address-ing these characteristics will pay dividends across *all* generations:

1. Mobile: Millennials and postmillennials are mobile beings. They spend approximately 25 percent of their waking hours accessing the internet from a mobile device (Statista 2018). If online content is not compatible with mobile devices, then they are less likely to engage with it.

2. Accustomed to ease and convenience: Millennials and postmillen-nials are reluctant to encounter friction. If a task is not as easy or as convenient as they think it should be or could be, then there is a real possibility that they will abandon it—even if the task was one that they were initially motivated to complete.

3. Frugal with their time and attention: Millennials and postmillenni-als are busy, surrounded by distractions (especially online), and prone to procrastination. If something does not seem urgent, fails to instantly capture their attention, or drags on without getting to the point, then they will lose interest and move on.

4. Social: Millennials and postmillennials grew up in the age of social media, and they are heavily influenced by their friends and peers. Peer pressure, social proof, and FOMO (fear of missing out) are powerful forces in their lives. If they know that members of their social network are doing something, then they are much more like-ly to do it themselves.

5. Expect personalization: Millennials and postmillennials are used to tailored experiences that account for their backgrounds, prefer-ences, and interests. If an appeal or call to action strikes them as generic, then they likely will not respond. This is especially true when it comes to interactions with their alma maters. They expect this institution to *know* them and are turned off when it offers them little more than an impersonal, transactional experience.

6. Motivated by impact, not loyalty: In contrast to earlier generations, millennials and postmillennials exhibit little affinity and loyalty to

organizations. Instead, they are loyal to people and causes and motivated by the opportunity to make a tangible impact. Solicitations framed around giving *through* their alma maters to drive meaningful progress are more likely to resonate than solicitations to give *to* their alma maters.

7. View educational institutions as worthy but not needy: Millennials and postmillennials care deeply about education, but many do not view educational institutions as *needing* financial support. By comparison, millennials and postmillennials view other nonprofits as both worthy *and* needy. Enhanced storytelling and communications, delivered by video and featuring personal narratives, are most likely to break through.

8. Lack trust in their alma maters: Millennials and postmillennials often are skeptical of their alma maters' management of its resources. They wonder where and how efficiently money is being spent and question whether additional funding is worthwhile. Increased transparency and improved stewardship are necessary to gain their trust and confidence.

9. Want to give back in multiple ways: Millennials and postmillennials do not want to be asked solely for money—and will resent what they perceive to be a unidimensional approach. They also want to be asked for time, advice, and talent. They are most likely to respond to holistic strategies that integrate multiple ways to give back and frame financial support as a necessary but nonexclusive component of philanthropy.

SOLUTIONS

Tactics that effectively capitalize on these characteristics typically exhibit seven high-level attributes:

1. Digital, social, and mobile channels: They are executed primarily via digital, social, and mobile channels—meeting younger alumni where they spend their time.

2. Deadlines: They include a prominently displayed deadline (normally measured in hours or days)—creating a sense of urgency and combating the tendency to procrastinate.

3. Public goal(s) and real-time progress tracking: They have a public goal (or goals), and progress toward this goal (or goals) is dis-

played in real time—delivering an element of transparency and a greater appreciation for how each individual's participation moves the needle.

4. Donor insights: They display a live feed of donor names and other data (e.g., locations, affiliations, class years)—providing instantaneous recognition, increasing transparency, and creating a sense of community (and even FOMO for some).

5. Peer-to-peer engagement: They incorporate peer-to-peer (P2P) engagement and solicitation—driving a more social and personal experience and introducing a degree of positive peer pressure. In some instances, this P2P component is executed by formally recruited volunteers; in others, it is organic. P2P engagement occurs via the channel(s) of communication selected by individuals as most relevant, alleviating the challenges that institutions face regarding channel selection and prioritization. P2P also creates opportunities to ask people to "give back" in a different way: by engaging their friends and peers.

6. Video: They use video as the primary storytelling medium. Many videos feature individuals addressing the audience and communicating the impact donations will have.

7. Donor centricity: Increased donor centricity can be accomplished in many ways but most often takes the form of allowing donors to designate their gifts (regardless of size). This provides transparency and connects donors with the tangible impacts of their philanthropy.

BEST PRACTICES IN ACTION

Short-term giving challenges (including giving days) and crowdfunding have emerged as the most popular manifestations of these attributes. They are today's most effective, widely used tactics for young alumni acquisition, retention, and reactivation.

Nonprofits began experimenting with giving challenges in the mid- and late 2000s, but the methods were relatively unsophisticated, and the challenges only partially reflected a subset of the attributes described in this chapter. By 2010 and 2011, community foundations and some nonprofits had begun conducting much more sophisticated, large-scale giving challenges like Colorado Gives Day and Give to the Max Day: Greater

Washington. They were joined by a handful of colleges and universities in 2011 and 2012—the same year that the Ninety-Second Street Y and the United Nations Foundation founded #GivingTuesday.

The early adopters realized strong results, but most educational institutions remained skeptical of giving challenges for several more years, even as their alumni participation rates declined and the return on investment (ROI) of other methods worsened. Some viewed giving challenges as a gimmick and suspected they were a novelty that would quickly wear off. Others worried that they were unsustainable methods and that the donors acquired would be difficult to retain.

For early adopters, the year-after-year results tell a different story. Davidson College began experimenting with giving challenges of varying lengths in the mid-2000s and held its first community-wide giving day in 2013. The success of the now-annual event has grown each year by virtually every metric imaginable. In 2018, the #AllinforDavidson challenge raised $1.86 million from 3,747 donors, all-time records for Davidson and almost inconceivable totals for a school with fewer than 2,000 students and approximately 24,000 living alumni of record. Thirty percent of donors were graduates of the last decade, and with the sole exception of $500,000 in challenge gifts that were solicited in advance, Davidson's totals only included gifts made within an 18-hour-and-37-minute window (Davidson College 2018).

College of the Holy Cross's first community-wide giving challenge drew national media attention when it garnered the support of more than 6,200 donors in early 2016. More than 75 percent of the donors acquired during the challenge were graduates of the last decade, and more than 50 percent of all donations came from alumni who graduated after 1990 (Douglas-Gabriel 2016). Overall, the challenge drove a 10 percent increase in young-alumni participation—an astounding result that Holy Cross repeated when it held its second community-wide giving challenge a year later (Morgan, Riendeau, and Saucier 2018).

One key to success for both Davidson and Holy Cross is the robust P2P component of their giving challenges. For example, at Holy Cross, 27 percent of all alumni donors and 38 percent of first-time donors acquired during the college's challenges made their gifts *in direct response* to an appeal from a peer. P2P drove approximately one-third of Holy Cross's website traffic and generated approximately 20 percent of all money raised. Further underscoring the significance of P2P, Holy Cross's retention of new donors year over year was directly correlated to its retention of the individuals who conducted the P2P outreach that drove the acquisition of those new donors (Morgan, Riendeau, and Saucier 2018).

Davidson and Holy Cross prioritize P2P and their approaches share many common elements: First, both institutions invest heavily in recruitment, tapping into existing volunteer networks and other engaged pockets of their constituency to identify individuals who will advocate for their giving challenges and help spread the word. Second, in the weeks immediately preceding their giving challenges, they offer short training sessions for volunteers. These sessions are focused on a limited number of specific actions they want volunteers to carry out during the challenge. Third, they provide their P2P volunteers with a variety of easy-to-use tools for engaging their social networks: tools for sharing on social media, by e-mail, and by text message; a repository of engaging content to share; tools to add their voices and faces to the challenge in the form of a "selfie" video; and tools that empower them to challenge peers with their own matching gifts.

Fourth, they incentivize their P2P volunteers with rewards tied to their impact, such as a "shout-out" on social media when their P2P outreach results in a donation. Lastly, they provide their P2P volunteers with real-time recognition and connect them to their impacts in a tangible way. Both colleges display a list of their P2P volunteers, showing how much traffic each one has driven to the giving challenge and how many gifts and dollars their outreach has generated. Combined with incentives tied to impact, this gamifies the experience for volunteers and introduces a healthy sense of friendly competition. The real-time feedback has a powerful effect on the volunteers and serves as a form of stewardship that deepens their connection with the institution.

Crowdfunding began to revolutionize the funding model for a variety of industries in the late 1990s and early 2000s, and by the late 2000s, it had become a mainstream method for raising funds on the internet—with platforms like Kiva, Indiegogo, Kickstarter, and GoFundme serving as fundraising channels for everything from music and film to real estate, loans, scientific research, personal medical bills, and donations. Donors-Choose, a crowdfunding platform for public school teachers, launched in 2000, but it was not until a decade later that colleges and universities began to experiment with crowdfunding. By 2015, several dozen institutions were crowdfunding, and the term *crowdfunding* had become a buzz-word at industry conferences.

By 2015, crowdfunding already had empowered tens of millions of people and organizations outside of higher education to efficiently reach supporters and raise billions of dollars. In the process, it had changed the way that people support causes and give to organizations and other people. The early adopters within higher education were the first to begin tapping into this shifting behavior. Through crowdfunding, they were giving donors more control, making giving more personal, and allowing donors to connect more deeply and directly with the impact of their philanthropy. In these ways, crowdfunding helped them create experiences for all donors akin to the experiences of major donors. Crowdfunding also helped them address needs that could not easily be funded through traditional fundraising channels, and it gave them a mechanism to corral "rogue" fundraising activities already occurring across campus (e.g., those being conducted by students and faculty members on Go-FundMe).

Fordham University turned to crowdfunding to increase donor acquisition and to address a phenomenon that is commonplace at institutions without a central crowdfunding apparatus. Fordham alumni were giving to areas of specific interest through nontraditional or unsanctioned channels, and as a result, the development office was not capturing vital donor information, and donors were not being stewarded or cultivated. In its first year alone, crowdfunding at Fordham generated more than three thousand gifts—double the number of online gifts that the university typically received in a year. Thirty percent of Fordham's crowdfunding donors are newly acquired (Ball, Meyer, and Ezrapour 2018).

The strength of Fordham's crowdfunding program starts with the partnerships that the development office has forged with stakeholders across campus, such as the Office of Student Life. These partners help identify crowdfunding candidates, who are vetted and trained through a process designed by the development office. This includes completion of a formal application and acknowledgment of a carefully curated set of guidelines and expectations. Candidates approved for crowdfunding are provided with a handbook and other training resources, and they are expected to create their own digital content, generate lists of alumni and friends to contact, share regular updates on their progress, and steward their donors.

This process is designed to ensure that students feel ownership, which breeds greater accountability and follow-through. By involving students directly in its crowdfunding program, Fordham also is educating its future alumni about the importance of giving back and the impact that philanthropy has on campus. Fordham's approach is a collaborative one on which the development office continuously iterates, recognizing that each round of crowdfunding campaigns offers an opportunity for learning and refinement.

Despite the proven value of the crowdfunding model outside of higher education and the early success of institutions like Fordham, many development offices have remained skeptical of crowdfunding well into the late 2010s. Similar to the doubts about giving challenges, some fear that crowdfunding will fade in popularity and effectiveness, that it distracts staff and donors from institutional priorities, that it risks cannibalizing the annual fund, and that it acquires donors who will be difficult to retain.

The data from early adopters paints a different picture. Especially at institutions that treat crowdfunding as a teaching tool with students and young alumni, crowdfunding has helped build broader bases of support within hard-to-reach populations. It has provided valuable insights about new donors, such as what they care about and to whom they are connected socially.

Finally, the idea that crowdfunding produces mostly one-and-done donors has been debunked as a myth. Retention rates are quite strong among crowdfunding programs that are focused on alumni (vs. those that target family members of current students) and those that consistently deliver high-quality stewardship. In 2018, Fordham retained 24 percent of all new donors it acquired in 2017—but it retained 45 percent of new donors acquired through crowdfunding (Ball, Meyer, and Ezrapour 2018).

OVER THE HORIZON

If short-term giving challenges and crowdfunding are today's most effective methods for acquiring and retaining millennial and postmillennial donors, then what comes next? Where do the trends suggest we are headed? How do we get *ahead* of the curve and position ourselves to more effectively acquire and retain future generations as loyal, lifelong donors?

First, advancement offices should study and learn from the ways that leading businesses and organizations allocate their resources to drive innovation and sustainable long-term returns. At the most successful organizations—including the companies that make the digital technology that students and young alumni use every day—innovation and discovery are prioritized through serious and sustained investments in research and development.

Executives foster a culture of experimentation and pride themselves on being early adopters of new technologies and approaches. They also embrace failure. Indeed, failure has been a stepping stone on the pathway to most of humankind's greatest achievements, and an organization that rarely fails is an organization that is not pushing the boundaries. Without failure, we rarely make discoveries before it is too late to fully capitalize on the truths they reveal. Failure is how innovation is unlocked, and for too long, too many advancement offices have been environments where every initiative is expected to succeed and every outcome is expected to be known in advance.

Second, advancement offices should spend more time talking to their target audience. Students and young alumni should be represented on every board and council, not merely to observe, but also to actively participate, to be listened to, and to vote. Young alumni who are not giving should be asked *why not*.

Most institutions do an excellent job talking to and soliciting feedback from alumni who *are* giving, and as a result, many strategies are optimized for existing donors. In some cases, this optimization leads to approaches that alienate nondonors and create a vicious cycle wherein certain segments are consistently retained while others are never acquired in the first place. Asking people why they have elected not to give can be a painful and humbling conversation, but it may be the most valuable.

Third, advancement offices must more seriously invest in initiatives focused on students and young alumni. Even at institutions that have created a dedicated position(s) for this purpose, it often is the case that the position will be filled by the youngest and least experienced member(s) of the staff—or that this staff member will be given meager resources and little autonomy (or both). This is a losing equation. We should prioritize staff and resources focused on students and young alumni and provide these staff members with substantial political capital and the freedom to experiment—and, if we are lucky, to fail.

Orienting an advancement office to anticipate and effectively act on the needs of younger generations requires buy-in from senior leadership, organizational discipline and alignment, and patience. The time horizons over which investments focused on students and young alumni pay dividends are often long.

CONCLUSION

Mike Bloomberg began giving to his alma mater, the Johns Hopkins University, the year after he graduated. His first gift was five dollars, and he gave the same amount each of the next two years. It was *seven years* before his total lifetime giving surpassed one hundred dollars. Today, he has donated more than $3.35 billion. That includes a $1.8 billion commitment made in 2018, the largest gift in the history of higher education (Anderson 2018; Bloomberg, Daniels, and Schroeder 2018). But what if he had never made that first five-dollar gift? What if Johns Hopkins had not retained him as a donor throughout his twenties? In hindsight, we all certainly can agree that the investments that produced that first five-dollar gift were well worth it. But did everyone deem them worthy at the time?

Successfully engaging millennials and postmillennials is vital. For the next six decades, members of these generations will be the owners and stewards of most of our world's wealth. They share an overwhelming commitment to social good, and they are genuine believers in the transformative power of education. By better understanding these younger donors and the most effective ways to engage them and by positioning ourselves to iterate on and improve this understanding over time through research, development, experimentation, and failure, we have an opportunity to usher in an exciting new era of philanthropy for education. The next generation of donors is waiting.

REFERENCES

Anderson, Nick. 2018. "Bloomberg Gives Johns Hopkins a Record $1.8 Billion for Student Financial Aid." *Washington Post*, November 18, 2018. https://www.washingtonpost.com/local/education/bloomberg-gives-johns-hopkins-a-record-18-billion-for-student-financial-aid/2018/11/18/8db256cc-eb4e-11e8-96d4-0d23f2aaad09_story.html?utm_term=.d4acb80c445c.

Ball, Susan, Robert Meyer, and Elaine Ezrapour. 2018. "Fordham University's Crowdfunding Journey." Presentation at the GiveCampus Partners Conference, Washington, DC, February 22, 2018.

Bloomberg, Mike, Ron Daniels, and Fritz Schroeder. 2018. "A Conversation with Mike Bloomberg." Presentation at the CASE (Council for Advancement and Support of Education) Summit for Leaders in Advancement, New York, NY, July 17, 2018.

Davidson College. 2018. "Fifth Annual #ALLINFORDAVIDSON Raises $1.86 Million in Less Than a Day." Press release, April 19, 2018. https://www.davidson.edu/news/news-stories/180419-fifth-annual-allinfordavidson.

Douglas-Gabriel, Danielle. 2016. "Colleges Are Going Online to Crowdsource Donations, and They're Raising Millions." *Washington Post*, April 16, 2016. https://www.washingtonpost.com/news/grade-point/wp/2016/04/19/colleges-are-going-online-to-crowdsource-donations-and-theyre-raising-millions/?utm_term=.b1c2d8b550f8.

Fry, Richard. 2018. "Millennials Are the Largest Generation in the US Labor Force." Pew Research Center. April 11, 2018. http://www.pewresearch.org/fact-tank/2018/04/11/millennials-largest-generation-us-labor-force/.

Lipsman, Andrew. 2017. "5 Interesting Facts about Millennials' Mobile App Usage from 'The 2017 US Mobile App Report.'" *Comscore* (blog). August 24, 2017. https://www.comscore.com/Insights/Blog/5-Interesting-Facts-About-Millennials-Mobile-App-Usage-from-The-2017-US-Mobile-App-Report.

Morgan, Greta, Christene Riendeau, and Kerri Saucier. 2018. "The Quest for 50%: How Giving Days Reshaped Holy Cross' Participation Strategy." Presentation at Give-Campus Partners Conference, Washington, DC, February 21, 2018.

Notte, Jason. 2018. "Why Millennials Are More Charitable Than the Rest of You." TheStreet. January 25, 2018. https://www.thestreet.com/story/14445741/1/why-millennials-are-more-charitable.html.

Statista. 2018. "Daily Time Spent on Mobile by Millennial Internet Users Worldwide from 2012 to 2017 (in Minutes)." https://www.statista.com/statistics/283138/millennials-daily-mobile-usage/.

THIRTEEN

Women and Philanthropy

Andrea K. Pactor and Debra J. Mesch

Women are driving philanthropy today. In this chapter, we discuss some characteristics of women's philanthropy and new approaches that colleges and universities are adopting to attract more support from women donors.

Women are more than 50 percent of the population and are the key decision makers on philanthropy in a majority of households. Moreover, women are twice as likely as men to want to use their wealth for charitable purposes (US Trust 2013). Rethinking how to engage with women as donors is essential to grow the resources to meet an institution's mission. There has been a paradigm shift, from stand-alone programs for women donors to fully incorporating women and men across the fundraising process. This change is encompassing alumnae engagement, annual giving, major gifts, planned gifts, and campaigns, and it is generating results and impact.

In a holistic fundraising approach, efforts are institutionalized, and the entire development team is responsible for engaging men and women. Earlier stand-alone women's philanthropy programs relied heavily on the leadership of one staff member, either in the alumni engagement or annual giving department. Staff turnover often caused the program to flounder or to be of a lower priority than other projects.

A broader, more comprehensive approach presents opportunities to fully involve women as leaders and donors across the university. The intent is not to create an entirely new fundraising strategy but rather to be inclusive, adjusting and tweaking existing programs, recognizing that demographics are changing and the donor pool is more expansive.

A wise person once said that fundraising is 80 percent listening. Two stories illustrate why that is good advice and why it is essential to pay more attention to women in every phase of the fundraising process:

- A prominent businessman in the community told a group of non-profit leaders in a public setting that the nonprofit would send *him* a thank-you letter when his wife would make a contribution. He commented, "They keep doing it and they keep making her mad. It's no doubt that it will cause a cessation of gifts. Furthermore, I watch it; it happens all the time. Whoever is advising nonprofits should advise them to pay attention to who is behind the gift" (McColl 2017).

- A large university hired a female planned-giving officer, who combed through the database looking to build her portfolio. She found that a male alumnus had died three years earlier, so the planned-giving officer went to visit the widow. The widow told her, "No one has called me in three years or written me a note. I had intended to leave everything to the university because my husband loved it so dearly but, as no one reached out to me, I am leaving it elsewhere" (Hampton Perez 2018).

Although women today have more access to education, income, and wealth, they remain underrepresented and under-asked as donors. These stories are among many that illuminate the urgent need to rethink, revise, and refresh fundraising strategies so that men *and* women are fully engaged at your institution.

For practitioners who rely heavily on data to drive decisions, research conducted at the Women's Philanthropy Institute (WPI) of the Indiana University Lilly Family School of Philanthropy offers insights about how gender differences affect every aspect of the fundraising process. What works for men may not work for women and other underrepresented donor communities. Donors' motivations, gender, marital status, generation, and other variables affect how households make charitable decisions. These variables have implications for fundraisers.

DONOR MOTIVATIONS

Fundraisers know that understanding a donor's motivations is crucial to deepening donor engagement. Women are more motivated by empathy for others than men; for men, giving is more often about self-interest (Mesch, Osili, Pactor, and Ackerman 2015, 5). This is a matter of degree and priority; it does not imply that men are not empathetic. However, because women are socialized from an early age into more helping, nurturing, and caring roles, these behaviors become ingrained and form the basis for many of their actions, including philanthropy. Empathy also drives women's deep engagement with nonprofits.

Research has shown that women are more likely to give to organizations where they have a personal connection or an alignment with political or philosophical beliefs. Single women are more likely than single men to cite being on a board or volunteering for an organization as motivations for their giving (Mesch, Osili, Pactor, Ackerman, Dale, et al. 2015, 24).

Asking donors about their motivations for giving is a productive strategy for engagement, cultivation, and stewardship. Answers to open-ended questions can provide rich insights. For example, a gift officer might ask, "What motivates your giving? Who are your philanthropic role models? What causes do you care about most? What do you want your legacy to be from your giving?" The answers will help major-gift and planned-giving officers craft thoughtful proposals that reflect the donor's philanthropic vision.

MARITAL STATUS AND GENERATIONS

Gender differences appear when looking at giving by single men and single women and also in the context of a marriage. Single women are more likely to give and give more than single men (Mesch 2010, 4–6). This holds true across all income levels and has been affirmed across numerous studies. Moreover, while giving makes us all happy, single men see the greatest increase in life satisfaction (happiness) when they become donors. For single and married women, life satisfaction increases most when they increase their giving as a percentage of income (Mesch, Osili, Okten, et al. 2017, 18–19).

The results of several studies suggest that one way institutions can grow charitable giving is to find new ways to appeal to single men, especially as they transition from college to the workforce. For women, there is a strong connection between their deeper involvement as volunteers and subsequent increased giving to those organizations.

Some research highlights generational differences among single women, single men, and married couples when each generation was the ages of twenty-five to forty-seven. The research found that single Generation X and millennial women are holding their own in giving, comparable to older, pre-baby-boomer women. Unlike the single women, giving by Generation X and millennial single men and married couples is lower than pre-baby-boomer single men and married couples (Mesch, Ottoni-Wilhelm, and Osili 2016, 4).

Creating a baseline understanding of donor giving by gender, marital status, and generation allows the gaps and opportunities to emerge; fundraisers then can develop strategies to grow the donor base accordingly. This important step provides a solid metric against which to measure the impact of the work.

For example, Dartmouth College knew that four women had made gifts of $1 million or more in their last campaign. The goal for the Dartmouth campaign launched in April 2018 is to identify one hundred women who will make gifts of $1 million or more. The baseline metric may also include the donor participation rate among male and female graduates; the average gift size by men and women; the percentage of assigned prospects who are women; and the percentage of visits to men, women, and couples.

What happens to charitable giving after marriage? The available data are mostly about heterosexual couples (new research is analyzing giving by same-sex couples), but overall, marriage is good for charitable giving. Married couples give more, and the more they give as a percentage of income, the happier they are (Mesch, Osili, Okten, et al. 2017, 15). Understanding the dynamics of how couples decide about charitable giving helps fundraisers tailor requests and send acknowledgments to the appropriate individual in the household, as the businessman earlier in the chapter encouraged.

Households decide about charitable giving primarily in four ways: the male decides, the female decides, they decide jointly, and they decide separately (Brown 2005, 78). Joint decision making is the norm for most American households.

These giving patterns may be shifting across generations. The study that analyzed two generations between the ages of twenty-five and forty-seven found that young Generation X and millennial married women have more influence in charitable decisions than their baby-boomer and pre-baby-boomer counterparts forty years earlier. When a woman influences a couple's decision making, those couples in the younger generation are giving higher amounts now than their counterparts in the older generation did forty years earlier (Mesch, Ottoni-Wilhelm, and Osili 2016, 4).

Fundraisers have repeatedly stated that, for major gifts, it is important to engage both the husband and wife throughout the process. Until the fundraiser knows for certain who is driving the giving to the institution, nothing should be taken for granted. Fundraisers should also pay attention to the power dynamic in the household. In one case, a woman donor called the director of a nonprofit whom she knew well and indicated she wanted to make a million-dollar gift. The director thanked her, hung up, and called right back to ask whether her husband approved of the contribution!

HOW MEN AND WOMEN GIVE

Lack of understanding about the differences in how men and women approach charitable giving may be one important reason women continue to be an untapped resource. As fundraising professionalized in the 1960s, white men were the major donor focus. Strategies to reach them, such as campaigns, recognition, giving levels, competition, and peer pressure, were effective and have raised millions of dollars over the years. But these strategies may not work as effectively for women and other underrepresented populations in the donor base.

Dartmouth College learned that, despite the long-standing success of its annual giving program, the Dartmouth College Fund did not appeal to all people. Dartmouth women donors to the Centennial Circle, established in 2014, said creating community and focusing on impact were more of a priority than the competitiveness of the annual fund (Laine 2018).

APPLYING NEW STRATEGIES AND METHODS

Fundraising today is complex, including efforts to reach donors using multiple communications channels and to connect with donors across multiple giving vehicles. New approaches used by donors include donor-advised funds, impact investing, and online platforms. Research has shown that gender should be considered in developing strategies in these areas.

Women give differently. To date, the research has identified four tangible ways in which the differences are manifest: Women (1) distribute their gifts more broadly, (2) often give together, (3) leverage technology, and (4) look at giving holistically.

Giving Broadly

Single women spread out their philanthropy more than single men (Mesch, Osili, Pactor, Ackerman, and Bergdoll 2015, 7). If a woman gives one hundred dollars to each of ten organizations, no one fundraiser will appreciate the full sense of her generosity. Because of this, women are less likely to appear on prospect lists for major or planned gifts. Careful review of the database for these hidden donors, especially women who have given gifts of one hundred to five hundred dollars for years, may well reveal significant gift potential.

Giving Collectively

Some women prefer to give collectively to fully maximize their impact. Giving circles appeal to women because of their collaborative and democratic process. Mostly community-based, occasionally they are part of a campus fundraising strategy. In a giving circle or collective-giving group, individuals pool their contributions and decide together how and where funding will be allocated. Giving circles are not to be taken lightly; the number of giving circles tripled from 2007 to 2017, and they have granted nearly $1.3 billion since 1982 (Bearman et al. 2017, 5–6). While women represent the majority of giving-circle members, the ecosystem is becoming more diverse with LGBTQ, men-only, Jewish, African American, Latinx, and Asian American groups forming.

The Sally Society at Wayland Baptist University in Plainview, Texas, is one example of a giving circle on campus. Established in 2011 and named for the university's cofounder, the Sally Society includes members who contribute $1,000 annually and select a project to support on campus. Originally viewed as an alumnae-engagement vehicle, the group has expanded to build support from the community; membership is now 75 percent alumnae or women with ties to the university and 25 percent community members. The Sally Society has raised more than $380,000 since 2011 to support special projects at the university. This giving circle started as a staff-driven operation; constraints on staff time have prompted a move to a more volunteer-led model, especially for special events (Young 2018).

At Miami University in Oxford, Ohio, the M.I.A.M.I. Women Giving Circle focuses on advancing, mentoring, and investing in Miami women. Originally envisioned as an annual leadership symposium to connect with alumnae, the initiative has expanded to include a giving circle with a unique feature. Donors contribute one thousand dollars annually to the giving circle and ultimately vote for projects that have advanced in the Hawk Tank, which is modeled after the popular *Shark Tank*. In this program, faculty, staff, and students learn how to fast-pitch ideas, receive guidance in developing their projects and pitches from the Miami Farmer School of Business Entrepreneurship, and then compete for grants. The funded projects enrich the campus culture; they are often projects for which university funding is not available. In 2018, the giving circle awarded ten grants totaling $104,000. Faculty, staff, students, and giving-circle members are involved throughout the process (Bortel 2018).

The giving circles appeal to women at both universities for similar reasons—the community that is created and the opportunity to be more involved in campus life. Women at Miami have cited meeting students as a draw and benefit of the initiative. For the fundraisers, the giving circle is an opportunity to reach out to women who have not given before or whose last gift was ten years earlier. A common concern is that giving circles can be labor intensive for staff and the advancement office, especially depending on how elaborate the grant-making process may be.

Using Technology

A third difference is how men and women leverage technology for their giving. A WPI study about #GivingTuesday donors found that women are more likely than men to give on that special day. While giving goes up sharply for both men and women on #GivingTuesday and they give approximately equal amounts, the greater participation of women leads to a greater total of donations from women. In this study, women donors gave 61 percent of the total dollars raised on #Giving-Tuesday (Osili, Mesch, Preston, et al. 2017, 8).

William & Mary found similar results from their 2018 day of giving, One Tribe One Day, to which 58 percent of the donors were women. As a result of higher participation rates, they gave more than men gave on that day (Cushman 2018). If an institution is eager to grow annual giving, then thinking creatively about reaching alumnae through social media or building or augmenting a designated day of giving is an option to explore.

Giving Holistically

The newest approach to leveraging the growing power of women in philanthropy includes deliberate and intentional strategies that are woven into the overall fundraising strategy and that are fully supported by leadership with dedicated staff. Recognizing that no one model is suited to every institution, evaluate your institution's readiness and commitment to the effort before embarking on this journey.

The following two case studies, one driven by alumnae and the other by the advancement leadership, are examples of the impact this paradigm shift is making to overall fundraising engagement and success.

Dartmouth College

In early 2014, several Dartmouth College alumnae developed a plan to recruit one hundred women to make gifts of $100,000 or more to honor the one-hundredth anniversary of the Dartmouth College Fund. That initial effort culminated in gifts from 114 women, totaling more than $14 million. The next year, the group organized and hosted a symposium for Dartmouth women.

What started as a single event to honor a milestone in the college's history has now been institutionalized as the Centennial Circle, with staff, resources, and the college's leadership behind it. The impact on Dartmouth fundraising has been impressive. Since 2014, Centennial Circle members have contributed more than $40 million to the annual fund and more than $100 million across the Dartmouth community. Furthermore, the Call to Lead campaign, launched in 2018, achieved balanced leadership by gender on its campaign committee through a collaborative effort among Centennial Circle members, university leadership, and staff (Laine 2018).

Through this process, Dartmouth reached out to women who had not been active or who had never been asked for gifts. The emphasis on women's philanthropic leadership—asks of $100,000 or more—made a difference in the college's ability to attract new donors. In this short time, Dartmouth has been closing the gender gap in giving across the board. The success of the Centennial Circle is based on (1) carefully listening to women and learning about their philanthropic vision and behaviors; (2) connecting with the women on multiple levels and platforms; (3) engaging women as volunteers in every facet; and (4) training the entire development staff on how to talk to women, either individually or as part of a couple.

A collaborative effort to engage all donors has become ingrained in the Dartmouth fundraising culture. One outcome is that Centennial Circle members have deepened their giving over time; many make multiple gifts across the college.

William & Mary

At William & Mary, the impetus to more fully engage women in philanthropy originated with the foundation board as they began planning for the next campaign. Familiar with the research about gender and giving, the board formed a task force to explore how best to involve women in the campaign.

Initial efforts led to a university-wide initiative to increase both women's leadership around campus and their giving. The timing coincided perfectly with the university's preparations to celebrate one hundred years of admitting women in 2018. The advancement team built strategies to leverage that anniversary, including training all 175 members of the advancement staff about women's philanthropy (Cushman 2018).

William & Mary has integrated their work with women donors across all fundraising strategies and involved all staff across advancement. Each department set measurable goals to hold themselves accountable for creating a more gender-balanced culture of leadership and giving. For example, prospect research places equal emphasis on single women and both members of a couple in their briefings. Frontline fundraisers have created strategies to engage alumnae. The marketing and communications department is working to ensure that female voices are represented in all communications.

William & Mary's vice president for university advancement, Matthew Lambert, was an early supporter of the work around women's philanthropy. Lambert has commented that the groundbreaking work with alumnae can serve as a model for engaging other underrepresented communities, such as LGBTQ and African American alumni (Cushman 2018).

The Society of 1918 is one facet of William & Mary's work with women donors. They envisioned recruiting one hundred donors to contribute a minimum of $10,000 annually to reach $1 million in a year. Achieving that goal within two months, they immediately set a higher goal of $1,918,000. As of mid-2018, the Society of 1918 had 350 members, who have contributed $2.6 million. The pent-up desire to support the institution prompted the leadership to raise the goal to $4 million by the end of the fiscal year.

Volunteers developed the group's vision and mission, identifying engagement, leadership, and philanthropy as the three guiding pillars and structuring the program to be by women, for women. No prospective member asked about the benefits of membership; each wanted to be part of something bigger, reflecting another distinctive feature of women's philanthropy. The volunteer leadership launched an endowment to ensure that the Society of 1918 would become permanent (Cushman 2018).

CONCLUSION

The examples in this chapter are proof that each institution must craft a women's philanthropy initiative according to its culture and needs. Initiatives are successful when the vision is bold, leadership is fully onboard, volunteers step up to lead, designated staff guide and coordinate efforts, the entire advancement office is aligned, baseline metrics are established, and sufficient time is allocated to build and nurture the effort.

Before campuses can fully leverage the power of women's philanthropy, it is essential to acknowledge that gender matters in philanthropy and that the one-size-fits-all fundraising model is obsolete in today's fast-changing world. Colleges and universities that step fully into creating welcoming environments for women as donors will experience their deeper engagement, increased giving, and loyalty. In addition, women often bring others along on the journey, whether family, friends, fellow alumnae, or the men in their lives.

Fundraisers cannot assume that what works well for men also works well for women. The goal is to work smarter, not harder. Tweaking existing strategies to ensure they are inclusive and reflect men's and women's patterns of giving will generate more and new resources to meet your institution's mission. Women's engagement and philanthropy are growing exponentially; make sure your institution is tapping into these powerful and influential donors.

REFERENCES

Bearman, Jessica, Julia Carboni, Angela Eikenberry, and Jason Franklin. 2017. *The Landscape of Giving Circles/Collective Giving Groups in the U.S.* Indianapolis: Women's Philanthropy Institute at the Indiana University Lilly School of Philanthropy. https://scholarworks.iupui.edu/bitstream/handle/1805/14527/giving-circles2017-2. pdf?sequence=4&isAllowed=y.

Bortel, Heidi. 2018. Interview by Andrea Pactor via telephone. August 10, 2018.

Brown, Eleanor. 2005. "Married Couples' Charitable Giving: Who and Why." *New Directions for Philanthropic Fundraising*, 50: 69–80.

Cushman, Valerie. 2018. Interview by Andrea Pactor. August 22, 2018.

Hampton Perez, April. 2018. Interview by Andrea Pactor via focus-group discussion, Southwestern University, July 11, 2018.

Laine, Mindi. 2018. Interview by Andrea Pactor via telephone. August 16, 2018.

McColl, Hugh. 2017. "Women Give 2017." Panel discussion at the Women Give 2017 launch, Charlotte, NC, October 17, 2017.

Mesch, Debra. 2010. *Women Give 2010: New Research about Women and Giving.* Indianapolis: Women's Philanthropy Institute at the Indiana University Lilly School of Philanthropy. https://scholarworks.iupui.edu/bitstream/handle/1805/6337/women_give_2010_report.pdf?sequence=1&isAllowed=y.

Mesch, Debra, Una Osili, Cagla Okten, Xiao Han, Andrea Pactor, and Jacqueline Ackerman. 2017. *Women Give 2017: Charitable Giving and Life Satisfaction: Does Gender Matter?* Indianapolis: Women's Philanthropy Institute at the Indiana University Lilly School of Philanthropy. https://scholarworks.iupui.edu/bitstream/handle/1805/14283/womengive17.pdf.

Mesch, Debra, Una Osili, Andrea Pactor, and Jacqueline Ackerman. 2015. *Do Women Give More? Findings from Three Unique Data Sets on Charitable Giving.* Indianapolis: Women's Philanthropy Institute at the Indiana University Lilly School of Philanthropy. https://scholarworks.iupui.edu/bitstream/handle/1805/6984/Do%20Women %20Give%20More%20-%20Working%20Paper%201%20-%20Sept%202015.pdf? sequence=4&isAllowed=y.

Mesch, Debra, Una Osili, Andrea Pactor, Jacqueline Ackerman, and Jon Bergdoll. 2015. *Where Do Men and Women Give? Gender Differences in the Motivations and Purposes for Charitable Giving.* Indianapolis: Women's Philanthropy Institute at the Indiana University Lilly School of Philanthropy. https://scholarworks.iupui.edu/bitstream/ handle/1805/6985/Where%20Do%20Men%20and%20Women%20Give%20- %20Working%20Paper%202%20-%20Sept%202015.pdf?sequence=4&isAllowed=y.

Mesch, Debra, Una Osili, Andrea Pactor, Jacqueline Ackerman, Elizabeth Dale, and Jon Bergdoll. 2015. *How and Why Women Give: Current and Future Directions for Research on Women's Philanthropy*. Indianapolis: Women's Philanthropy Institute at the Indiana University Lilly School of Philanthropy. https://scholarworks.iupui. edu/bitstream/handle/1805/6983/How%20and%20Why%20Women%20Give%20-%20Literature%20Review%20-%20May%202015.pdf?sequence=4&isAllowed=y.

Mesch, Debra, Mark Ottoni-Wilhelm, and Una Osili. 2016. *Women Give 2016: Giving in Young Adulthood: Gender Differences and Changing Patterns across the Generations*. Indianapolis: Women's Philanthropy Institute at the Indiana University Lilly School of Philanthropy. https://scholarworks.iupui.edu/bitstream/handle/1805/11446/WomenGive16%20Final%20Single%20Pages%5b1%5d.pdf?sequence=1&isAllowed=y.

Osili, Una, Debra Mesch, Linh Preston, Cagla Okten, Jonathan Bergdoll, Jacqueline Ackerman, and Andrea Pactor. 2017. *Gender Differences in #GivingTuesday Participation*. Indianapolis: Women's Philanthropy Institute at the Indiana University Lilly School of Philanthropy. https://scholarworks.iupui.edu/bitstream/handle/1805/14782/Giving.Tuesday.Report.Final.Web.pdf?sequence=1&isAllowed=y.

US Trust. 2013. "Insights on Wealth and Worth: Women and Wealth." Bank of America Corporation. https://www.ustrust.com/publish/content/application/pdf/GWMOL/ARS7ME57.pdf.

Young, Teresa Cox. 2018. Interview by Andrea Pactor. August 7, 2018.

FOURTEEN

Engaging Underrepresented Communities

Rachel E. Vassel

The US Census predicts that American minority groups will be the majority population by 2044, with Latino Americans and African Americans becoming the top two ethnic groups in the country (US Census Bureau 2015). Because diverse populations in the United States are growing, American universities have become some of the most diverse communities in the country. In fact, top colleges tend to be more diverse because they enjoy endowments that allow admissions to be need-blind and meet the full need of students (Schifrin 2015). As diversity in higher education grows, advancement professionals will need to understand all of the segments of their alumni base to ensure that engagement strategies are appealing across cultures and that giving opportunities are meaningful.

Leveraging a targeted approach to alumni engagement and development, universities can increase their overall fundraising goals and drive great enthusiasm among underrepresented communities that often feel marginalized. This marginalization can cause diverse alumni to remain uninvolved in their alma maters postgraduation. However, when diverse alumni are made to feel that they are valued and that their alma maters understand their specific experiences and interests, it is possible to count on their participation—as donors, event attendees, volunteers, and advocates for the university.

Consider how society operates in our current digital age. Because today's consumers now have access to targeted information—that is, information specific to culture, life stage, interests, politics, or gender—they
are much less willing to filter through general content to find the information that is most important to them. One of the best examples of this
change is the television industry, which now offers hundreds of narrow-
cast cable television networks in addition to the original big three broadcasting networks. The viewer's perspective is now "Why watch the six
o'clock news on a broadcast network and wait for the sports updates,
when I can go directly to ESPN, which offers all sports, all the time?"

Actually, consumers today do not have to wait for targeted information at all because the internet allows us to access specific content that
interests us at any time of day. Content is targeted in the digital age, so
we can always find the viewpoint that we desire, the perspective that we
prefer. This makes us all less interested in one-size-fits-all programming.

In higher education, understanding this phenomenon from an alumni-engagement standpoint is hugely important. Increasingly, alumni
want the ESPN experience—specific, targeted engagement. All segments
in the alumni population—diverse, young, LGBTQ, Latino, international,
and others—come with unique insights and campus experiences that universities can leverage to drive their connection to the institution. The
most progressive universities are building targeted programs for audiences that result in increased participation, engagement, giving, and loyalty. These programs can also complement long-standing general programs for all alumni.

ENGAGING ALUMNI

How can universities develop an outreach model that is specific to underrepresented populations? The program at Syracuse University (SU) offers
one example. SU has enjoyed an independent multicultural alumni engagement and fundraising office since the early 1980s. Originally called
the Office of Program Development, this office was renamed as the Office
of Multicultural Advancement in 2019.

The office was founded by the then–vice president of public relations,
who was an African American leader. Recognizing the need for black
alumni to connect with one another, the office launched SU's first targeted alumni reunion. Today, the renamed office sits within the univer-

sity's advancement and external affairs division, with the distinct goal of increasing engagement and giving among African American and Latino alumni. It hosts a triennial reunion called Coming Back Together (CBT), an on-campus alumni weekend built specifically for diverse alumni.

During CBT, everything—including the food, session topics, speakers, and the music—is culturally relevant, relatable, and nostalgic. While all alumni are encouraged to attend SU's annual homecoming, known as Orange Central, CBT holds a special place in the hearts of diverse alumni because it is so specific to their tastes and experiences. Engagement during CBT is extremely high as a result. Alumni of color who participate have indicated over the years that CBT is a very special reunion that takes priority in their lives.

Because of the high engagement during CBT, the reunion offers a tremendous platform for fundraising. Messaging is integrated throughout the reunion, encouraging giving toward culturally relevant campus priorities, such as the Our Time Has Come (OTHC) Scholarship Program. OTHC benefits African American and Latino students through more than forty endowed funds. CBT has been very successful over the years, resulting in significant giving among SU's diverse alumni groups—at giving levels not achieved previously. Since the inception of OTHC, 1,300 minority scholarships have been given, and millions of dollars have been raised.

CBT 2017 was the largest CBT ever. More than one thousand alumni of color returned to campus for the exciting four-day event, filled with industry panel discussions, an SU football game and tailgate, an awards gala, a community-service project, a concert, and several receptions and celebrations. Many VIPs and prominent alumni were part of the programming, which included forty events in four days.

As an added fundraising opportunity, SU launched the first-ever CBT celebrity basketball game, which drove the return of athletes, who played in the exhibition game. Ticket sales benefited the OTHC Scholarship Fund. Latino alumni were particularly thrilled by the Hispanic Heritage Month parade and reception as well as the unveiling of the National Association of Latino Fraternal Organizations (NALFO) plaques, located just off the quad and honoring the nine traditionally Latino fraternities and sororities on campus.

What underrepresented communities like most about the CBT reunion is that it celebrates the best of them, in a world that rarely does so. It says to them, "You came to Syracuse University and made an impact. We're proud to call you Orange." Attendees consistently tell us that CBT is a special time when the university they love welcomes them home with honor, respect, and acceptance. Most importantly, it provides an opportunity for diverse alumni to connect with one another as well as current students—to whom they can give their time, talent, and treasure to ensure the success stories of the next generation of diverse alumni.

In addition to our programs and events, we consistently celebrate our African American and Latino alumni within our diverse alumni magazine, *Syracuse Manuscript*. The magazine features underrepresented alumni; discusses student, faculty, and staff success stories and student programs; celebrates diversity; and promotes university initiatives important to the groups we seek to engage. This kind of positive content goes a long way in communicating that the university values diverse alumni and ways that they can take part in key university initiatives and volunteer activities. Advancement professionals certainly know that building a relationship is the first step in getting alumni connected, involved, and giving.

Several universities now have programs that target and engage diverse alumni. Many offer diverse alumni events as a component of their overall university homecoming activities. That is a great way to get started with targeted engagement, particularly if the budget doesn't exist for a stand-alone diverse-alumni weekend.

For example, Northwestern University connects with African American alumni through their Northwestern University Black Alumni Association (NUBAA), which hosts the NUBAA Homecoming. In 2018, the weekend reunion program kicked off with a welcome-back reception at the university's Black House (black student union facility); followed by a tailgate cosponsored by Kappa Alpha Psi, a traditionally African American fraternity; and a homecoming party.

The weekend closed with a brunch and screening of the *Takeover* documentary, which tells the story of the Bursar 100, a group of black students who protested the university's policies in 1968 by holding an administration building sit-in. By revisiting historical moments in NU's black history, the university is able to promote healing and acknowledge progress over the years.

Similarly, the University of Pittsburgh's African American Alumni Council (AAAC) offers an annual Sankofa Homecoming, which provides culturally relevant events for black alumni during Pitt's annual home-coming. (*Sankofa* is a word in the Twi language of Ghana that means "go back and get what was lost," but African American scholars have adopted the term to mean "remembering our past to protect our future.")

The 2018 Sankofa events included a screening of *Blue Gold and Black*, a documentary highlighting 180 years of black achievement at Pitt; an awards banquet; a community-service project; the debut of the Dr. Bebe Moore Campbell Memorial Collection (honoring the deceased African American author and alumna); a National Society of Black Engineers student–alumni mixer; and a panel discussion celebrating the fiftieth an-niversary of the Black Action Society (BAS) at Pitt. Both Northwestern and Pitt, in partnership with alumni affinity groups, have developed targeted events that resonate well with black alumni.

Along with strong alumni engagement, diverse alumni associations also provide support for multicultural student recruitment and scholar-ship fundraising. For example, the UCLA Latino Alumni Association hosts the Fiesta de Inspiracion Scholarship Reception to raise dollars for Latino scholarships, which have been offered at UCLA for twenty-seven years. UCLA Latino alumni also host Raza Weekend, which encourages admitted Latino students to choose UCLA through connections with their future UCLA classmates and by promoting key cultural activities, Latino leaders, and organizations available on campus.

Similarly, Harvard's Latino Alumni Alliance (HLAA) offers several student-focused gatherings, from a Latino graduation ceremony to a Lati-no students retreat to a Thanksgiving *pachanga* (party or gathering) held at the home of a Harvard alumnus. Harvard's Latino alumni raise money for the HLAA Scholarship, which provides financial support for stu-dents, as well as opportunities for HLAA scholars to spend time with prominent Latino alumni. Connecting alumni of color with current stu-dents and creating opportunities for them to support diverse scholarship creation is one of the best ways to keep them involved.

UNDERREPRESENTED COMMUNITIES IN THE LARGER UNIVERSITY

Members of underrepresented communities experience a certain duality as alumni of predominantly white universities. They would like to see greater support of black and brown students, greater recruitment from underrepresented communities, and more focus on matters of diversity and inclusion. However, they are also pleased to have been accepted into the university family and to enjoy all of the privileges, connections, and successes that alumni status brings. The more that predominantly white universities can tap into these insights, the greater their success in engaging underrepresented alumni.

One of the questions that colleagues, alumni, and friends sometimes ask is, "Doesn't your program exclude others?" The response is in the negative. At Syracuse, all alumni are welcome to attend CBT and the university's other targeted events. No one is ever excluded. We build the events based on marketing insights about our diverse alumni audience, but we do not check anyone's ethnicity at the door.

We simply cater to the interests of the African American and Latino alumni in our efforts and are intentional about displaying diverse alumni and students in the programming. If you are not a member of either the African American or Latino community but want to experience cultural food, music, traditions, and perspectives, you may feel free to participate in CBT. Our focus is to ensure that diverse alumni are at the center of our engagement events and activities because that is the kind of engagement they desire. That is a donor-centric approach, similar to what we might do to meet the needs and interests of other alumni groups.

Students of color experience challenges, including financial aid shortfalls, isolation within the student body, institutional racism, and sometimes mistreatment by faculty and staff. These conditions can negatively affect their interest in supporting their alma maters as alumni. Additionally, these students often seek to find their own traditions, social networks, and cultural organizations in their student experiences. That requires comfortable spaces and much-needed support and camaraderie on campuses that often overlook their needs. Alumni outreach that considers these insights and sends the message that diverse alumni are understood and valued can make a world of difference in building relationships with these individuals.

PROVIDING RELEVANT GIVING OPPORTUNITIES

Beyond targeted outreach, it is important to provide programs and culturally relevant giving opportunities that allow diverse alumni to celebrate their shared experiences and support their communities through university involvement. According to Blackbaud's *Diversity in Giving* study (Rovner 2015), African American donors, more than any other group, are interested in supporting their unique heritage and community. Latino donors are likely to give consistently when the giving benefits their community because this is where they see the greatest need.

Universities should offer scholarship funds benefiting students of color (or, if university policies do not allow this, first-generation students), as well as opportunities to give in support of programs that enrich the diverse student experience and facilities that serve the needs of multicultural students, faculty, and staff. Giving opportunities like these provide diverse donors the opportunity to support their cultures and build a legacy on campus. Universities can leave money on the table if they choose not to offer these kinds of philanthropic programs. A generic annual-giving appeal is just not as interesting to underrepresented communities.

Another crucial issue universities must understand is that underrepresented communities are often ignored when appeals are made. Blackbaud's *Diversity in Giving* study (Rovner 2015) found that Latino donors want to help nonprofits they care about but often don't know how to do so. That same report found that African American donors would give more if they were asked. If you are a major-gift officer, you might ask yourself how many prospects you personally manage who are alumni of color. Universities should also ask themselves how many of their front-line fundraisers are people of color who can easily connect with underrepresented communities. Finally, as advancement professionals we must offer giving opportunities that will motivate diverse donors.

Some of these points are illustrated by another example, from outside higher education—the Smithsonian Institution and its recent fundraising experience. Their donor base has never been as diverse as it is today. Why? Because the National Museum of African American History and Culture is now a driver for gifts from African American donors. During the museum's fundraising campaign, the Smithsonian "discovered [African American] families who weren't on commonly shared donor lists" (McGlone 2016).

In the end, 74 percent of the individuals who each gave $1 million or more were African American, a figure almost double their early expectations (McGlone 2016). Furthermore, the museum received significant support from African American organizations, including black sororities, fraternities, and civic groups. For many of the museum's diverse donors, the gifts are personal. The required $540 million goal came in easily because the museum mattered to African American donors (McGlone 2016).

This success is partly attributable to the fact that there was an African American development officer at the Smithsonian who knew how to connect with donors in that community (Sandoval 2017). Without diversity within our development teams, as well as a culture of inclusion and cultural awareness related to prospects and donor opportunities, universities will not be able to enjoy full alumni support.

Like the Smithsonian's National Museum of African History and Culture, Syracuse's CBT 2017 also broke records. Attendance reached one thousand (up from three hundred attendees in 2014), and gift presentations quadrupled during the CBT Gala, where $1 million in gifts and pledges were secured for the university. SU also received the Council for Advancement and Support of Education (CASE) Circle of Excellence Gold Award for Diversity Programs. But our biggest win was that diverse alumni felt welcomed and at home on campus, and left the reunion knowing that they could make a significant impact for the university—and their community—by staying involved and giving back.

CONCLUSION

Targeted engagement of underrepresented communities is not easy work. It requires a steady drumbeat of culturally relevant communications and out-of-the-box ideas, the ability to uplift communities that often have negative history with the institution, as well as lots of executive support and investment. However, we can all do more, and it can be done. As the demographics of our country continue to change, we have to pay attention to the needs and desires of all segments of our campus communities so that we can be successful in reaching our common goals.

REFERENCES

McGlone, Peggy. 2016. "How the African American Museum Is Raising the Bar for Black Philanthropy." *Washington Post.* May 24, 2016. https://www.washingtonpost.com/entertainment/museums/african-american-museums-fundraising-touches-deep-history-among-donors/2016/05/23/bc2cbc94-1613-11e6-924d-838753295f9a_story.html?utm_term=.cce5311a5655.

Rovner, Mark. 2015. *Diversity in Giving: The Changing Landscape of American Philanthropy.* Charleston, SC: Blackbaud. https://institute.blackbaud.com/asset/diversity-in-giving/.

Sandoval, Timothy. 2017. "From Zero to $40 Million: Elite Fundraiser Explains How She Did It." *Chronicle of Philanthropy*, September 6, 2017. https://www.philanthropy.com/article/From-Zero-to-40-Million-/241065.

Schifrin, Matt. 2015. "Diversity at Top Colleges: Here's the Proof." *Forbes Magazine*, December 20, 2015. https://www.forbes.com/sites/schifrin/2015/12/20/diversity-at-top-colleges-heres-the-proof/#50c0d9b06d3f.

US Census Bureau. 2015. "New Census Bureau Report Analyzes US Population Projections." Press release, March 3, 2015. https://www.census.gov/newsroom/press-releases/2015/cb15-tps16.html.

FIFTEEN

International and Global Fundraising

Ivan A. Adames

In September 29, 2010, Bill Gates and Warren Buffett hosted a dinner like no other. They invited fifty of China's wealthiest entrepreneurs to dinner in Beijing to discuss and encourage large-scale philanthropy among the country's newest billionaires. Buffett, Gates, and his wife, Melinda, had just launched the Giving Pledge—an open invitation to the most affluent citizens worldwide to publicly commit the majority of their wealth to philanthropy in order to help address society's most pressing problems.

At its launch, forty American individuals and couples joined in this commitment. Today, the Giving Pledge counts 183 members from 22 countries, whose pledges total more than $365 billion. Members give to a diverse range of issues that are important to them, from global health and arts and culture to criminal justice reform, education, and more (Giving Pledge, n.d.). Few can argue that the Giving Pledge has elevated the conversation about philanthropy among many of the world's richest individuals and families. In addition, it has helped diminish the misconception that a commitment to philanthropy is an exclusively American or Western ideology.

Global philanthropic dollars are often invested close to home, but US higher education is seeing a growing level of giving from international alumni and donors. This growth in international philanthropic giving reflects a roughly 40 percent increase in the number of millionaire households outside the United States since 2010. It has led to a spike in transformational gifts to US colleges and universities. (Staff Writer 2017). Some examples include:

- The Chan family's 2014 gift of $350 million to Harvard University's School of Public Health to honor their late father, T. H. Chan, who staunchly supported education and research to alleviate human suffering (Harvard T. F. Chan School of Public Health 2014).
- More than $150 million to Boston University from alumnus and trustee Rajen Kilachand ('74) for projects ranging from the formation of an honors college, capital improvement projects, and an interdisciplinary center for research at the intersection of the life sciences and engineering (Jahnke 2017).
- Drs. Kiran and Pallavi Patel's gifts of $225 million to Nova Southeastern University in Florida to expand its programs in health sciences, including a new campus for the school's College of Osteopathic Medicine and a $50 million scholarship fund (Candid 2017).

Over the last decade, international student enrollment in US colleges and universities has nearly doubled, and the percent of total US enrollment by international students has risen from 3.4 percent to 5.3 percent in 2016–2017 (Institute of International Education, n.d.). The 2017–2018 academic year saw the first, albeit small, decline in international enrollment in twelve years, potentially due to the current political climate and uncertainty about US immigration policies (Redden 2018).

However, there are still nearly 500,000 international undergraduate students, many coming from elite preparatory schools and families with considerable wealth, whose parents should be strongly considered part of an institution's parent and family program. The number of alumni from US institutions abroad is at its highest point in history, presenting vast opportunities for engagement and cultivation of donors and prospects, now and for years to come.

Today, it is not a question of whether an institution should have an international advancement strategy but how to have one that is efficient and effective and leads to success in the long term. A robust international advancement strategy should not be a separate entity but rather part of the overall strategy for a college or university—linked to enrollment, corporate relations, and parent and alumni programs, as well as the development operation.

DETERMINING WHERE TO START

When starting or refining an international advancement program, it is essential to begin by determining where in the world to expend your energy (and your budget), cataloging the resources you have at hand, and devising processes and tactics for getting your leadership in front of great prospects abroad. There is not a requirement to start these efforts in any particular season or year, but many find that a campaign provides the momentum to get these fundamentals in place, linked to broader university strategic plans.

Just as you would for your domestic advancement program, it is essential to look geographically at where the majority of your prospects live abroad. Include in your analysis:

- Alumni and donors
- Parents of current students (particularly undergraduates)
- Forecasts of future alumni populations—based on your enrollment trends, where your alumni hotspots will be in five and ten years
- Grateful patient prospects
- Corporate partners abroad

It is very likely that you will have prospects and alumni communities scattered across the globe, and the question will quickly become how to prioritize your focus. Beyond providing alumni and parent concentrations, prospect researchers can flag known prospects and begin the process of working internally and with vendors to identify others.

Your decisions will need to reflect the resources you have available to commit. These include financial resources, human and academic resources, and leadership. What will your budget support? If you have a few great prospects but they are scattered far and wide, how can you be creative with your dollars? International advancement is not for the budgeting faint of heart; trips are very expensive, and it is important to be realistic about projected expenses.

Things to consider include the following: Are there areas of the world where your institution has both prospects and specific expertise? Perhaps faculty travel there regularly, the country is the focus area of a department, or you have a large population of faculty or staff who speak the language and are culturally fluent? Does your senior leadership have connections—academic, cultural, or otherwise—in a certain region of the world?

Selecting the regions for focus requires some strategic decisions. For example, Canada may be covered by your existing regional development officers, who perhaps can just expand their territories to include Canadian cities near the United States. Many globetrotting prospects in finance and other fields are very accustomed to regular travel to some of the world's largest cities: London, New York, San Francisco, Hong Kong, and Miami. You can be quite efficient and effective by using these as regional hubs.

Importantly, think big. Invite alumni in Asia to events in San Francisco, alumni in Europe to events in New York City, and Central and South American alumni to your Miami events. In addition to these popular locations, you might add, if resources allow, a city or region or two where *your* institutional map points you, whether Greece, India, Brazil, Malaysia, or somewhere else entirely.

INVENTORY YOUR HUMAN RESOURCES

Your human resources are essential when considering the scope and direction of your international advancement operation. Create an inventory of your resources, people who may be helpful in the following areas. Consider staff, students, faculty, administrative leadership, volunteer leaders, corporate partners, and others.

Many programs rely heavily on volunteers for their valuable cultural insights, as well as on-the-ground help as liaisons and more. A volunteer abroad can play a myriad of important roles; they can become a member of alumni leadership (chapter lead, local contact for alumni); identify and, as appropriate, qualify prospects; act as a cultural attaché; serve as a guide or host; provide diplomatic assistance when navigating local regulatory matters; offer pro bono banking and legal advice; and serve on committees or councils for campaigns. Just remember that, like domestic volunteers, international volunteers need clear expectations and sufficient training and management to be successful as an important part of your advancement team.

What do you need most from your various partners? Consider the following areas:

- Cultural guidance: It is important to have people you can call on for coaching on important cultural differences, especially as it relates to engagement and philanthropy.
- Prospect identification: Beyond your research team, there may be others who are able to point to good prospects. These may include faculty members, corporate- or alumni-engagement staff who have relationships abroad, or high-level volunteers. In addition, your admissions office can be an extremely valuable partner in identifying parent prospects.
- Prospect qualification and cultivation: Identify people in your sphere who may be able to play a valuable role in the qualification and cultivation of prospects abroad. These may be faculty members, volunteers, or even students or young alumni deployed to engage prospects abroad.
- Other assistance: You may have senior volunteers who can leverage their multinational connections abroad for corporate-hosted events or open doors in countries with considerable bureaucracy. Perhaps you have a business or law professor who specializes in a region with many prospects and can help craft talking points for development staff. There are many ways that you might find help in your efforts abroad if you think creatively and leverage the diverse community of your college or university. Faculty can be notoriously independent, but some may become allies and provide helpful leads.

PROACTIVE PLANNING

Before you begin planning events and donor meetings, it is essential to discuss the best way to schedule international trips with senior leaders. Often, key faculty members, deans, and presidents have plans a year or more in advance for overseas conferences or events, and that can be a starting point for discussions about scheduling advancement activities in the region.

Keep in mind that you are not the only part of the university with an international plan—trips may need to be coordinated with admissions, corporate relations, and possibly other institutional stakeholders. However, those events can also be fantastic events for advancement, providing opportunities to meet parents and interface with alumni at corporations abroad.

Even with much hard work and established processes, sometimes you will find out that a key faculty member or university leader is going abroad at the last minute. Think creatively! You might ask if the faculty member can extend his or her trip by one day and set up a meeting with a donor who is interested in his or her research, for example. Keep your communication open and regular with your campus partners, and you will help encourage a culture of collaboration around international advancement.

SETTING METRICS AND GOALS

Measure your success and analyze it. Be realistic and consider a start-up period of at least one year to learn and set reasonable goals for the short term and long term. Each institution will have a slightly different set of objectives when determining return on investment, but some key metrics for international advancement include:

- Productivity: number and amount of gifts coming from abroad
- Donors: number of international donors
- Attendees: number of people who attend your international events and gatherings
- Qualifications: prospects identified and qualified for major-gift work
- Visits: one-on-one prospect meetings abroad

PROSPECTING AND RESEARCH ON A GLOBAL SCALE

Identifying good major-gift prospects in the United States today is one part art, two parts science, and one part good fortune. Identifying good major-gift prospects abroad often has a different formula. Further complicating matters for American institutions with alumni across the Atlantic, the European Union established new privacy rules in May 2018.

The EU's General Data Protection Regulation (GDPR) requires that nonprofits have a legal basis to collect, hold, and process European donor and alumni data (Rock 2018). Institutions can demonstrate that they have a legitimate interest in an individual or get consent from alumni and donors to possess and use personal data. Both processes can be time-consuming, and fines for violating the new rules are steep. Colleges and universities would be wise to employ a task force—including staff in research, data compliance, legal, and development—to ensure not only compliance but also an understanding among staff members what GDPR means for their organization and their day-to-day work.

International prospect research is not doomed—far from it. It is evolving constantly from the data perspective, but some core principles still apply, with a little adjustment:

- Time: Research takes time. International research requires additional start-up time. Your researchers need to learn about the market and wealth in other countries.
- Family matters: Research has substantiated that family ties positively influence a domestic donor's likelihood to give (Edmonson 2011). For international students and alumni, this importance is often heightened. Work with admissions and your in-house data and development directors to identify current students or alumni whose parents, grandparents, or other relatives also attended your institution.
- Intelligence: The best intelligence is human intelligence. Volunteers are crucial and not only for referrals. They often have insights into an individual's lifestyle and social circle that can help indicate wealth, and they can pick up on local-language news that may be helpful.

Finally, do not forget about your expatriate alumni. Many expats are on temporary assignment abroad with multinational corporations. These alumni are often on a leadership track. It is crucial to establish relationships with them early because they have US assets, which make giving seamless. In addition, they may help open doors for advancement or recruitment activities for the institution.

CHINA

A common refrain in any business today is "What's your China strategy?" Higher-education advancement is no different. The growth of wealth in China has accompanied a rise in Chinese enrollment in US educational institutions and an increased awareness of Western traditions of philanthropy. There is tremendous opportunity for institutions that craft a thoughtful and strategic approach to Chinese alumni and prospects.

Higher education sits at the nexus of two important cultural values for many Chinese families—education and community—and it is becoming a common place for philanthropic investment. Parents of Chinese undergraduates are accustomed to sending their children to elite and often costly boarding schools, again representing a sizable market of opportunity.

While rich in opportunity, China can be a daunting place to begin. Cultural differences, language barriers, governmental hurdles, and more can make the landscape tricky to navigate, but with some basics under your belt, you can launch with confidence:

- Study the charity laws in China regarding foreign NGOs and how money can be raised. In September 2016, the National People's Congress (NPC, the country's parliament) of the People's Republic of China passed the country's first charity law, calling for significantly more transparency. All global charities, including US colleges, are finding it challenging to navigate, so consult with your legal teams and professional associations who are monitoring these policies.
- When you are working with a prospect in China, it is important not to shy away from the question of where the donor's liquid assets lie. The Chinese government has a cap on the amount of currency that a donor can legally export from the mainland (as do governments in India, Korea, and elsewhere), and it may be challenging for a donor to make a significant gift to a US institution if all the donor's assets are local.
- China is vast, but you can think of it more simply as a three-market country: Beijing, Shanghai, and Hong Kong. If you are looking for one area on which to focus, consider Hong Kong, both for its location as a financial and business hub and for its resident alumni and friends. Wealthy individuals from Hong Kong are by far the top Chinese donors to American universities, and some of the Chinese laws regarding currency exports do not apply to assets in Hong Kong, which may make major gifts less complex.

ENGAGING INTERNATIONAL ALUMNI AND FRIENDS

Once you have identified your key markets and regions, have some great prospects, and are collaborating with leadership and other campus units, the rubber meets the road—most likely on the tarmac at your local airport—and it's time to begin strategically planning engagements with your international alumni and donors. Where you begin or how your program grows is determined by your budget, timelines, institutional traditions, and more—there are many avenues to explore.

Create Local Traditions and Signature Events

Alumni often have a tradition-based routine when it comes to events with their alma maters—homecoming, reunions, game-viewing parties, and so on. For alumni and friends abroad, create periodic events in your key markets that encourage habitual engagement. Schedule larger events far enough in advance to allow travel planning for alumni, as well as your campus leadership. Around such events, your team can plan VIP engagements, donor meetings, happy hours with younger alumni, visits with local corporate offices, and more.

Just as with regional events in the United States, it is crucial to consider the content, timing, and audience when investing heavily in a signature event:

- Content: While spirit-driven events (such as student send-offs or homecoming parties) can bring a loyal, local crowd and a university update is an important element at any large gathering, globetrotting alumni whom you would like to attract to a regional signature event will often greatly appreciate being engaged intellectually. Consider how you can include cutting-edge researchers or economists, entrepreneurs from the region, or other fascinating presenters to bring content of value to your audience members.
- Timing: Consider your audience as well as your locations when planning the ideal timing for events that will draw broadly from the region. For instance, August is not a good month to draw European alumni and friends to an event—too many will be on vacation and not planning business trips to London or New York.
- Audience: We often consider alumni and donors as the sole audience for advancement events. However, when devoting resources

to substantial events abroad where leadership will be present, consider other stakeholders when planning. These could include parents of current students from the area; admissions, who may want to cultivate relationships with local top schools; or corporate relations, who may have local leaders they would like to engage.

Let's take a look at two examples of programs that illustrate some of these principles. Thunderbird School of Global Management at Arizona State University has more than 170 active alumni chapters around the world. On the first Tuesday of every month, Thunderbird alumni (who call themselves T-Birds) gather across the globe to connect, bring potential students to learn more about the school, and network professionally.

T-Birds feel a strong sense of connection to one another and the institution and often find first-Tuesday happy hours or events where they are traveling. It provides a built-in community in any corner of the globe. Such a tradition is not created overnight. However, once established, such a tradition provides alumni a regular connection to the institution, as well as personal and professional benefits that many standard chapter meetings do not.

Since 1993, the Wharton School at the University of Pennsylvania has held more than fifty global forum events around the world. These semiannual flagship events feature high-profile keynote speakers from business and government, Wharton faculty who are global thought leaders, and social events and networking where "Wharton alumni and global business leaders can engage in thought-provoking dialogue" (Wharton School 2018). Each event brings together hundreds of attendees and leaders over a three-day period, many but not all Wharton alumni.

Devise Ways to Give Locally

Despite the fact that business and communication are truly global today, sometimes the campus and its priorities seem quite distant for alumni on a different continent. Think creatively about opportunities to engage alumni at all levels in giving locally, that is, giving to an aspect of the institution that feels closer to home.

Use alumni chapters across the globe to raise funds among local alumni for scholarship funds that benefit students from that area. This is an excellent way to solicit annual gifts from donors overseas, and the experience can provide top-notch stewardship for those donors, resulting in better-than-average donor retention.

Mine your key faculty and staff contacts for ideas related to student travel or faculty research abroad, and find major-gift opportunities to support those initiatives. Donors can sponsor travel programs that bring students to the region (and can often provide contacts and other valuable support) or can support a faculty member's research that is affecting the area.

Connect Back to Campus

While it is unrealistic for all alumni worldwide to make it back to your campus regularly, it is ideal to maintain the connection. This is possible through traditional means—conference calls, physical visits—or through such virtual means as video conferencing, social media, and other evolving online tools.

Boards, committees, and councils have long been a key engagement tool for advancement. Ensure that your institution is thinking globally and recruiting members to these valuable groups who live beyond US borders. Annual meetings on campus are a fantastic way to bring a prospect to campus to reconnect and tour, and the common giving requirement can be an entrée to a broader philanthropic conversation. Regional councils can also provide a valuable engagement tool, with such simplified assignments as advancing the brand of the institution by hosting faculty or students or admissions events.

For top international prospects, consider periodic opportunities to engage with campus leadership via conference or video calls, where they are able to not just listen but also ask questions and chime in. The content of these exclusive-access calls can be tailored to alumni and donors of a certain region in either the information being shared or the opinions and considerations being sought by your leaders, providing a highly valuable interaction for all parties.

Do you use WeChat or WhatsApp? When planning online engagement abroad, you must think beyond Facebook, Instagram, Twitter, and LinkedIn; you must also think beyond the PC to the most popular mobile platforms because that is where you will find your international alumni. Increasingly, web traffic is now on mobile devices, and it is crucial to know what the most important platforms are in your common markets.

CONCLUSION

The field of international advancement is still young, but the dynamics of the moment necessitate that colleges and universities invest in this growing philanthropic market. International student enrollment in US colleges and universities has nearly doubled over the last decade, and numbers of alumni abroad are growing each year. Global wealth creation and philanthropy are on the rise. Institutions of higher education are well positioned to speak to prospects across the globe about education, transformative research, entrepreneurship, health care, and more.

These realities make it imperative to take a global perspective. But remember, building a program takes time and a long-term view; waiting a few more years will result in significant lost opportunity. There are also other dynamics that must be taken into account, including regulatory environments, economic cycles, and political changes that effect working with donors abroad. But without a doubt, the opportunity vastly outweighs the uncertainties. If you have been considering launching an international advancement program, then get out there and do it!

Safe travels!

REFERENCES

Candid. 2017. "Patel Foundation Commits $200 Million to Nova Southeastern University." September 26, 2017. http://philanthropynewsdigest.org/news/patel-foundation-commits-200-million-to-nova-southeastern-university.

Edmonson, Lauren. 2011. "Explaining the Alumni Relationship and Giving Tendencies of Multigeneration Alumni Legacy Families at Marquette University." College of Professional Studies Professional Projects. Paper 39. https://epublications.marquette.edu/cgi/viewcontent.cgi?referer=https://www.google.com/&httpsredir=1&article=1033&context=cps_professional.

The Giving Pledge. n.d. Accessed December 15, 2018. https://givingpledge.org/About.aspx.

Harvard T. F. Chan School of Public Health. 2014. "Harvard University Receives Transformational Gift for the School of Public Health." Press release, September 8, 2014. https://www.hsph.harvard.edu/news/press-releases/transformational-gift-for-school-of-public-health/.

Institute of International Education. n.d. "Enrollment." Accessed December 13, 2018. https://www.iie.org/en/Research-and-Insights/Open-Doors/Data/International-Students/Enrollment.

Jahnke, Art. 2017. "Four Generations of Philanthropy behind BU's Largest Gift." *BU Today*, September 14, 2017. http://www.bu.edu/today/2017/rajen-kilachand-philanthropy/.

Redden, Elizabeth. 2018. "International Student Numbers Decline." *Inside Higher Ed*, January 22, 2018. https://www.insidehighered.com/news/2018/01/22/nsf-report-documents-declines-international-enrollments-after-years-growth.

Rock, Kerry. 2018. "The Key to Understanding GDPR." *Currents* (March/April). https://www.case.org/currents/x74387.

Staff Writer. 2017. "How Many Millionaire Households There Are in South Africa. Business Tech. June 19, 2017. https://businesstech.co.za/news/wealth/180043/how-many-millionaire-households-there-are-in-south-africa/.

Wharton School. 2018. "Global Forums." https://alumni.wharton.upenn.edu/global-forums/.

VI

Understanding Institutional Settings

As Michael Worth describes in chapter 2, the roots of advancement lie in private institutions in the early years of the nation. But in the twentieth and twenty-first centuries, advancement has become a vital activity in both public and private institutions, and advancement professionals now work at all levels of those institutions. Indeed, as Matthew Lambert discusses in chapter 1, many institutions may be evolving into hybrids that combine the features of both private and public entities.

In chapter 16, James Moore explores the role of institutionally related foundations that serve public colleges and universities. Focusing on the relationship between the foundation and the institution, Moore discusses potential issues, as well as strategies that have created successful partnerships. Looking ahead, he analyzes for foundations the implications of trends in higher education and offers best practices for the governance, management, and funding of foundations.

In chapter 17, Lauren Brookey observes that declining public support, tax law changes, increased demands from society, and other forces have caused many community colleges to adopt advancement strategies from four-year institutions. Brookey emphasizes the importance of building the advancement program on institutional planning so that fundraising priorities reflect real institutional needs and the potential for impact. She concludes with a prediction of continued growth in community college advancement programs.

Advancement programs and professional staff now work at all levels in complex universities, including schools and units, as well as central administration. In chapter 18, David Welch provides the perspective of a school chief development officer who works primarily with the dean. Welch emphasizes the importance of forming a relationship with the dean, understanding the dean's role and perspective, working with the

faculty, and creating a partnership with the university's central administration. Welch also considers the implications of various organizational
models from his perspective as a school advancement officer. In chapter
19, in the next section of this book, Nuvyn Peters further explores these
various models from the perspective of a university vice president.

SIXTEEN

Institutionally Related Foundations in Public Colleges and Universities

James H. Moore Jr.

Multibillion-dollar endowments, behemoth fundraising campaigns, the emerging higher-education funding model, and increasingly sophisticated donors are just a few of the issues affecting the characteristics and operations of institutionally related foundations (IRFs). The development of a plan to ensure that the IRF and institution are positioned as partners in their success will require a commitment from leadership of both entities and the ability to manage the head- and tailwinds that can make the sailing smooth or blow you dangerously off course.

The IRF exists to support the public university or college. Understanding and accepting that it is fundamental to the relationship between the institution and the foundation. If the appropriate time and attention is given to defining the scope of services the IRF will provide and if there is a clear alignment of mission and vision between the two partner organizations, both the IRF and the institution should spend most of the time in calm waters or, when necessary, navigate effectively through the choppy seas.

Building a successful relationship between the foundation and university requires that leaders of both entities be engaged and equally passionate partners. The university is the ultimate beneficiary of the charitable assets managed by the IRF, and the foundation is the trusted entity that must exercise a duty of care to invest and steward gifted assets for the benefit of the university.

Distinguishing the roles of each party is necessary to position the relationship for success. Knowing what each organization is responsible for doing and how and where they intersect on issues, practices, and policies can mitigate problems and conflicts before they occur. Knowledge and acceptance of the ground rules by the institution and the foundation will also provide important guidance to faculty, staff, and donors, who all benefit from a well-functioning partnership.

DEFINING AND MANAGING THE RELATIONSHIP

Foundations or related organizations have existed for more than a century, yet they are still not well understood by the general public. Some university and foundation leaders may even wonder how well foundations are understood by those who work in higher education. The notion that the IRF is not a formal or legal arm of the university is surprising to many people. In fact, sometimes the foundation is referred to as the "alumni association" and is believed to be responsible for managing alumni programs in addition to fundraising.

Externally, donors and alumni are equally unfamiliar with the legal, operational, and governance structures of IRFs and how important they are to the future of public higher education. However, foundation and university administrators are aware—sometimes painfully so—of the growing significance of these nonpublic organizations that for decades have primarily been repositories of gifted assets and custodians of donor data.

Throughout their history, issues affecting the campus at large have affected foundations, as well. That includes campus crises and unrest, budget and fiscal challenges, and other events that may have a negative impact on the reputation of the university. Likewise, bad behavior by foundation administrators and board members often spills over to the university. So, despite the legal bright line that may separate the foundation from the university or college, the line that separates their respective identities is faint.

Success in any partnership requires open and effective lines of communication. It is imperative that the foundation and partner institution are both acutely aware of what the university requires of the foundation.

Though IRFs are indeed nonpublic bodies, they typically serve a single client, and it is incumbent on the leadership of both entities to be aligned in their expectation of services, consideration provided for such services, and respective fiduciary and governance responsibilities each entity has.

If there is a secret sauce in a recipe for success, then it is a commitment to being partners who are synchronous in their belief that all decisions are taken with a focus on advancing the university. University and IRF leaders change seats often, as do board members, volunteers, and even donors, but our universities have been designed to withstand the test of time.

As stewards of these organizations, we shoulder a heavy burden to remain focused on the horizon and to ensure that our institutions are well positioned for those who will follow in our footsteps. The burden is made even more arduous due to the shifting sands that universities and IRF leaders find themselves while traversing today's rapidly changing and politically charged environment.

UNDERSTANDING DIFFERENCES AND DISTINCTIONS

Before attempting to discuss new strategies for IRFs to consider in support of their respective institution partners, it is important to be mindful that no two foundations are exactly alike. Since the establishment of the Kansas Endowment Association in 1891, thousands of related organizations and foundations have been created to advance public university philanthropic agendas (KU Endowment 2018). While they may all be similar in purpose, it is important to recognize that innovations and strategies that work for one organization may not be the right solution for another. Size, governance structures, resources, and legal facts and circumstances that vary from one state to the next are a few of the reasons it is difficult to write a single recipe for success.

When assessing the impact IRFs have on their public partners, it is also important to point out that not all public universities have a related organization or foundation (perhaps most notably the University of Michigan). If a particular state enables the public university to manage their philanthropic assets and partnerships without fear of sweeping intervention from the state, then a foundation may not be necessary. Public records laws and the preservation of donor intent have typically been the two biggest issues that have influenced public universities when determining if a foundation was needed or appropriate.

The University of Illinois (UI) Foundation was established in 1935, when alumni and friends determined it was necessary to have an entity separate from the state to manage and administer private gifts. The following excerpt from the UI *Bulletin*, published in 1937, articulates the value proposition of the foundation, even in its earliest beginnings:

> This new organization in the rather short time it has been going has demonstrated its value in soliciting and administering gifts to the University. When the alumnus or other citizen fully realizes that one man gave, for instance, to a Midwestern University a $90,000 gift at an actual cost to him of only $23,400 (the government taking 74% in taxes otherwise) one will give the matter of donations extra careful thought before deciding what else to do with his money. (University of Illinois 1937)

Beyond creating an entity to manage gifts, the establishment of the UI Foundation was also a statement (or restatement) of the importance of alumni and community engagement on the growth and success of public institutions.

As is the case at other institutions, the UI Foundation is not the only independent nonpublic body associated with the UI, nor was it the first. The UI Alumni Association was established in 1873 with a similar purpose (University of Illinois Alumni Association, n.d.). Because many alumni associations preceded their foundation sister organizations and, in some cases, foundations were spun out of the alumni associations, it is reasonable to confuse the two organizations as one and the same.

For decades this dual structure—with alumni engagement being managed by the alumni association and the foundation serving as the manager of gifted assets—has been the commonly accepted model for most public colleges and universities. More recently, some institutions have challenged this convention by merging or joining these entities under one corporate umbrella. This approach is examined more closely later in this chapter.

THE CHANGING LANDSCAPE

The higher-education industry is facing significant challenges, all of which affect IRFs. University foundations remain committed to their historic missions. But in light of changes affecting universities, many new and emerging IRFs are being asked to do more than hold and manage gifts.

Reduced Public Support

State spending on higher education in the United States has been declining for years. According to the US Government Accountability Office, a 2016 report published by the Center on Budget and Policy Priority concluded that "forty-six states—all except Montana, North Dakota, Wisconsin and Wyoming [spent] less per student in the 2015–2016 school year than they did before the recession" (Mitchell, Leachman, and Masterson 2016). The result of this pendulum swing has meant students and families are paying or borrowing more to cover education costs, and universities are leaning on philanthropy for financial assistance or even to shore up budget cuts to core programs.

Tuition and fees are at record highs for most public institutions, raising the question of how much more of the cost burden are students and families able and willing to carry. If access and excellence are to remain top priorities for our American public universities, then philanthropy will undoubtedly become more imperative. So, too, will the responsibility of the IRF to appropriately steward those gifted and invested assets.

Shifting Donor Expectations

Donors have definitely changed how they give and what they expect from the foundation when they invest in the college or university through the foundation. Gifts are larger and more complex, and documentation often involves multiple legal and financial advisors. Additionally, many donors now use donor-advised funds, community foundations, or their own personal family foundations to manage their philanthropy. The days of the greatest generation simply and privately bequeathing their life's treasures to institutions to do with as they deem appropriate are long gone. Donors to universities are motivated by many factors and influences.

The competition for charitable gifts is also unprecedented and will likely continue to grow. As discussed in chapter 5 of this book, integrated and well-resourced university-advancement programs are necessary to help create and leverage philanthropic opportunities. The synchronous planning and integration of fundraising; alumni, parent, and community relations; and marketing and communications efforts, along with appropriately engaging the foundation, will continue to shape and change how IRFs support their partner institutions.

Demands for Transparency

Last, an unquenchable thirst for transparency in the court of public opinion has led to questions from public officials about the relationship IRFs have with their partner institutions. Recent court cases in some states have challenged the nonpublic-body status of IRFs to gain access to records associated with donors and their gifts (Dyer 2018). Some foundations have even had to stave off state officials who believed the state had a right to direct or redirect the funds held by the foundation.

More recently, foundations have had to respond to questions from members of Congress about the not-for-profit status of IFRs. Charitable giving and endowment management continue to be top-of-mind issues for many federal legislators and a variety of watchdog organizations.

Philanthropy is indeed big business, and the IRF must evolve to meet the needs of its institution and donors. A plethora of known and unknown issues and opportunities will require IRFs and university leaders to be entrepreneurial and forward thinking. Changes in public policy, political ideology, tax laws, and the economy may create pitfalls or windfalls. Foundations must look for opportunities to add value to the college or university and support the institution's mission and needs. In doing so, they will need to address new issues and concerns in three broad areas: (1) governance, (2) organizational structure and services provided, and (3) resources and funding.

GOVERNANCE

Updating or amending bylaws, drafting and revising service agreements, and managing and mitigating risk, along with a host of other corporate-governance issues, have always been important topics for foundation leaders and boards. With a heightened level of interest in foundations, IRF and university leaders will need to be more diligent and forward thinking about governance matters.

The University of New Mexico Foundation in May 2018 was instructed by the courts to release closely guarded records in response to legal challenges. Court cases challenging the nonpublic-body status are on the rise, with many plaintiffs positing that the foundation is indeed a public body. Very often these cases are attempting to require the foundation to comply with public-body freedom of information (FOIA) or state sunshine laws (Dyer 2018). While it is always wise to be as transparent as possible, it may be equally important to be able to conduct foundation business without undue influence from the state.

It is essential to make governance a top priority for management and the board. It is not the most exciting part of the job, but if not properly managed, the consequences could compromise both the foundation and the university. Some of the central issues involve board membership composition, risk management, corporate documents and documentation, and donor confidence and the preservation of donor intent.

Board Membership Composition

University leaders often serve as members of the foundation board. There are some crucial questions every foundation should consider, including: When and where should university leaders be involved in setting foundation policies? (In most cases the answer is that they may advise but should not be formally involved in setting foundation policies.) How many university leaders serve on the board, and what is the percentage of their membership compared to nonuniversity directors? What is the role of university leaders on the foundation board? Are they directing the use of foundation assets? Do they have direct influence or management responsibility for foundation staff?

Risk Management

Enterprise risk management (ERM) should no longer be that project that is always next on the to-do list but never gets done. It is essential to make ERM a priority. Regularly assess and track liabilities; develop mitigation plans; and stress-test your financials, policies, and procedures to identify weaknesses.

Corporate Documents and Documentation

Having updated and current bylaws, articles of incorporation and services agreements, or contracts that clearly spell out the services being provided by the foundation and the consideration being provided to the foundation by the college or university for such services is vital. In addition to documentation, honest and direct dialogue at the top of both organizations is important to ensure the spirit of the governing documents is fully aligned with the intent.

Donor Confidence and the Preservation of Donor Intent

The reputation of the foundation may be the foundation's most valuable asset. If donors question the foundation's capacity to deliver on the promise made when accepting the gift, then future contributions likely will be compromised. It is essential to establish model gift agreements and conduct regular audits of gifts and gift funds.

Getting a handle on your governance model is often an arduous and painful task. It forces uncomfortable and sometimes-contentious conversations between university and foundation leaders and takes time. It is useful to engage experts, to use resources from professional associations and colleagues, and to not compromise getting it right for simply getting it done.

ORGANIZATIONAL STRUCTURE AND SERVICES PROVIDED

Trying to establish a standard organizational design or structure for all foundations is not realistic. As previously stated, no two foundations are exactly alike. The historic discussion about organizational design has focused on how independent the foundation is or should be and whether the foundation provides any other services beyond custodial asset management, most notably fundraising.

Maintaining legal separation from the state institution should remain an important priority for the foundation and the public body. As a side-car organization, the foundation is able to do things that have a beneficial impact to the university. Some foundation leaders have begun to explore new roles for the foundation beyond fundraising and asset management that will add value to their public partners.

For example, in 2016, Arizona State University Foundation reorganized its nonprofit entities with a new structure and organization called ASU Enterprise Partners. The model "moves the university beyond traditional fundraising and towards comprehensive resource raising" (Arizona State University 2016). Created to generate sources of revenue for Arizona State University, "it looks much like a holding or parent organization made up of separate 501(c)(3), not-for-profit organizations. . . . This model allows [ASU] to add new entities for diverse revenue as those opportunities come along" (Arizona State University 2016).

The ASU Enterprise model also speaks to the value of synchronous communication strategies within and among partner entities. Transitioning to the enterprise model has allowed ASU and its related organizations to improve what donors know and understand about a variety of investment opportunities across the university.

With tightening budgets and pressure to increase efficiency, many foundations are also working more closely and collaboratively with campus partners. The natural partners are the traditional university-advancement functions: external relations, communications and marketing, and alumni engagement. Going forward, foundations may also find a need or opportunity to align operations more closely with a variety of nonadvancement partner units, departments, and programs. For example, student financial assistance operations within university administration have naturally been engaged with the related foundation-administration teams.

These relationships have typically centered on accounting, gift administration, and donor stewardship issues. Securing and managing scholarship funds, however, is not the only way some foundations are supporting students and families today. Some IRFs are stretching their organizations to do more than hold and manage scholarship gifts by actually providing a plethora of financial services to students and families to help bridge the gap between the cost of attending and their financial capacity to pay.

Foundations have managed donor-funded loan programs for years as a way to help students and families. In recent years, other programs like income-sharing agreements (ISAs) have been introduced. For example, the Purdue University Back a Boiler Program is an example of a foundation working with its public body to help students who may not otherwise have been able to attend their university (Purdue Research Foundation 2016). Purdue is providing students with financial support in consideration for future earnings that will be paid to the foundation when the student graduates.

Innovations like ISAs are not the only innovations in the IRF sector. Particularly in the large public research university space, foundation leaders find themselves in conversations with university partners discussing such things as P3s (public–private partnerships), construction partnerships, technology commercialization, and corporate research parks. Traditionalists may argue that these alternative ventures should be viewed as mission creep. Yet, if the core purpose of the foundation is to support the institution and the foundation can legally and prudently step in to help the institution's funding position or perhaps improve efficiency, then it would be irresponsible not to do so.

With public scrutiny of university administrative operations on the rise, efficiency and costs of advancement programs are also under the microscope. Universities have made clear the need for more engagement from their alumni, parents, community partners, and donors. Foundation and university governing boards have echoed this same sentiment, and some boards have actually challenged the leaders of their alumni associations and foundations to consider alternative operating models.

While the notion that advancement units work more efficiently and optimally when they are coordinated is not a novel or new concept, it is not uncommon for advancement units to operate more autonomously than synchronously. As these functions have evolved and have become more integral to university finances, some university and IRF leaders have formally tethered or merged these entities within the foundation to leverage resources and economies of scale.

For example, in 2017 the University of Iowa realigned its foundation and alumni association as a single entity called the University of Iowa Center for Advancement (an operational name for the University of Iowa Foundation) to better organize and manage alumni engagement and philanthropy programs (University of Iowa Center for Advancement, n.d.). Several other universities have adopted similar models, and many more have recognized the benefits of stronger collaborations and partnerships among advancement units.

University-advancement programs use sophisticated contact- or customer-relationship management (CRM) systems and complex multichannel marketing strategies. For this reason, more attention is also being given to strategic engagements with nonuniversity-advancement partners. Solicitations, event promotions, celebrating successes, and even crisis communications are a few examples of times when having well-established strategic partnerships with academic leaders, senior university officials, and even community advocates can affect the work your foundation or advancement programs manage.

Foundation leaders need to be proactive network builders. By establishing formal and informal circles of influence, the foundation will be seen as a partner that adds value and is an important resource dedicated to the advancement of the institution it was established to serve.

The scope of services the IRF provides to the university and the consideration it receives for such services needs to be clearly articulated and agreed on by all parties. Terms and conditions should be reviewed and refreshed annually to reflect changes in leadership agendas, funding, or unforeseen and unplanned circumstances.

Documentation to review and assess performance is also imperative and should be a standard annual practice. Accepting that institutions will undoubtedly continue to rely more heavily on their IRF partners, it is also likely that the future will present new unforeseen partnership opportunities.

RESOURCES AND FUNDING

Making the case for the resources foundations need to do their important work is a crucial conversation among university and foundation leaders. From talent management to strategic program investments, foundations and university-advancement programs struggle with funding human capital and operational expenses. Fundraising produces revenue, yet development offices and foundations do not always have direct access to that revenue to meet the costs of doing business. Figuring out how to pay for foundation and development programs has always been a challenge.

Foundation operations are typically funded from direct payments from the public institution partner (fee for services), fees on endowed funds, fees on restricted funds, unrestricted expendable funds, unrestricted endowments (UR endowments established for the benefit of the IRF—if they exist), direct gifts to the IRF (typically rare or small), and gift fees on current gifts.

Because donors are typically not fans of gift or transaction fees, the tendency is to push fees down or, if possible, avoid them altogether. It is reasonable to ask whether foundations or advancement programs can be sustained, much less grow, relying only on these traditional funding sources. Despite the negative associations with gift fees, foundations and university-advancement programs that don't currently charge gift fees may have no choice but to consider adopting them if they intend to maintain or increase productivity and effectiveness.

A 2011 *Currents* article on this topic states, "Whether you call it a gift or administrative fee, a tax, or an assessment, using a portion of a donor's gift to support the administrative costs of development work has become common practice. Many public university foundations have been doing it for years, but the current economic climate has prompted more public and some private institutions to explore the possibility" (Collins 2011).

As mentioned previously, some foundations are proactively exploring alternative lines of business. Real estate ventures have been fairly common and in some cases can be a win-win for the university and the foundation. For example, the Virginia Tech Foundation has been a leader in this space for years, with more than two million square feet of real estate under management and properties throughout Virginia and in Switzerland. They operate and manage academic, research, and commercial properties, including a hotel and golf course (Virginia Tech Foundation 2018).

Technology commercialization and research initiatives are also related areas of business that could possibly serve as opportunities for IRFs to create structures that yield financial reward for the foundation and the public partner institutions. Tread carefully in the tech commercialization space, though. Early-stage investments are exciting and risky. The headlines tend to only focus on the big wins, but far too often, investments in university technology-transfer programs yield minimal results and require time-consuming governance and oversight. That said, universities are bastions of innovation, and there may be reasonable and positive net revenue opportunities for the foundation if you are willing to invest the necessary time, attention, and resources.

Foundation and university leaders have long acknowledged the need to invest in fundraising and donor-engagement programs. Whether driven by the economic realities of increased costs, the cost to invest in excellence, or the market opportunity of the thousands of unengaged alumni, it makes sense for institutions to grow their advancement enterprises. Making the decision to either direct or redirect institutional funds, ask the donor to share a larger percentage of the costs, or diversify the foundation operations with alternative revenue sources requires a commitment from leadership and a well-conceived strategic framework.

CONCLUSION

Accepting that the new (or not-so-new) normal public higher-education-funding model requires alternative sources of funding, what does that mean for IRFs and organizations? How can IRFs further support their partner institutions? What will donors expect from the charitable entities responsible for managing and stewarding their gifted assets? How will the court of public opinion judge or weigh in on the services and support IRFs provide their public partners? What impact will negative headlines about IRFs accused of wrongdoing have on laws that govern IRFs? Unpacking these and many similar questions is necessary to develop strategies that will advance your foundation and university or college.

Some of these questions are addressed in this chapter. Many more should be considered and asked regularly. The public university landscape is indeed changing, and foundations and leadership of the public and nonpublic bodies need to be thoughtful, nimble, and entrepreneurial to best leverage the precious resources needed for our public universities to flourish.

REFERENCES

Arizona State University. 2016. "Introducing Enterprise Partners: A Resource-Raising Innovation." *ASU News*, July 18, 2016. https://asunow.asu.edu/20160718-asu-news-enterprise-partners-resource-raising-organization.

Collins, Mary Ellen. 2011. "Seeding Growth." *Currents* 37, no. 1 (January). https://www.case.org/Publications_and_Products/2011/January_2011/Seeding_Growth.html.

Dyer, Jessica. 2018. "Judge: UNM Foundation Records Subject to Public Records Laws." *Albuquerque Journal*, May 24, 2018. https://www.abqjournal.com/1176241/judge-unm-foundations-records-are-subject-to-states-public-records-laws.html.

KU Endowment. 2018. "About Us." http://ku.imodules.com/s/1312/endowment/index.aspx?sid=1312&gid=1&pgid=572.

Mitchell, Michael, Michael Leachman, and Kathleen Masterson. 2016. "Funding Down, Tuition Up: State Cuts to Higher Education Threaten Quality and Affordability at Public Colleges." Center on Budget and Policy Priorities. August 15, 2016. https://www.cbpp.org/research/state-budget-and-tax/funding-down-tuition-up.

Purdue Research Foundation. 2016. "Back a Boiler Program Overview."https://www.purdue.edu/backaboiler/overview/index.html.

University of Illinois. 1937. "Illini, Here We Go—All Together." *Bulletin* 34, no. 39:1.

University of Illinois Alumni Association. n.d. "University of Illinois Alumni Alliance." Accessed October 16, 2018. https://uialumniassociation.org/.

University of Iowa Center for Advancement. n.d. "About the University of Iowa Center for Advancement." Accessed October 16, 2018. http://www.foriowa.org/about/.

Virginia Tech Foundation. 2018. "About Us." http://www.vtf.edu/about-us.html.

SEVENTEEN

Raising Funds for Community Colleges

Lauren F. Brookey

Community colleges are benefiting from a series of national policy and economic factors driving a need to grow their fundraising and advancement functions, while at the same time providing the job-ready graduates who are the essential building blocks for a new economy. On the surface, it might appear that community colleges are hamstrung by a lack of fundraising tradition. However, the budget instability created by state and local funding reductions has inspired community college leaders to turn to advancement functions to diversify revenue streams quickly and fill funding gaps. This sense of urgency has resulted in a surge of interest in development models practiced by their university and college colleagues. Today, there is an opportunity for community college advancement offices to adapt, redefine their strategic direction, and reimagine operations to provide significant donor investments in community colleges at previously unseen levels while laying the foundation for a future of fundraising success.

RESPONDING TO NEW CHALLENGES

Public higher education has experienced a host of tremors, including changes in federal tax policy, sluggish state economies with accompanying declines in support for higher education, significant questions about the affordability of higher education with rising student debt, and challenges to the conventional belief that higher learning improves society.

Overall state funding, adjusted for inflation, for public two-year and four-year colleges in 2017 was nearly $9 billion below its 2008 level (Mitchell, Leachman, and Masterson 2017). In addition to state-level changes in funding, federal tax reform is anticipated to cut federal funding for education in order to pay for the tax cuts and have an impact on the nation's trillion-dollar-level debt.

Funding losses have forced colleges and universities to raise tuition, limit course offerings, reduce faculty and staff, and in some cases close campuses. The environment of depletion has turned fundraising and advancement from a competitive advantage on college campuses to economic essentialism.

In the face of reduced revenue and the need to raise tuition, diversifying resources has become a crucial budget tool. Fortunately, the drop in state and federal support is countered by rising support for higher education at large: Communities, foundations, and individuals increasingly appreciate the role of higher education as the economic driver for their area workforce.

In 2017, total fundraising support for higher education grew 6.3 percent, for a total of $43.6 billion in support. This was the highest fundraising total recorded in a six-decade history (CASE 2018, 2). Corporations drive a significant portion of that giving at 15 percent of the total. Foundations and alumni combine to provide 56 percent of private support (CASE 2018, 24). This trend in giving has encouraged presidents, advancement leaders, and college finance officers to increasingly look to private support in order to compensate for the drop in public funding.

The private sector has tremendous confidence in higher education to fill workforce needs and drive positive social and economic outcomes. However, this confidence comes with the expectation that higher education's impact on the workforce must come sooner rather than later. This impact *heightens* the appeal of the community college mission to provide training and education in order to close workforce gaps and promote social mobility for members of society who have been untapped for workforce needs. That is where community colleges come in and where community college advancement leaders have the best story to tell.

BUILDING A COMMUNITY COLLEGE ADVANCEMENT PROGRAM

A demonstrated community need is foundational to inspiring and engaging donors through storytelling. Community college advancement leaders can adapt to the new environment of urgency and need defined by our community; assemble a team, both external and internal; and develop a strategy that addresses crucial needs for the community and aligns with the community college mission. With urgency comes engagement, and engagement can result in the establishment of support to be repeated and reinforced for decades to come.

Filling a community need is likely to have the most transformative impact on a community college advancement office's success. The crucial first step in this process is to develop a board that reflects leadership from the community. By placing key community leaders from the sectors identified in addressing the community need—such as the workforce, local degree attainment, or economic readiness—the campaign establishes a foundation of credibility.

The impact of strong members for a foundation board or campaign advisory cabinet cannot be understated, especially if that college is already playing a vital role in the community, because leadership weaknesses cannot be easily unwound or retooled midcampaign. For many community colleges, credibility that their fundraising goals are worthy, achievable, and part of an overall community plan is a key factor in generating success. Having members of the community emphasizing those points can move a campaign forward significantly.

It can be instinctive for community college development officers to rely on corporate representatives who have played a valuable role in identifying training needs and developing curriculum. However, in many cases, those are not the same individuals who can make convincing arguments for large gifts. They may not have made similar contributions of their own in the community, or they may lack the peer relationships necessary to open doors.

High-level leaders, such as corporate presidents or chief financial officers, are capable of having discussions with high-capacity donors and should be invited to serve on community college boards. Failing to aim high and aim true when identifying potential leaders, especially by failing to including those who have strong affinity to your mission, is a commonplace community college error.

In this environment of demand for a ready workforce and improved community conditions for underemployed citizens, the environment is stronger than ever to align with leaders who see the imperative and hear the challenges among their own peers and internal executives. With corporate-giving trends up, engaging the company leader on a board or campaign creates a window of opportunity for strengthening the donor base and creating a pattern of giving that can be sustained for many decades. The competitiveness that drives that business sector can be turned to the college's fundraising advantage as leaders challenge leaders for higher levels of fundraising success.

STRATEGIC PLANS AND FUNDRAISING STRATEGIES

It is important to note that campaigns rarely fail because of lack of vision or hard work. Typically, strong storytelling and relationships build excitement, momentum, and success. The foundation of your campaign should be selecting high-level corporate or thought leaders who are respected and enjoy numerous community or corporate relationships. However, in addition to having a fresh perspective on who should and will support the community college mission at the leadership level, there is also a need for a new strategic plan and fundraising strategies.

Strategic planning informs and galvanizes high-performing leaders, aligns board leaders with the college president or advancement leader, and focuses scope. It also provides an opportunity to match identified needs in the current environment with a fresher fundraising perspective. For example, community colleges have historically had an access mission that married well with scholarship campaigns. Today's missions are following the agenda set by national community college funders.

The goal is to ensure student success through proven retention and graduation strategies that require operating funds—not endowed funds—to accelerate and demonstrate measurable impact. Industry and opinion leaders identified to serve as community college volunteer leaders can accomplish these new goals and guarantee success by enlisting future volunteers who are their leadership peers.

The strategic plan can be an essential next step for growing development efforts at the community college level. It is tempting to jump into a fundraising program without a big-picture strategy to show results, fund an essential project, or demonstrate staff leadership. Instead, having a master plan that board members have discussed, had the opportunity to create, and reflects the needs of the community and college will serve staff on many levels. The comprehensive strategic plan for advancing fundraising is easy to bypass or point to as cumbersome and unnecessary, but the reality is, it will save significant time in the long run.

The well-built strategic plan should have the following goals: to engage and excite the institution's support base; to mesh college and foundation or advancement goals; to create support from both the foundation board and the executive college leadership; to differentiate who would and would not be appropriate for board membership; to plan responsibilities to ensure distribution of effort and resources; to generate confidence from donors; and ultimately, to demonstrate progress, which builds on future support and success.

Strategic plans come in many formats and are developed in various settings. Essential elements include participation by both college and foundation staff and leadership; typically, a facilitator familiar with the strategic planning process; information that reflects both community and college needs; data on key operational elements of the foundation and college; and a focus on multiyear planning.

The collaboration and goal setting found in conducting a strategic session with individuals who care about the success of the institution will be invaluable for future fundraising initiatives. It will also demonstrate the need for specific staffing, resources, and relationships to achieve results. Once an advancement office has effective and committed leadership, clear goals, and articulation of essential resources, the path to fundraising success is at hand.

ESTABLISHING OPERATIONAL SYSTEMS

A mature advancement office that is poised for success has key operational systems in place to research, solicit, and steward donors. Community colleges are still emerging in advancement; in many cases, these essential functions are impoverished and understaffed. Because fundraising is not a core activity for most two-year colleges, the case for funding development staff—where top talent is expensive and in high demand—as well as technology and crucial marketing resources are low on the budget priority list. The bread and butter of sophisticated university-advancement teams, alumni databases, and donor research are beyond the reach of many community colleges. The investments have to be significant in order to cross the chasm of years of neglect.

Most college presidents and policy makers believe the return of substantial public-higher-education funding to community colleges is unlikely. Economic conditions make it essential for a high-functioning advancement office that diversifies the revenue for the community college. However, colleges should plan for at least a three- to five-year window for cash flow from fundraising.

The arguments on behalf of a higher investment can be convincing—decreasing public appropriations, rising rates of philanthropy and alumni giving, and a fairly high return on investment are the strongest. Yield rates show that a twenty-four-cent investment generates one dollar of new private revenue, though the rates can fluctuate depending on the maturity of the development function (Benefactor Group 2018). However, most education and finance officers agree that an investment in fundraising is almost guaranteed to yield positive outcomes.

One of the strongest positive outcomes for community colleges is increased morale and confidence as a result of private support and engagement. Public and private universities have enjoyed attention and engagement with alumni and donors for years, and the expectations rise every year, with multimillion-dollar and, in some cases, billion-dollar goals. In comparison, community colleges are the Cinderellas of the fundraising world.

In light of this reality, community college administrators, faculty, and staff consider each gift from small to large a sign of confidence and respect for the institution. In times of diminishing resources, a donor gift can make an incredible difference to a faculty member, dean, or other administrator hoping to affect students' lives. Increasing morale and opportunities for expansion and investment for community college faculty and staff can lead to increased creativity among employees and more positive outcomes for students. While hard to measure, these results are visible and speak to the importance of capitalizing on the current economic climate to tell prospective donors just how transformational a gift can be in their community.

Early operational investments need to focus on qualified and experienced staff, robust customer-relationship management systems, and marketing materials sufficient to keep alumni and prospective donors informed—assuming a database of alumni even exists. Staffing today's advancement office is harder than ever due to the high demand for individuals capable of managing the fundraising function with sufficient relationships to build that essential voluntary leadership team. Nevertheless, the cost of not making that early investment in appropriate staffing is years of missteps and possibly broken relationships due to insufficient stewardship and attention.

Technology has changed the landscape for fundraising professionals in terms of research, donor record keeping, relationship management, social media, grant making, scholarship management, and reporting. The same technology that facilitates the role of a fundraiser can also measure their effectiveness by providing key performance indicators to management and donors for confidence or shoring up gaps. Bringing on highly qualified staff requires community colleges to equip that staff with sufficient resources to inspire confidence in the community and the donor.

A staff of two or three can have tremendous impact with sufficient technology and resources to build a major-gifts operation. Big results require big investments, and the evidence is clear: Fundraising can yield big results for colleges strapped for resources and facing an uncertain future.

CONCLUSION

Despite the common perceptions that community colleges are handicapped in the fundraising arena—with disconnected alumni, minimal development infrastructure, shrinking budgets, and inexperienced staff—there remains much to be excited about for the future. Communities are clamoring for a trained workforce and for strategies to address the unemployed or underemployed. Private support for higher education is on the rise, and the mission of community colleges to increase the social mobility of all sectors of society resonates now more than ever.

Reaping the benefits of fundraising and strengthening the college's advancement efforts requires adapting, investing, and engaging the community quickly and at higher levels than before. The good news is the rewards are higher than ever before if the commitment is made to essential practices and strong leadership.

REFERENCES

Benefactor   Group.   2018.   "Fundraising   Return   on   Investment."   https://
    benefactorgroup.com/fundraising-return-on-investment/.
CASE (Council for Advancement and Support of Education). 2018. *Voluntary Support
    of Education 2017*. Washington, DC: CASE. https://cae.org/images/uploads/pdf/
    VSE_2017_Sample_Pages.pdf.
Mitchell, Michael, Michael Leachman, and Kathleen Masterson. 2017. "A Lost Decade
    in Higher Education Funding: State Cuts Have Driven up Tuition and Reduced
    Quality." Center on Budget and Policy Priorities. August 23, 2017. https://www.
    cbpp.org/research/state-budget-and-tax/a-lost-decade-in-higher-education-
    funding.

EIGHTEEN

Raising Funds for a School, College, or Unit within a University

David T. Welch

Working as a frontline fundraiser is rewarding. It provides exposure to many individuals whom you likely would never have known if it were not for your affiliation with an institution they love and value. If you are a fundraiser working on behalf of a school or unit, then you are able to provide those individuals with a connection to their university, as well as to the specific component of it where they have had the deepest experience. In order to advance that connection, it is essential that the chief development officer (CDO) assigned to a school have a close relationship with the dean. That relationship is crucial to the ability to advance the school's priorities and address the interests of the school's constituency.

BUILDING A RELATIONSHIP WITH THE DEAN

The collaboration between a CDO of a school and the dean offers many rewards and challenges and requires a high degree of trust between the two. The travel, the donor meetings, and the back-and-forth discussions on academic priorities all build a level of understanding and respect but also require both flexibility and effort. Each partner has strengths in the various skills needed to build productive, philanthropic connections with those outside the academy.

When their collaboration is strong, the dean and development officer operate together in balance and provide each other with capabilities neither possesses alone. It is a dance where each one has to let the other lead at different times, believing that it will bring about the shared outcome of increased support for the priorities of their school.

The strength of the relationship between the dean and CDO has a significant impact on the success of the entire development team and on the school more broadly. The effectiveness of this partnership determines more than just how much is raised. It also helps define and communicate a shared vision for the institution. The fact that the development operation is a priority for the dean encourages others in the organization to also become engaged in fundraising and helps to develop a culture of fundraising and philanthropy throughout the school.

The connection between the dean and CDO is often nurtured on the road. That is where they get to know each other and test how their personalities function together. Time on the road can be full of nerve-wracking situations—the last-minute meeting cancellation, the canceled flight, the crummy hotel room—but it can also be an extremely productive experience.

Once the calls and e-mails are done; the visits are set; and the flights, hotels, and rental cars are reserved, then the CDO can look forward to more relaxed conversations with the dean. These conversations often explore the current state of the academic unit, the dean's priorities beyond advancement work, what lasting impact she wants to make on the school, and crucial insights about how she makes decisions. Collectively, these conversations help the development team better understand how to work effectively with the dean.

At the College of Arts and Sciences at the University of Oregon, the advancement team has a regular practice of maintaining a list of topics to discuss with the dean during trips in order to gauge his thinking. Team members also share with each other what they have learned on such trips through how the dean describes the priorities to donors and handles questions and objections. Sometimes this is helpful to provide a critique of the dean's messaging, but often it helps to inform the advancement team members about the themes they should communicate when working with donor prospects.

While there are many individuals who work with the dean, the CDO often gets to know the dean in a unique way. It is a more personal partnership than many will have. A dean can delegate many things, but ensuring that his vision is understood, funded, and brought to fruition is a task that requires the dean's personal engagement and attention. The CDO is the one who most closely supports the dean in these activities.

UNDERSTANDING THE DEAN'S ROLE

It is important for development officers to recognize that deans come from different backgrounds and disciplines, which shape the way they approach their leadership. Most have spent their professional lives focused on their teaching and research before moving into administration. They may do a stint as a department chair before becoming a dean, but the demands and expectations placed on them change significantly when they become head of a major unit of the university. They are no longer evaluated on their teaching and research but on leadership, management, fundraising, and institution building. The accomplishments that led to the deanship, particularly teaching and publishing, are quite different from establishing a new program or securing a significant gift. The transition requires adopting a different mind-set.

Higher education has seen limited success when bringing in leadership from outside academia, resulting in high demand for skilled academic leaders. This is because being a successful dean requires a deep understanding and connection to the work and passion it takes to be a productive faculty member. They are responsible not only for the successful education of students but also for nurturing the development of their faculty. At the same time, they are required to perform as managers of a substantial enterprise, visionaries who identify new opportunities, and entrepreneurs who pursue new areas where investment will allow the institution to thrive in the future. It is essential that development officers understand these complex challenges of the dean's role, in order to best support the dean in accomplishing her goals for the school.

DEVELOPMENT IN THE ACADEMIC CULTURE

Universities have a culture and style of management and leadership that has been established over centuries. However, as discussed in chapter 1 of this book, the field of advancement is still relatively young; this is especially true for certain types of institutions. The presence of a CDO near the top of an academic unit's organizational chart, interacting direct-ly with the dean and other academic leaders, is a relatively new phenom-enon in many cases.

The advancement culture and academic culture are different. Creating an effective relationship between development and academic leaders—and the faculty—requires efforts by all parties. But responsibility lies primarily with the CDO.

The key requirement for a successful relationship is clarity about pri-orities and roles. The basis for a successful collaboration between the CDO and academic leaders, starting with the dean, requires a shared vision for the institution and a shared understanding of what areas can be addressed through philanthropy. The dean needs resources to fund his or her vision, and the CDO needs a vision in order to attract the funds.

Deans need to identify and articulate the academic priorities of the unit. They are involved in the larger university-management structure and also have their pulse on the faculty, staff, and students. They are closest to the daily academic enterprise and many times can see emerging opportunities and funding needs in advance of central leadership. The CDO knows the views and interests of the external constituency and is responsible for providing those insights to the academic planners while also respecting the values and traditions of higher education.

Sometimes fundraising priorities are influenced from the top down, set by the university's central administration. However, in most cases, deans are expected to identify the funding priorities of their schools. This is a role that has emerged within the past few decades. In the past, deans were often viewed as primarily academic leaders who interacted with the faculty and students but did not have a broader responsibility for ad-vancement of the institution. Deans are now asked to look beyond the day-to-day operations, think in the long term, and take a more active leadership role in the growth and development of their units. They are also expected to provide leadership in fundraising, engaging with do-nors, and soliciting significant gifts to advance their priorities.

This expanded role of deans in fundraising provides them with the opportunity to build a legacy, but it requires a long-term perspective. A dean may benefit from the fundraising efforts of previous deans, but he or she also may spend time developing relationships that will primarily benefit future deans. In many cases, deans may secure philanthropic commitments they will never see come to fruition and that will not have impact during their administrations.

Although there may not be immediate impact on the priorities of the current dean, there can be satisfaction in knowing that increased resources are being developed for the future. Fundraising is thus an opportunity to shape an institution and leave behind a meaningful and long-lasting legacy.

WORKING WITH THE FACULTY

The faculty are the heart of the institution. Because they are close to the students and research, they can help fundraisers identify relevant gift opportunities. They also can describe to donors the impact philanthropy can make to their work. In addition to helping cultivate and solicit donors, they can be vital in providing meaningful stewardship after the gift is made.

Deans play a crucial role in the successful interaction between the faculty and the development team. The dean can help prioritize the requests for support that may come from faculty and their departments, communicate to the faculty the areas in which the development team is focused, and sometimes help find alternative sources of funds to address their needs. The dean's support in this way is important for keeping fundraisers productive and for making clear to the faculty that the fundraisers do not have a bias toward one area or another.

When the dean helps build healthy, productive relationships between the faculty and the development team, the development officers can carry more of the fundraising workload. That allows the dean to attend to other priorities and use his or her time in fundraising most effectively. For the fundraiser, being able to develop these deep relationships with the faculty provides more assets at their disposal and can provide important insights on academic priorities. That is especially important when there are changes in leadership, which can occur midstream in a campaign or fundraising cycle.

ROLE OF THE CHIEF DEVELOPMENT OFFICER

It is the daily role of the CDO and her team to build and shape relationships with individuals outside of the school—including alumni, parents, donors, and friends. This requires the CDO continually to search out and engage supporters who can understand the complex priorities of an academic institution and to translate those priorities to a nonacademic audience.

These constituents are essential to implementing the dean's vision and priorities, and they sometimes may also shape them. They may provide a perspective that helps academic leaders look beyond internal day-to-day responsibilities and identify emerging opportunities presented by the wider environment.

Higher education, and institutions in general, are frequently slow to change. However, consistent and relevant interaction can develop meaningful priorities that align the unit's goals with the needs and interests of its constituencies. Orchestrating this interaction is the role of the CDO, and it is one important way in which the CDO contributes to the broader success of the school.

Development officers are accustomed to having their work evaluated by metrics, and they use these metrics to manage their own time and effort. But for deans, having to make one hundred visits during the year or devoting 40 to 50 percent of their effort to development may be a real shift from how they would prefer to prioritize their time. It is the role of the CDO to keep the dean focused on such goals and to push, even if gently, to ensure this activity happens.

Good intentions do not raise money. Although metrics can be seen as a way to make sure deans are active, it is also a powerful tool for explaining the commitment it will take to be successful. For that reason, metrics need to be developed and consistently reviewed with the dean to make sure they see the progress and the areas where there needs to be improvement. Some deans may at times find this kind of input from their CDOs annoying, but most will appreciate the need for discipline in their own fundraising efforts. Again, a relationship of trust between the dean and the CDO is crucial.

Specific metrics can help the dean to see how the many different steps in fundraising can be tracked, how they lead to gifts, and how tracking activity ultimately leads to progress. The use of metrics does more than ensure activity; it also helps the dean explain to the faculty and staff why he or she needs to be on the road so much and to demonstrate progress toward the academic goals that the school is trying to accomplish.

VARIOUS ORGANIZATIONAL STRUCTURES

The reporting lines between CDOs and their deans vary depending on what sort of system they are working under: centralized, decentralized, or hybrid. Development operations are usually structured according to the culture of the institution and its funding model. Resources to pay for development officers and other advancement functions may be centralized at the university level, decentralized for the academic or administrative unit, or shared between the two. How these positions are funded can have a significant impact on the working relationship between the CDO and dean.

In a centralized structure, there is one division responsible for managing the many development operations, and resources come from either the president or institutionally related foundation. This approach can save money by avoiding duplication throughout the university, create clear expectations for everyone involved, and enable consistent and more responsive decision making.

But, in a centralized model, the school-based CDO normally does not report directly to the dean. That can reduce the amount of influence and input the dean has in the process. The dean may even be concerned about whether the CDO assigned to work with the school fully shares his priorities or whether that CDO is distracted by requirements coming from the central administration.

Decentralized units within a university also bring benefits and challenges. They are often funded directly by the school, and their responsibility to serve the school's priorities is thus very clear. School-based teams in a decentralized model are usually larger than they would be in a centralized model, and the CDO and dean often manage more than just major-gifts fundraising. They may also have their own communications, alumni engagement, and foundation staff. Given their strong alignment with the dean and his or her priorities, these teams can have a greater understanding of their academic area and control of the messaging to their stakeholders.

From the perspective of the CDO working in the school, there also are drawbacks of this model. The CDO's focus may be pulled away from core fundraising duties due to the need to manage larger staff at the school level, some of whom are involved in activities that may not directly affect fundraising. "Other duties as assigned" by the dean can vary widely and often have little to do with development work in a decentralized model.

A school CDO in a decentralized model also may find that the lack of a strong reporting line to other development professionals at the university level provides them with less guidance and assistance in their work. There also can be a duplication of functions that could be shared over the larger advancement operation in a centralized model.

The hybrid model provides many advantages. It facilitates the collaboration of all involved. In this scenario, the CDO has strong connections to both the academic unit and central advancement administration because of dual reporting lines to the dean and, usually, an associate vice president. Because funding of development staff positions is typically shared between the unit and the central administration, all parties have a stake in the relationship and depend on each other to manage and shape the outcomes.

Generally, crucial support functions, such as research and gift processing, are centralized. That frees the unit CDO and their teams to focus on building connections and pursuing major gifts. It can also provide an opportunity for central university priorities to be integrated with the unit's specific priorities and to deliver more unified communication to alumni and donors across the university.

One drawback of the hybrid model, compared with the other two models, is that the school has less direct control over development decisions. Another is that the CDO can get trapped in a negative situation if there is disagreement about the development vision between the dean and the president or the provost.

Any of these models can create a successful and rewarding collaboration between the dean and their development teams. The best outcomes will occur if all parties involved focus on implementing the key benefits of the hybrid approach. This requires that all participants at every level make sure that there is a respect for each other's position, that the dean has agency in shaping priorities and management of the school-based development team, that the school's CDO has support and endorsement from the dean in their work with the academic leadership and faculty, and that there is a shared responsibility and desire to accomplish the development goals.

MAKING RELATIONSHIPS WORK

As a development professional, your external relationships are only as strong as your internal ones. The internal relationships can be tricky—not all personalities are a perfect fit. But if an honest, working relationship can be established and metrics are used to both inform and gain agreement on the use of time, then the CDO has the opportunity to move the dean's vision forward and have an impact on the institution. Success also depends on deans creating strong and clear visions for their schools. If all of this can come together, then the dean and CDO can also benefit from a central advancement leadership that recognizes the important role of the dean–CDO relationship in the creation of academic priorities. Their investment of time and effort to make sure these relationships develop across campus can produce significant benefits.

CONCLUSION

Many former deans, when looking back on their time in the position, have said that development work was one of the most enjoyable parts of the job. Seeing new places, having intelligent and thought-provoking conversations with alumni and donors, and hearing personal stories are rewarding experiences. These opportunities to interact with those in the external constituency who care about the school provide insights that can be brought to bear on internal leadership of the institution and contribute to the overall success of a dean or other unit head within a university. Development officers who serve schools and units have the privilege of making these experiences possible and advancing the priorities and goals of the institutions they serve.

VII

Managing and Supporting
Advancement Programs

In chapter 9, Jeff Comfort writes that planned giving should be viewed as a combination of science and art. Indeed, that perspective could apply to all of institutional advancement. As many of the authors in this volume emphasize, there is an element of art in all that advancement professionals do, including skillful listening and creative thinking. But the application of management *science* also is essential in order to ensure that advancement programs are both effective and efficient. The two chapters in this final part of the book address the important topics of managing advancement staff and providing quality advancement services.

In chapter 19, Nuvyn Peters explores the pros and cons of alternative organizational structures from her perspective as a university vice president, providing further insight on some of the points discussed by David Welch in the preceding chapter, who writes from the perspective of a school development officer. She also explores the important topic of metrics and argues for goals that go beyond the simple totals of dollars raised and visits secured, offering examples from some innovative institutions that are using a broader array of performance measures. Expanding on some of the points advanced by Armin Afsahi in chapter 6, Peters also considers strategies for building culture and motivating advancement staff.

In the book's concluding chapter 20, Caroline Chang discusses advancement services. Although some people may think of the activities carried out under the rubric of advancement services as the "science" part of the field, Chang argues that, indeed, "Advancement services is both an art and a science." In other words, it is not all about systems and processes; there are crucial judgments that advancement-services professionals need to exercise.

NINETEEN

Structuring and Managing the Advancement Staff

Nuvyn Peters

Coke or Pepsi? Rent or buy? Decentralized or centralized? Every few years the pendulum swings. Hire fundraisers dedicated to schools and units, or hire central fundraisers? Some institutions explore a combination of both centralized and decentralized functions and employ a hybrid model. But the debate is ongoing: What is an effective way to structure an advancement team?

PROS AND CONS OF MODELS

As David Welch notes in the preceding chapter, there are benefits to both decentralized and centralized staffing environments. Often, fundraisers are embedded in the school or unit, with a direct reporting line (or joint reporting) to a dean, vice president, or faculty leader. These decentralized fundraisers are well versed in the strategic priorities of the faculty, school, or unit they represent. They can articulate clear and compelling giving opportunities that benefit their unit and have ready access to faculty leadership.

Given the size and scope of an institution, unit-based fundraisers may have their own prospect researchers, craft annual-giving appeals, manage stewardship, and plan events. Those may be advantages. However, decentralized fundraising staff may become so deeply embedded in the faculty setting that they find themselves isolated from the general campus experience and narrative.

Centralized fundraisers have the benefit of a macroview of the university and a strong connection to university leadership, such as the president, provost, and vice presidents. They often manage principal gifts and multidisciplinary opportunities and are well connected to other advancement functions, for example, central prospect research teams, advancement services, and communications. As an institution contemplates or approaches a university-wide campaign, it is often the responsibility of the central fundraising team to help articulate campaign priorities and represent the various pillars or aspects of the campaign.

In larger, more complex institutions, there often exists a hybrid model, in which there are both decentralized and centralized fundraisers functioning within an advancement office. This approach is often developed with an aspiration that these two fundraising structures will coexist and function in a harmonious environment, where tension, ambiguity, and competing priorities and interests may otherwise abound.

Hybrid organizational structures often expand fundraising expertise into multiple institutional areas, with staff members organized in various ways, including:

- Regional fundraisers: This model can work well for large institutions with geographically diverse alumni and prospects. Often these fundraisers carry broad portfolios and can speak to multiple institutional priority areas. At some institutions, once a prospect identifies a particular area of interest, they might be transferred to a unit-based portfolio for further engagement, stewardship, or both.
- Initiative-based fundraisers: Sometimes individuals are hired to represent a specific initiative or priority of the university, for example, scholarships, entrepreneurship or innovation, medical research, campaign priorities, athletics, and others.
- Fundraisers assigned by portfolio capacity: Fundraisers manage portfolios of a certain size based on donor capacity, for example, annual giving, major gifts, and principal gifts. Such portfolios are managed based on financial capacity, regardless of a donor's affiliation or area of interest. Fundraisers often enter the profession by managing annual giving or prospects with relatively modest capacity and, with experience, move their way up to major- and subsequently principal-gift portfolios.

- Fundraisers assigned by types of giving: Portfolios are divided based on types of giving, such as annual and legacy. This allows fundraisers to become subject-matter experts in specific, sometimes complex, areas or giving vehicles and develop engagement and stewardship strategies that resonate with multiple donor interests. For example, articulating annual-giving benefits or launching a legacy society for those who indicate the university as part of their estate plans are often activities associated with portfolios aligned by giving type.
- Fundraisers assigned by constituency: This fundraising structure is often built to complement a decentralized fundraising model. In this approach, fundraisers carry portfolios of prospects representing specific constituent types, for example, undergraduate or graduate alumni, parents, and foundations or corporations.

COMMON PITFALLS AND THE PENDULUM

Unfortunately, because of its complexity, a hybrid model can sometimes spiral into an acrimonious working environment that includes misunderstandings and a lack of communication. This often results in staff turnover and low morale. It is not unusual for the pendulum to then swing; a new organizational structure is created in reaction to the problems that existed in the previous structure. This often comes every few years with a new campaign cycle or with a leadership change. Some advancement vice presidents are partial to the central model, while others believe wholeheartedly in a decentralized shop.

The ways in which leaders can structure an advancement team are virtually limitless. It is not surprising that tensions or feelings of territoriality arise among staff. Tensions often arise around prospect strategy, fundraiser credit, and engagement. Fundraisers may feel ownership over donors and make an effort to steer philanthropy toward their faculty, school, or unit. In a working environment motivated by metrics; dollars raised; and, in some cases, incentive pay, fundraisers can be tempted to close gifts without donor intent at heart. At the same time, with so many competing interests and philanthropic priorities, it is often difficult to coordinate appropriate donor-engagement strategies.

The importance of coordination is highlighted by one real-life case. One principal-gift donor was invited to no less than fifty university events over the course of a twelve-month period. The invitations often appeared haphazard, uncoordinated, and disconnected and seemed to reflect little regard for the donor's philanthropic interest. Through these multiple invitations, the voice of the institution was lost. As this example illustrates, metrics sometimes pit fundraisers against each other in a quest to raise as much money as possible, regardless of the cost, seemingly turning advancement into a competitive race rather than a profession that seeks to raise money for the greater good.

ESTABLISHING RULES, POLICIES, AND GUIDELINES

Advancement leaders often change the organizational structure to address and respond to negative staff behaviors, such as the destructive competition for donors. Yet organizational changes alone rarely solve all the problems. As a result, managers create rules, policies, and principles to guide activity, including, for example:

- Before reaching out to a prospect, a fundraiser must get clearance from the portfolio manager.
- Engagement strategies must be captured and entered into a central database.
- Proposals must be vetted before presented to donors.
- Credit must be divided between solicitors if there is more than one fundraiser.
- Fundraisers have authority to tell a dean or volunteer that they cannot visit with a prospect or donor.

We set up processes to manage a system that is inherently in conflict, yet through these processes and layers, we expect different results. We now have teams of data analysts to track donor behavior, monitor trends and giving frequency, track e-mail open rates, capture solicitation closure rates, quantify the moves-management philosophy, assign portfolio capacity, demonstrate average gift per solicitation, and measure other variables. But through these layers we too often lose track of the goals and outcomes we are seeking to measure. The world is not divided into silos, yet academic institutions often adhere to very traditional models of learning and development. As a result, we often structure our advancement teams in the same manner.

If someone graduates from the faculty of economics, then we assume that they must be interested in giving to economics, and therefore a fund-raiser focused on economics should approach them to determine capacity and engage them in subsequent donor conversations. If the prospect indicates that they are not interested in supporting that fundraiser's area (in this example, economics), then sometimes the prospect might be removed from the cultivation cycle or may linger in the fundraiser's portfolio without a specific engagement strategy. Our advancement structures are often at odds with the donor experience we seek to create.

When performance is lackluster or a campaign lags, advancement leaders often restructure the team in the hopes that a new model might yield a different result. But in the absence of a well-defined vision or goal, advancement teams risk alienating staff and donors in their quest to develop the best organizational structure. Examining organizational structure through a goals-based or outcomes-based lens can be a helpful tool to refine or enhance a team structure. However, the organizational structure itself is not the outcome; rather, the goals and culture are the outcome. Without clearly defined goals and metrics, it is no wonder that fundraisers develop a territorial orientation.

Donors lose confidence in an institution when the right hand doesn't know what the left hand is doing. Fundraisers are set up to compete with each other, not to complement the work of their colleagues. How do you build a solid foundation without compromising an outcomes-based approach?

USING METRICS TO GUIDE ORGANIZATIONAL CULTURE

One size doesn't fit all. This goes for goals, too. Many of us have heard the common admonition "If you want to do it, you've got to measure it. What doesn't get measured, doesn't get done." Advancement leaders often set goals and targets for dollars and face-to-face visits. Although they sometimes vary by unit, fundraisers are treated equally for the most part. This may set up an "eat-what-you-kill" environment, in which a fundraiser might act self-servingly and not in the best interests of the donor or the institution.

Irrespective of the advancement model used, leaders ought to explore fundraiser metrics that go beyond dollars raised or visits secured. In addition to these traditional targets, some innovative institutions have begun to pioneer the following goals for their fundraisers:

- Referral goals: In order to build a culture of collaboration, fundraisers have targets for the number of prospects referred to another fundraiser. For example, through the course of a fundraiser's face-to-face visit, they might determine that a prospect is particularly interested in a specific area of the institution that lies outside of that fundraiser's area of expertise. Rather than keeping the prospect in their portfolio, the fundraiser would refer that prospect to be managed by a fundraiser who is better qualified to advance the gift conversation.

- Collaborative proposals: Fundraisers are recognized for building multidisciplinary proposals that present giving opportunities beyond specific units. These multidisciplinary proposals not only result in stronger working relationships between fundraisers but also may facilitate deeper dialogue between academic leadership on innovative program developments.

- Entrepreneurial activities: *Innovation* is the new buzzword. Whether it's pitch competitions, seed funding, crowdfunding, venture philanthropy, or commercialization, it seems as though entrepreneurial development is the next big thing. Some institutions have fundraisers dedicated to the development of entrepreneurial activities and giving opportunities, but all fundraisers can be recognized for innovative initiatives.

The advancement team at the University of Calgary recently was challenged to examine the characteristics of entrepreneurs, specifically the qualities of resiliency, perseverance, commitment, and passion that often make entrepreneurs so successful. As part of their annual business plans, fundraisers were asked to articulate three to five entrepreneurial initiatives that they would explore this year. This encouraged fundraisers to examine their profession through a different lens and gave them permission to try something new.

The results were inspiring. Rather than being narrowly focused on how much money was raised, fundraisers were given the freedom to pioneer new ways to pursue donor engagement and gift opportunities. They collaborated and communicated more frequently, shared successes, and celebrated efforts. This goal breathed vigor and camaraderie into our working environment.

- Tiered portfolio: Built on a moves-management system, fundraisers' portfolio targets are often set with the goal of achieving or maintaining a certain percentage of prospects in various stages of engagement. These goals are based on the age or stage of the fundraiser's portfolio. For example, a fundraiser managing a mature major-gift portfolio might have goals aligned by the following prospect stages: 20 percent cultivation; 40 percent intent to solicit; 30 percent solicitation; and 10 percent stewardship.

  In contrast, a junior regional fundraiser may have a portfolio more heavily weighted toward prospects in qualification and cultivation. Rather than tracking the number of prospects through the investment cycle (as one might see with a moves-management system), fundraisers are incentivized to adhere to a set portfolio breakdown. This encourages well-seasoned fundraisers with major portfolios to ensure they remain outward facing by holding a high solicitation target, while junior fundraisers who are building relationships with new prospects focus on qualification and cultivation.

- Number of proposals submitted and proposals closed: Fundraisers set targets at the beginning of the fiscal year of the number of proposals they seek to present to prospects. This keeps fundraisers focused on solicitation. Complementary targets for closure rates and yield also are often included. As a result, not only are fundraisers presenting proposals to donors, but also the percentage of proposals closed (i.e., closure rate) as a result and the amount funded (i.e., yield) is quantified.

Articulated fundraising metrics, whether implemented in a decentralized, centralized, or hybrid environment, will directly affect the culture and behavior that an advancement leader is seeking to create. By expanding the focus from purely dollars raised and visits completed, fundraisers are empowered and granted permission to focus on the life cycle of development and the building of strong relationships, the essence of true philanthropy.

Key elements in the development of fundraising metrics are consistency and transparency. In some advancement teams, goals are known by and communicated to the individual fundraiser and their manager, while other teams have a more open philosophy. Some even post goals on a staff intranet. Regardless of which method works for the culture of the team, it is important that goals are consistent, understood, and justifiable.

MOTIVATING AND MANAGING STAFF PERFORMANCE

It is the responsibility of the leader to set the tone, pace, and culture of an organization and to emphasize the behaviors that will be recognized and rewarded. Having proactive conversations with fundraisers around institutional culture and expectations is crucial. Before articulating and implementing fundraiser annual plans, it is important to consider the following:

- What are the qualities or characteristics of a successful fundraiser on your development team?
- Is this ideal well articulated and understood?
- What are the expectations around collaboration and team building?
- How should fundraisers engage beyond their area of expertise?

When fundraisers understand the qualities and expectations of a strong member of the team, they will work to achieve those goals.

With relatively high turnover rates in the advancement profession, retention of top-performing fundraisers is an important concern. Strong fundraisers know their worth and their value in the market. Advancement leadership often prioritizes managing those fundraisers who are not performing through the development of performance plans, mentorship and coaching, and other methods. These efforts can result in unintentionally neglecting the top performers, which can lead to their feeling undervalued by the institution.

If you have top performers on the team, then tell them. Be open and transparent in recognizing the behaviors and outcomes that are valuable to your organization. Professional-development conversations ought to focus on goals, strategy, and opportunity rather than resolving current problems. When concerns arise that warrant intervention by management, the sooner the better. Don't delay performance conversations until the end of the year.

True philanthropy is based on and nurtured through personal connection. It results from a relationship that is built over time. It is for this reason that fundraiser turnover can be so paralyzing to development.

When a fundraiser departs, the institution is at risk of losing its connection to the donor or prospect.

Fundraisers often view themselves as gatekeepers, whereby they control access to the donor. In development vernacular, it is common to use the term *relationship manager*, which implies a certain element of control. While ensuring that a donor's interests are honored and that they are appropriately engaged, it is important to reiterate that the role of the fundraiser is to facilitate a connection to the institution, not to manage it. Introducing donors to multiple university and development leaders, thereby creating multiple connection points on their journey of engagement, serves to strengthen and enhance the donor's connection to the institution. That helps to alleviate the impact of fundraiser turnover.

Younger professionals have different expectations of what their workplace will deliver. They expect to rise through the ranks faster and work on strategic initiatives and proposals. In an attempt to retain and attract fundraisers to our teams, we often hire or promote before an individual is ready or has the experience required to lead and inspire a team. Being transparent with fundraisers and new hires on expectations for advancement and milestones to be achieved before promotion will help manage expectations around career trajectory.

Consider including performance metrics as part of job profiles during recruitment. Promotion is a two-way street. If staff members understand from the outset how they will be evaluated, how they will be expected to contribute to the culture of an organization, and what future opportunities for advancement look like, then a leader can appropriately guide and mentor the fundraiser.

Staff members demand a creative and innovative workplace. When the University of Calgary needed to get fundraisers excited about the university's annual giving-day blitz—a twenty-four-hour online campaign to raise money for student scholarships—we created a short video that articulated expectations of each fundraiser and the role they play in ensuring a successful giving day. That was followed up with a live video webinar, where fundraisers could ask specific questions about giving day, for example "How should I engage my major-gift prospects?" "What if a donor wants to support giving day but doesn't want to make a gift to scholarships?" "Can a donor make a gift to an existing scholarship endowment as part of giving day?" Each question was answered and discussed live through the webinar. Fundraisers didn't have to leave the convenience of their offices to attend a time-consuming meeting, yet the video helped create a common connection. In order to attract and retain top performers, it is the responsibility of leaders to promote creative and entrepreneurial working environments.

Within an advancement team, there are multiple ways for fundraisers to contribute as thought leaders within the organization. These can include collaboration task forces that explore opportunities for fundraisers to deepen their working relationships and "lunch-'n'-learns," where fundraisers share experiences and insights, such as best practices, challenging gift conversations, and exciting new initiatives.

There are multiple ways to engage fundraisers in organizational dialogue to enhance their commitment to the institution. When we create a culture of empowerment and innovation among advancement team members, we help to increase their commitment to their roles and responsibilities. At the University of Calgary, the advancement team is encouraged to get to know each other through a monthly "coffee challenge." Once per month every person on the team must go for coffee with someone whom they don't know or don't work with regularly—the caffeine is optional, but the activity is not. This helps to build understanding and collaboration across the team.

One prominent Canadian institution holds monthly workshops for fundraisers, deans, and other university leaders, the purpose of which is to examine new trends in philanthropy and donor behavior, from crowdfunding and giving-day campaigns to multidisciplinary transformational gifts. These regular sessions provide opportunities to deepen understanding of and appreciation for fundraising while cultivating and exploring new ideas and opportunities.

COMMUNICATING AND CELEBRATING SUCCESS

Equally as important as informing and creating a culture of curiosity and learning is the importance of communicating and celebrating success, particularly beyond the walls of development. To varying degrees, all deans, department heads, university leaders, and campus partners ought to be kept informed of development progress toward annual or campaign goals while reiterating the impact that philanthropy has on the institution.

Within the development framework at many institutions, it is common to develop stories of impact, particularly when it comes to donor stewardship. We highlight examples of scholarship recipients, research discoveries, and innovative advancements. We understand that stewardship deepens donors' connection to the university. We communicate the importance of philanthropy to our donors through regular communications and updates, from events to e-newsletters to annual reports. Yet, we too often overlook the importance of engaging our faculty ambassadors and university champions.

As fundraisers, we ought to be reaching out to deans and other university leaders to inform them of campaign progress; highlight examples of noteworthy gifts; detail ongoing initiatives; and outline, at a high level, the philanthropic focus ahead, whether legacy gifts, year-end appeals, giving day, or others. It is imperative to communicate and celebrate success while highlighting examples that reflect the organizational culture and tone you as the leader seek to create. By engaging university leaders in a broad conversation about the impact of development on the life of the institution, advancement leaders can help create and support an appreciation of philanthropy.

CONCLUSION

This chapter focuses on organizational structure and metrics, but these are secondary to goals and culture. Without metrics and goals, clearly articulated and tracked within a culture of collaboration and innovation, advancement leaders will fall into the trap of addressing organizational performance through a debate around structure. Regardless which unit fundraisers represent or to which region they travel, we are all honest brokers of our institutions and must be guided by donor intent and desire. When we sway from those guiding principles, we are no longer adhering to the fundamental tenets of our profession. At its core, philanthropy is about seeking opportunities to connect potential donors with opportunities to make a difference.

It is the responsibility of fundraisers to guide donors to engagement opportunities that resonate with the donor's animating passion. It is the responsibility of development leaders to guide and shape the culture of the organization and to lay the framework of expectations, metrics, and goals, thereby creating an environment where curiosity and innovation thrive.

TWENTY

Advancement Services

Caroline S. Chang

What is advancement services? It's called many things: operations, information technology services, donor services, and more. There are as many variations for what comprises advancement services as there are institutions, and that variety is what makes it hard to define what advancement services is. Advancement services can be comprised of any of the following areas:

- Gift processing or administration
- Biographic or demographic information
- Prospect research
- Prospect development and management
- Stewardship
- Donor relations (events)
- Communications
- Information technology (systems)
- Reporting
- Analytics and business intelligence (BI)
- Training and support
- Budgeting
- Human resources
- Facilities
- Grants

Advancement services is the heart of advancement. The transactions and data, the reporting and analysis, the research and stewardship are all intertwined with advancement services. We cannot engage our constituents, connect them to our institutions, or solicit them without these areas. We synthesize the data received, convert information into actionable intelligence, and then disseminate it to the front lines. We manage constituent data securely, and at the same time, we record and report fundraising activities accurately, according to standards. We translate accounting rules for fundraisers and fundraising definitions for accounting. We translate donor desires for finance and requests for information into reports and analysis.

ART AND SCIENCE

Advancement services is both an art and a science. One might think that what we do is black and white; in reality, what we do is subject to interpretation. The definition of *science* is "the state of knowing—knowledge as distinguished from ignorance or misunderstanding." *Art* is "skill acquired by experience, study, or observation" (Merriam-Webster 2018b, 2018a). In our context, consider the following examples.

1. What is a gift? A "science" definition might be the IRS (2017) definition: a charitable contribution for the use of a qualified organization, made voluntarily and made without getting or expecting to get anything of equal value. The "art" definition could mean a commitment (gift or pledge), the full amount of a gift annuity check, tangible personal property, or a student calling pledge that is paid by the end of the fiscal year.
2. For prospect management, the science could be a wealth-screening-capacity score, whereas the art could be about the relationship, inclination, timing of the cultivation and solicitation, and engagement and affinity levels.
3. The science of contact information could be the addresses, e-mails, and phone numbers for constituents, whereas the art could be about knowing what is the most effective and preferred way to contact and communicate with constituents.

As these points demonstrate, the role of advancement services is complex and multilayered. We need to know and understand all parts of the advancement organization in order to provide excellent service. We need to be able to interpret what is really needed, to read between the lines of requests and not simply provide what's written in the request. Our support of the entire organization allows us to see the whole picture and to anticipate needs and challenges.

Our unique view of the advancement enterprise means advancement services should be at the executive leadership table. Our involvement is crucial to the success of advancement precisely because we can provide much more than just service behind the scenes.

We can aid with strategic vision and planning, especially during campaign planning. We can help the organization become more efficient by analyzing business processes and suggesting technology where appropriate. We can be proactive in analyzing data and providing business intelligence so the organization can make informed decisions, and we can use data to help drive fundraising strategies, either for individuals or for the organization as a whole.

LANDSCAPE OF ADVANCEMENT SYSTEMS TODAY

We are in a remarkable time and space for advancement systems. Most institutions need to replace their aging systems, but there are not a lot of options. The landscape is further complicated by a workforce that expects everything to be Amazon-like in its delivery—easy to use (smartphone only!), seamless, requires no training—and has little patience for anything else. At the same time, we are asking our advancement systems to be more than just a system of record. Our systems need to be able to personalize outgoing communications, provide meaningful data for decision making, and yet also be as efficient as possible.

The fundraising databases of the past tried to be everything to everyone in an advancement shop—from a casual, occasional user to the power user who knows every screen and table, from those who are less technically inclined to those who understand relational databases. These databases had only limited success. Now, the landscape has changed. What we have now is a different way of thinking. We can now think of the core database as just that—a system of record for biographic information, gift and pledge transactions, contact reports, correspondence, and other documentation.

What's exciting about today's landscape is that you can overlay or extend the core database with a whole host of tools to help with personalization, communication, segmentation, relationship management, reporting, and data analytics. These powerful software tools enable you to conduct business in the way that is important to you.

One way we think of advancement system needs is in a form similar to Maslow's (1943) hierarchy of needs, as shown in figure 20.1. We need basic functions like servers and internet, authentication, and security before we can think of anything else. Core data needs, such as biographic data and what is done with it (e.g., mailings) signify low engagement. Belonging needs, or beginning engagement, are gifts and pledges and research. Esteem needs, or substantive engagement, are stewardship and prospect management. Self-actualization is realized with self-renewing engagement.

Tools overlaying or extending a core database creates an ecosystem: If you have the right integration tools, then you can swap out tools as new ones are developed or as business needs change. Figure 20.2 illustrates an advancement ecosystem as a layer cake. Before you have your core customer-relationship management (CRM) system, you need to ensure you have a solid technology infrastructure. Security, system and database administration, and cloud services (if needed) are just a few of the areas you need to make sure are running smoothly. Then you can layer on a core CRM, a system of record where transaction processing occurs. Transaction processing of biographic and gift information is at the heart of an advancement system; without accurate biographic and gift information, we cannot contact, engage, or solicit our constituents.

TO CLOUD OR NOT TO CLOUD?

Today, more core CRMs are being offered as cloud-based platforms. There are advantages to a cloud solution. For one, the institution does not need to purchase or maintain servers on-site, and therefore the security of the data and database is the responsibility of the CRM vendor. The disadvantage is that upgrades and updates are not in the control of the institution. The vendor will upgrade or update on its own schedule, and while vendors allow for some customization, there can be far less customization of the base product.

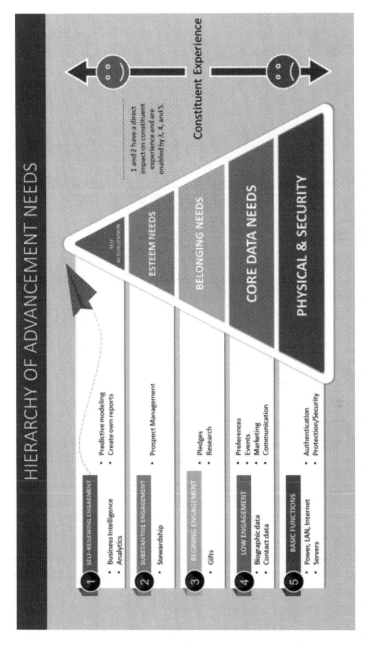

Figure 20.1. Hierarchy of Advancement Needs. *Source:* Transforming Solutions, 2017. Used with permission.

The cost for cloud-based platforms is not necessarily less, especially over a time period like five years. With self-hosted CRM solutions, there is an initial cost to purchase the software and then an annual mainte-nance fee that typically increases over time, so years 1 and 2 of a five-year contract are front-loaded for costs. With a cloud-based solution, costs are spread out more evenly over five years.

The trend is to move to cloud-based solutions, and eventually on-premises solutions will no longer be offered. Cloud-based solutions may reduce the need for a database or system administrator, but there is still most likely the need for developers and report writers, so appropriate expectations for costs and staffing need to be recognized.

FUTURE STATE ECOSYSTEM

With a layer-cake ecosystem, we can do more to take advantage of tech-nology and be nimbler to react to constituent and business needs. This nimbleness requires a data-integration strategy that is easier to maintain than the system currently in place at most institutions. Most institutions program multiple feeds—one feed (inbound/outbound) for each use or application that needs the data. There are several solutions to simplify this data exchange; one is to have middleware and a publish or subscribe model for the most commonly requested data elements. The IT staff then is freed from having to program, schedule, and maintain feeds and from having to troubleshoot when feeds fail.

Once a simplified system of data integrations and exchanges is in place, you can decide what additional functionality you prefer or if you would like the "best of breed" functionality that your CRM may not offer. You can also feel more comfortable trying out a product and then swap-ping out products if the result is not what you expected or hoped.

Fortunately, there are quite a few niche products that can overlay or extend your core CRM, and the market is growing. For example, artificial intelligence (AI) or machine learning is making its way into advancement technology. IBM's Watson has been around since 2010, but only recently have vendors taken advantage of Watson and AI to provide new features and technologies in advancement. Technology that incorporates machine learning cannot only automate marketing and communications, but it can also provide *curated* communications, which continues to be refined with more opportunities for the constituent to interact with the institution.

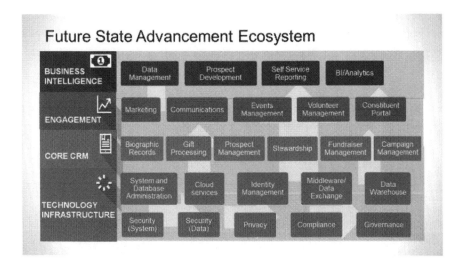

Figure 20.2. Future State of Advancement Ecosystem. *Source:* **Transforming Solutions, 2017. Used with permission.**

Can AI be used to help fundraisers decide where next to turn their attention, to determine "who's next" to be targeted for cultivation and solicitation? Absolutely. AI will eventually be able to help fundraisers figure out not only who to ask but also how much to ask and which initiatives are important to both the institution and the constituent. AI is already being used to remind fundraisers to contact prospects and craft a draft e-mail that is personal and relevant to the prospect.

Artificial intelligence, like Watson, is moving what we can do with analytics and business intelligence forward. Whether providing a reporting module that allows users to change a parameter and immediately see the effect on a chart, graph, or results or refining our data models for segmentation and fundraising, analytics and BI have come a long way from the time of waiting five business days for a list of prospects. These tools allow us to be forward looking and predictive rather retroactively reporting results. Today's tools also happen to allow us to display results in a more visual, consumable way for the typical user.

Other niche products include tools for social media integration and social listening. Many people visit Facebook at least once a day (Duggan et al. 2015). Aside from having a comprehensive social media strategy, we need a way to cull the information about how our constituents are interacting with our social media posts and link that information back to information we already have, such as whether the constituent is a donor. Social listening, performed by monitoring digital conversations, is another component. What are our constituents saying about the institution? How can these insights help us to better understand our constituents?

While these tools allow us to do our work differently and to offer more and different insights than ever before, the effect is that the skills needed by our workforce is evolving. Today's advancement services leader needs to recognize this change and think strategically about how to move the organization forward.

OUR CONSTITUENTS

The preceding discussion is internally focused, covering technology to help us work more efficiently to engage and solicit our constituents. What do our constituents want? They want to feel that we know them on a personal level, even though they might be 1 of 100,000 alumni. This is only possible by having a robust database in which we can have a complete 360-degree view of our constituents, storing information from the very beginning as prospective students and continuing through to our interactions with them as alumni.

We need to have degree and major and minor information—that's a given—but we also need to know where they lived on campus, including any fraternity or sorority information. What student groups did they join? Who was their advisor? What internships did they have? Did they receive financial aid, and was part of that aid from an endowed scholarship? Did they meet the benefactor of that scholarship? Can we find out who their friends and peers are?

However, acquiring information about our constituents' lives as students is often a challenge. Even if the information exists, it is located in disparate parts of campus and possibly not in an electronic format that can be fed and integrated into our system. For example, student-group information is often spotty at best. We need to work with our campus partners to gather and store this information in such a way that it can later be passed onto us, which is not always an easy task. Our campus partners may not see the importance or relevance of why we need this information.

In our own systems, we also need to gather and store as much information as possible to have a complete view of our constituents. What touchpoints do we have with our constituents? Have they met with the president, faculty, or board members? What communications are they receiving and in what format? How do they prefer to be contacted, and does the format vary depending on the content? Are they members of any groups, such as alumni clubs, the campus museum, or the radio station? How long have they held these memberships? Do they volunteer for the institution? What are their interests, and what do they support? If we have all this information (and more!), then having the right tools can help us interact with our constituents in the manner that is most meaningful to them.

We can also provide ways to make it easier for our constituents to interact with us. Many of us have an online alumni directory; what does the rest of their online experience look like? A constituent portal would make it easier for our constituents to interact with the institution. Elements of a portal could include not only an alumni directory but also a way to be served up curated content about the institution—information relevant to that particular constituent.

For example, event information and an easy way to register for events of interest plus a way to see past events the constituent has attended would be a logical feature, as would ways to volunteer. Ways to volunteer could include signing up to be a mentor to a student, as well as how to contact and interact with that student—all of which can be stored in our core CRM. The portal could be the place where the constituent interacts with career services, from a job board to posting job offerings. What affinity groups and regional clubs can the constituent join, and are they a member currently? What local events sponsored by the regional club are available?

In the area of privacy, a portal is a perfect place to provide the constituent with a way to indicate how they wish to be contacted, communications they wish to receive, and which information can be displayed on the alumni directory and a way to update their biographic information. With the advent of General Data Protection Regulation (GDPR) for the EU and forthcoming privacy changes, such as those in California, we need to have a strategy for how to work within the legal limitations.

For fundraising, a portal is the place where our constituents can view their giving history, including past and present pledges. The portal should provide an easy way to make a pledge payment and view and print tax receipts. Stewardship information, from financial reports to impact reports to information about the students who benefit from a constituent's endowed fund, should be part of a portal.

The portal, once a constituent is logged in, should be relevant and personal. If the constituent is a parent, then information and ways to interact with the institution as a parent would be viewable and accessible. If the constituent is not an alumnus, then the alumni directory would not be viewable and accessible; neither would alumni clubs, unless those clubs are available to nonalumni. These are just a few examples of how a portal could be personalized and relevant for our constituents. Of course, all of the content on the portal needs to be mobile-friendly.

These tactics and more need to be put in the context of an overall digital strategy for fundraising and engagement. The desire for our constituents to be engaged in the manner of their choice is a signal that the ways in which our constituents give to and interact with our institutions are changing.

For many institutions, the number of donors is down while dollars are up. Could it be that they want to be engaged, cultivated, and solicited in a different way—specifically, through digital only? Could traditional student-calling programs be augmented or replaced by texting? There already is a product that has this capability, and results are positive. Digital strategy should include information, stories, and ads on social media to keep your organization in your donors' feeds and keep your institution on top of your donors' minds. We need to be ready for this change by embracing the digital world fully.

CONCLUSION

This is an exciting time to be in advancement services. We no longer feel that we are the "back shop"—we can truly be partners with our fundraising and alumni-relations colleagues to advance our organizations. In order to make that partnership work and provide excellent service, we need to know and understand all parts of the advancement organization. That broad view of the advancement enterprise also suggests that advancement services should be at the executive leadership table. Our involvement at that level is crucial to the success of today's advancement programs.

REFERENCES

Duggan, Maeve, Nicole B. Ellison, Cliff Lampe, Amanda Lenhart, and Mary Madden. 2015. "Frequency of Social Media Use." Pew Research Center: Internet & Technology. http://www.pewinternet.org/2015/01/09/frequency-of-social-media-use-2/.

IRS (Internal Revenue Service). 2017. *Publication 526 (2017), Charitable Contributions. Publication 526 (2017), Charitable Contributions.* https://www.irs.gov/publications/p526.

Maslow, A. H. 1943. "A Theory of Human Motivation." *Psychological Review* 50, no. 4: 370–96.

Merriam-Webster. "Art." 2018a. https://www.merriam-webster.com/dictionary/art.

———. "Science." 2018b. https://www.merriam-webster.com/dictionary/science.

Transforming Solutions. 2017. "Current Landscape of Advancement Systems." *TSI Blog*, December 14, 2017. http://transforming.com/2017/12/14/current-landscape-of-advancement-systems/.

Conclusion

Michael J. Worth and Matthew T. Lambert

There are few earthly things more splendid than a university.
In these days of broken frontiers and collapsing values,
when the dams are down and the floods are making misery,
when every ancient foothold has become something of a quagmire,
wherever a university stands, it stands and shines;
wherever it exists, the free minds of men,
urged on to full and fair enquiry,
may still bring wisdom into human affairs.
> —John Masefield, poet laureate of the United Kingdom
> at the installation of the chancellor of the University of Sheffield
> June 25, 1946

John Masefield spoke in the aftermath of World War II, when the global power structure was being redefined. Economies and societies devastated by the war were just beginning to rebuild. Millions of men were returning home to pursue their lives, delayed by years of service in the military. It was a time of upheaval and uncertainty. Masefield portrayed universities as essential anchors of stability and reason in that turbulent world.

Although perhaps less dire, the environment we face today is also one of upheaval and uncertainty due to the powerful forces mentioned throughout this book—globalization, information and communication technologies, changing demographics, and evolving public attitudes toward traditional institutions. Now as then, universities are important anchors in a turbulent time, but they face challenges and will require leadership to remain strong and relevant.

Higher-education institutions need to adapt to the changing circumstances and new opportunities that the authors in this book describe. The years ahead likely will see new models for how education is provided and financed and changes in the curriculum in many disciplines—and certainly more growth in the interdisciplines, breaking down silos. Most

255

importantly, however, universities will need to sustain the confidence and support of the society and the many and diverse constituencies they serve, ensuring that advancement leaders will have a central role and increasing responsibility in the decades ahead.

In ways discussed throughout this book, advancement leaders already have been in the forefront of embracing change within their own fields, applying new technologies and innovative ideas for building and maintaining relationships. They have developed programs to engage increasingly diverse constituencies and have expanded their efforts into the international arena. They have examined their own roles and are developing new skills and management systems to increase the effectiveness of their work. They have adapted traditional models to current conditions, keeping what works and undertaking revision as demanded by new realities. In these ways, the advancement profession offers an example for all of higher education as it faces the future.

We hope that this volume expands the horizons of many readers, that they gain new insights and ideas from the examples the authors provide, and that they have come to further consider the wider implications of their work. Institutional advancement is more important than ever, and it is about more than engaging individuals, communicating messages, and raising money. Advancement professionals will play a vital role in ensuring that our universities continue to stand and shine as footholds of community, freedom, fairness, innovation, and wisdom in a time of historic transformation.

REFERENCE

The University of Sheffield. 1946. "A Legacy to Sheffield." Accessed December 14, 2018. https://www.sheffield.ac.uk/polopoly_fs/1.169730!/file/Legacy_Brochure.pdf.

Index

About the Contributors

Ivan A. Adames is chief development officer at DePaul University, the largest Catholic university in the country. He was previously the executive director of schools and programs at Northwestern University. He has served as the director of development for international programs at Johns Hopkins University and has held professional positions at The Ohio State University, Imperial College London, and the University of Massachusetts Foundation. He is a former Fulbright scholar (Germany) and CASE fellow, a past board member and advisor of the Science of Philanthropy Initiative at the University of Chicago, and a member of the CASE Commission on Philanthropy. He is a graduate of the Johns Hopkins University Carey School of Business.

Armin Afsahi is vice chancellor for advancement at the University of Denver. He was previously associate vice chancellor and chief alumni officer at the University of California, San Diego, where he built a new model for university advancement. Programs created under his leadership increased alumni engagement by 73 percent over five years. Alumni and student philanthropy grew by 427 percent and 450 percent, respectively. Afsahi holds an MBA in finance and strategic management from the University of San Diego.

Jenny Bickford has served as director of foundation giving at University of California, Davis, since 2012. She has worked in higher-education-foundation fundraising for nearly twenty years, with previous appointments at Arizona State University (ASU) and Penn State. She has a bachelor's degree from ASU.

Shaun Brenton serves as the associate vice president of corporate and foundation relations for the Arizona State University (ASU) Foundation, a position she has held since 2004. Her career in development spans more than twenty-five years and includes prior appointments at the University of Arizona and Centenary College of Louisiana. She holds a bachelor's degree from the University of New Mexico.

Lauren F. Brookey, APR, PRSA fellow, is vice president of marketing and communications at the University of Oklahoma. She was previously vice president of external affairs at Tulsa Community College and president of the Tulsa Community College Foundation. She has had a thirty-five-year career in public relations, marketing, and development. As of 2018, Brookey is a member of the CASE board of trustees. She is a graduate of the University of Oklahoma.

Caroline S. Chang is vice president, advancement solutions, for UC Innovation, a Salesforce CRM and consulting company. Previously, she was associate vice president for advancement services at Santa Clara University, director of operations at Stanford University, and director of annual giving for the Stanford Medical Center. She holds a BA and MA from Stanford University and an MBA from Santa Clara University.

Jeff Comfort has more than three decades of gift-planning experience. He is vice president of principal gifts and gift planning at the Oregon State University Foundation. Before moving to Oregon State, he served for eighteen years as head of planned giving at Georgetown University and for eleven years at the National Jewish Medical and Research Center. As a volunteer leader of the National Association of Charitable Gift Planners, Comfort served as president, chaired the tenth national conference, and was a member of the national board of directors for five years. Additionally, he was a member of the ethics committee and chaired the task force on gift valuation. He was a founding board member of the Colorado Planned Giving Roundtable and past president and board member of the National Capital Gift Planning Council.

Michael C. Eicher is senior vice president for advancement at The Ohio State University and president of The Ohio State University Foundation. Prior to joining Ohio State in 2012, Eicher served for six years as senior vice president for external affairs and development at Johns Hopkins University. He began his career in higher education at the University of California, Los Angeles, where he rose from associate director of development in the School of Medicine to vice chancellor, external affairs. At

Ohio State, he led the But for Ohio State Campaign, which raised more than $3 billion from more than 750,000 donors. He is a graduate of the University of California, San Diego.

Daniel H. Frezza is associate vice president for lifetime philanthropic engagement and annual giving at William & Mary, where he oversees the strategic leadership and execution of a comprehensive annual-giving approach that includes fundraising priorities for thirteen schools and units. William & Mary boasts the highest undergraduate-alumni participation rate among the public ivy universities and leads all top fifty national public universities, as ranked by U.S. News & World Report. Frezza received his bachelor's degree in communications and marketing from Western Carolina University and his master's degree in higher-education administration from North Carolina State University.

Matthew T. Lambert has served as vice president for university advancement at William & Mary since 2013. He oversees all William & Mary efforts related to alumni engagement, private fundraising, philanthropic outreach, university marketing, and alumni communications. From 2009 to 2013, he was associate vice president for university development at Georgetown University, with responsibility for leading the university's development team toward successful completion of a historic $1.5 billion campaign. He teaches at William & Mary's School of Education and Public Policy program, with undergraduate and graduate students. He is the author of *Privatization and the Public Good: Public Universities in the Balance* (2014). He earned his undergraduate degree in psychology and sociology at William & Mary, a master's degree from The Ohio State University, and a doctorate in higher-education management from the University of Pennsylvania.

James M. Langley is president of Langley Innovations, based in Frederick, Maryland. He previously served as vice president for advancement at Georgetown University; as vice chancellor for external relations and president of the UCSD Foundation at the University of California, San Diego; and as vice president of external affairs at Georgia Tech. He has published four books and dozens of articles and has conducted many seminars, workshops, and speeches. His most recent book is *Comprehensive Campaigns: A Guide for Presidents and Boards*.

Kestrel A. Linder is cofounder and CEO of GiveCampus, a digital-fund-raising and volunteer-management platform used by more than six hundred nonprofit educational institutions, including approximately 15 percent of all colleges and universities in the United States. Linder advises advancement leaders around the world on digital best practices and the future of philanthropy amid rapid technological change. He holds a bachelor's degree from Johns Hopkins University and a master's degree from Georgetown University.

Debra J. Mesch is professor of philanthropic studies at the Lilly Family School of Philanthropy at Indiana University and holds the Eileen Lamb O'Gara Chair in Women's Philanthropy. She was the director of the Women's Philanthropy Institute (WPI) from 2008 to 2018. She and her colleagues have written numerous reports for the signature Women Give series about the factors that shape gender-based giving patterns. Mesch received both her MBA and PhD in organizational behavior and human resource management from Indiana University Kelley School of Business.

Felicity Meu is the director of partner success at GiveCampus, where she supports the digital-fundraising and volunteer-management activities of more than six hundred nonprofit educational institutions, including approximately 15 percent of all colleges and universities in the United States. Previously, she spent nine years with Stanford University's Office of Development. As Stanford's inaugural director of next-generation giving, she worked closely with individual donors and volunteers and helped craft the university's vision for engaging its next great generation of philanthropists. Meu also spent time consulting for Stanford's Effective Philanthropy Lab, working on a project dedicated to understanding the needs of millennial donors.

James H. Moore Jr., president and CEO of the University of Illinois Foundation, provides strategic oversight and support to a comprehensive fundraising operation for the University of Illinois and its three campuses in Urbana–Champaign, Chicago, and Springfield. He previously served as president and CEO of the University of Arizona Foundation and the University of Northern Colorado Foundation. He also held senior-level positions at Northwest Missouri State University, Clarkson University, the University of Arizona, and Iowa State University. Moore has served on CASE's National Committee on Institutionally Related Foundations, as well as the CASE Commission on Philanthropy. As of 2018, he is chair-elect of the CASE board of trustees. Moore is the 2015 recipient of the CASE Commonfund Institutionally Related Foundation Award. He earned a master's degree in management systems from Clarkson University and a bachelor's degree in marketing from Northwest Missouri State.

Andrea K. Pactor is interim director (as of 2018) of the Women's Philanthropy Institute at the Indiana University Lilly Family School of Philanthropy, where she has worked since 2005. She is coauthor with Dwight Burlingame of a chapter on the history of donor education. She is also coauthor with Debra Mesch of *From Donor to Philanthropist: The Value of Donor Education in Creating Confident, Joyful Donors*. She is also coauthor of chapters on women and philanthropy, notably in the books *Fundraising Principles and Practice, Leadership in Nonprofit Organizations*, and *Achieving Excellence in Fundraising*. She has served arts, education, and faith-based organizations as a professional and volunteer. She has a BA from American University, an MA from the University of Michigan, and an MA in philanthropic studies from Indiana University.

Nuvyn Peters is vice president, development and alumni engagement, at the University of Calgary. Prior to joining the University of Calgary in 2014, she was the associate vice president of development and campaign operations at Georgetown University. She was named one of Canada's top newsmakers of the week by *Maclean's* magazine and was named as one of Canada's "Top 40 under 40." She holds a bachelor of arts in political science from the University of Saskatchewan and a master of arts in conflict resolution from Landegg International University in Switzerland.

Ronald J. Schiller, founding partner of the Aspen Leadership Group, is a nationally recognized advisor to nonprofit leaders. He has held leadership positions in seven educational and cultural institutions, including the University of Chicago, where he led a team of more than 450 that completed a $2.3 billion campaign and facilitated two nine-figure gifts. He serves on the faculty of the annual CASE conference, Inspiring the Largest Gifts of a Lifetime, and has served as cochair of CASE's Winter Institute for Chief Development Officers. He is a regular speaker on philanthropy at national and international conferences and is the author of three books: *The Chief Development Officer: Beyond Fundraising* (Rowman & Littlefield, 2013); *Belief and Confidence: Donors Talk about Successful Philanthropic Partnership* (2015); and *Raising Your Organization's Largest Gifts: A Principal Gifts Handbook* (2018).

Fritz W. Schroeder is vice president for development and alumni relations at Johns Hopkins University, which concluded its most recent campaign, Rising to the Challenge, in October 2018 with more than $6 billion in commitments. During his twenty-three years at Hopkins, he has held various leadership positions, including executive director of the alumni association and director of annual giving. Prior to Johns Hopkins, he spent seven years in annual-giving roles at the University of Maryland. He is a frequent speaker and conference leader and has authored *Annual Giving: A Practical Approach* and several other fundraising book chapters. As of 2018, he serves on the CASE board of trustees. He is a graduate of James Madison University and earned an MBA from the University of Maryland.

Rachel E. Vassel is assistant vice president, Office of Multicultural Advancement, at Syracuse University (SU) in Syracuse, New York. She also has served as an adjunct professor at the S. I. Newhouse School of Public Communications at SU. Previously, she was nationwide director of multicultural marketing at the American Cancer Society and held strategic marketing and sales leadership positions at Turner Broadcasting, the Weather Channel, Music Choice, and Young and Rubicam. Vassel is author of the book *Daughters of Men: Portraits of African-American Women and Their Fathers*. She holds a dual BS in public relations and marketing from SU.

David T. Welch is executive director of development of the College of Arts and Sciences at the University of Oregon, a position he has held since 2011. Previously, he was senior director of development at Georgetown University, senior director of development at the Kenan-Flagler Business School at the University of North Carolina at Chapel Hill, and associate director of development at the University of Washington Business School. He holds a BA in international relations and political science from Marquette University.

Michael J. Worth is professor of nonprofit management and former vice president for development and alumni affairs at the George Washington University, Washington, DC. He also is principal, Michael J. Worth and Associates, LLC, a fundraising consulting firm serving higher education and the nonprofit sector. He was previously director of development at the University of Maryland, director of development at DeSales University, and assistant to the president at Wilkes University. He is author or editor of several books, including *Leading the Campaign: The President and Fundraising in Higher Education* (Rowman & Littlefield, 2017). He was previously a member of CASE's Commission on Philanthropy. Worth holds an AB from Wilkes University, an MA from American University, and a PhD from the University of Maryland.

Darrow Zeidenstein is vice president for development and alumni relations at Rice University, where he has served in this capacity since 2007. Prior to his arrival at Rice, Zeidenstein was the founder of the analytics practice and a managing director at the consulting firm of Marts and Lundy, Inc. His development experience spans nearly twenty-five years and includes leadership positions at the Stern School of Business at New York University and the University of Texas at Austin. He holds a PhD in social anthropology from the University of Texas at Austin. He was a Fulbright Scholar in Syria and a Social Science Research Council postdoctoral fellow in Morocco.

Made in the USA
Middletown, DE
14 February 2024

49711933R00168